IMAGES
of America

MASON COUNTY

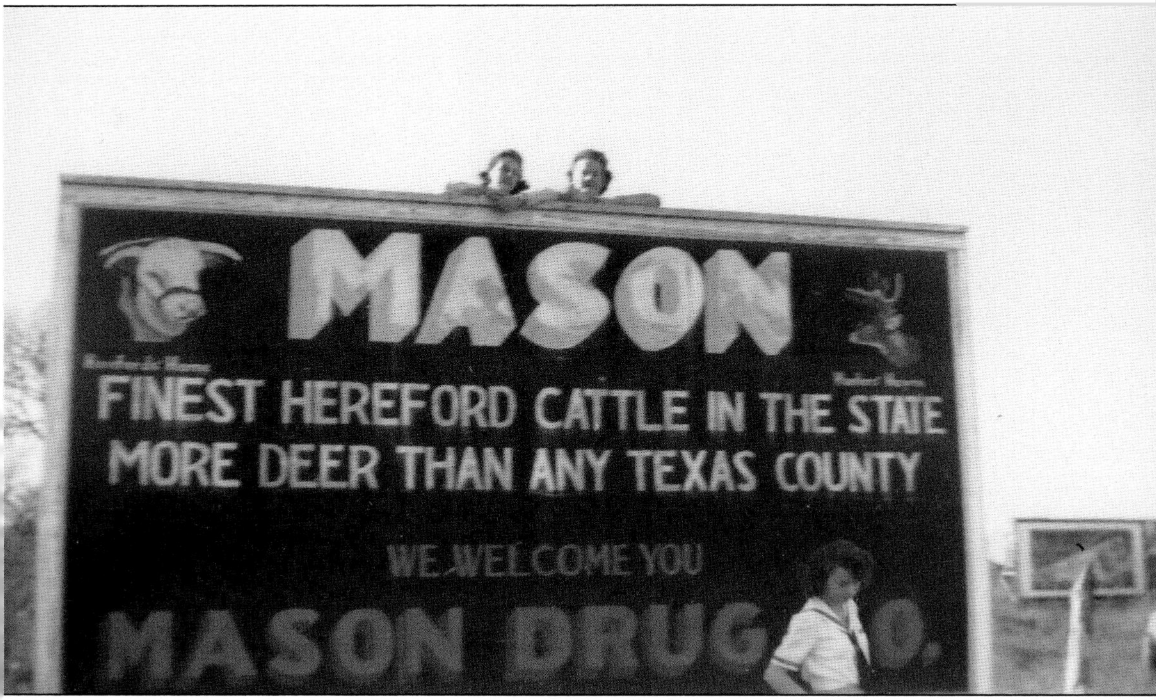

These very tall girls, Sybil Schmidt (left) and Sadie Mae Schuessler (McMillan), peer over the top of this billboard, which was located near the present-day entrance to Fort Mason City Park. Alice Ruth Runge (Alsup) stands at the base of the sign. Actually, the girls were standing on ladders in the bed of a pickup truck while posing for this photograph, taken in 1942 by Shirley Beth Grote (Lyles). (Courtesy of Shirley Beth Lyles.)

On the Cover: Leo Zesch's motorboat, the first of its kind to operate on the Llano River in Mason County, is pictured on July 4, 1911. The owner charged 10¢ to ride from his launch site about half a mile upstream from the James River Crossing to the mouth of Peters Creek. He also had a dance platform in the pecan bottom near Fritz Martin's field, which was a popular site for holiday gatherings. From left to right are Othello Traweek, Ruby Payne, Seth Martin Sr., Beulah Mebus Jennings, Harold Lemburg, and Will Lemburg. Boat pilot John Eastman is not shown. (Courtesy of MCHC.)

IMAGES
of America

MASON COUNTY

Mason County Historical Commission

ARCADIA
PUBLISHING

ISBN 978-0-7385-7931-3

Published by Arcadia Publishing
Charleston, South Carolina

Printed in the United States of America

Library of Congress Control Number: 2010926993

For all general information, please contact Arcadia Publishing:
Telephone 843-853-2070
Fax 843-853-0044
E-mail sales@arcadiapublishing.com
For customer service and orders:
Toll-Free 1-888-313-2665

Visit us on the Internet at www.arcadiapublishing.com

The Mason County Historical Commission dedicates this book to two of its pillars, Jane Hoerster and Julius DeVos, in appreciation of their inexhaustible patience in answering questions about the county's past and their decades of painstaking work to rediscover and preserve its stories for the future.

CONTENTS

ACKNOWLEDGMENTS

The Mason County Historical Commission (MCHC) is grateful to all those who provided photographs and information for this collection: Jan Appleby, Beverly Baker, Charles Banta, Sara Banta, Bobbie Baze, Ron Birk, Veleda Boyd, June Brandenberger, Leighton Brown, Sally Capps, Victor Castillo, Mary Jo Cockrell, Brenda Comer, Carolyn Copeland, Jack Crouch, Gerry Daniel, Doris Dannheim, Ruth Dannheim, Fae Danz, Elvie Donop, Kenneth Durst, Charles Eckert, Gaelyn Fisher, Bobbye and Marshall Frazier, Gerry Gamel, Eddie Garza, Yolanda Garza, the Arthur Geistweidt family, the Homer Geistweidt family, Reuben Geistweidt, Beck Gipson, David and Cynthia Gipson, Alex Grosse, Helen Habecker, Dick Hahn, Kelsey Hickok, the Hilda Methodist Church, Fran Hoerster, Jane Hoerster, Sam and Maribelle Hoerster, Florene Hofmann, Joyce Holloway, Harold Hudson, Rene Ince, the Ischar family, Emma Gene Jackson, Dorothy Johnson, Ron Johnson, Spider Johnson, Dolores Keller, Geneva Keller, Steven B. Kensing, Charles Kettner, Rex Klingelhefer, the Koock family, Don Kothmann, Lester and Cindy Kothmann, Rosemary Kruckemeyer, Eva Lang, Peggy Laverty, Jack and Laverne Lee, Judy Lehmberg, Roy Lehmberg, Pearl Leifeste, Carolyn Loeffler, Candy Luna, Shirley Beth Lyles, Marilyn Mahon, Hazel Martin, Seth and Kathryn Martin, Irene Martinez, the Mason County Museum, the M. Beven Eckert Memorial Library, the Alfred Menchaca family, Dolores Menchaca, Sandy Miller, Rebecca Moneyhon, Patty Moss, Carolyn Nixon, B. H. and Julie Nobles, Elaine O'Neal, Amanda Orozpe, Linda Owen, Charles Pluenneke, Lila Jo Polk, Norman and Kay Ponder, Pat Reardon, Shirley Cottle Reed, Charles Reichenau, Glenn Ruthven, Judy Schoenfeld, Wilburn Shearer, Tommy Splittgerber, Dalton Stephens, Dorothy Tartt, Mary Velez, Doug and Sherry Willmann, Christy Wright, Jane Zavala, Gene and Patsy Zesch, and Jordan Zesch.

MCHC also thanks Kristie Kelly and Hannah Carney at Arcadia Publishing for their helpful guidance and cheerful support.

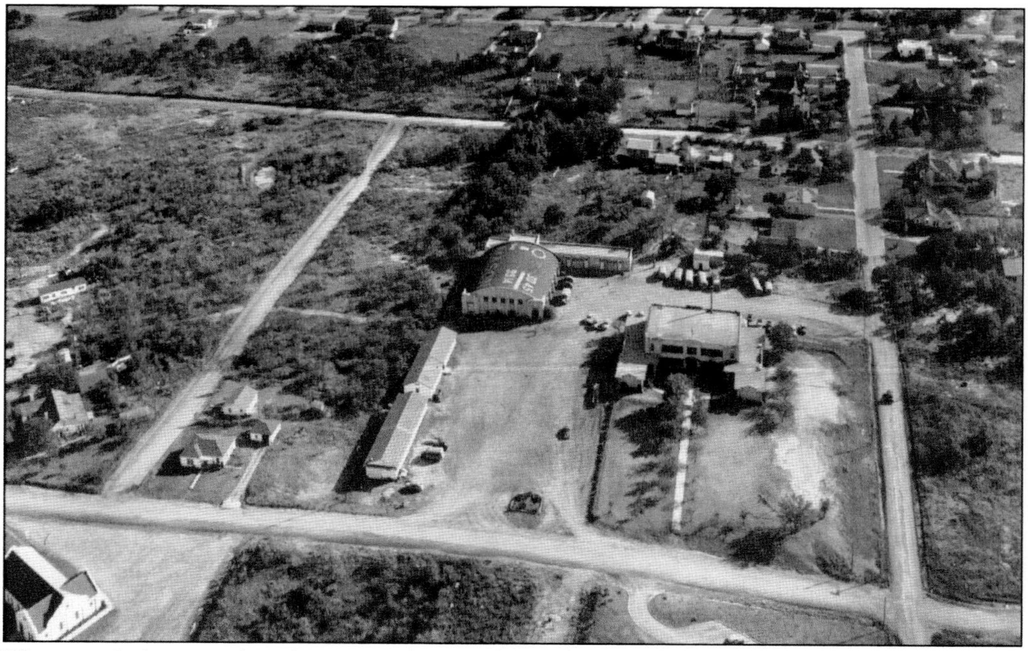

This aerial photograph, taken around 1956, shows the block bordered by (clockwise from the bottom) College, Wren, Kettner, and Post Oak Streets. The Church of Christ is on the bottom left, and the high school campus is in the center. (Courtesy of Carolyn Loeffler.)

Introduction

Mason County is a relaxed and welcoming place today, with its nostalgic courthouse square and its neighborly traditions. Yet its first decades were times of tension, fear, and even armed conflict between the different peoples who lived here.

At the time the Republic of Texas was formed in 1836, this area was part of the huge county of Bexar. It became part of Gillespie County in 1848. As a practical matter, these lines on the map meant little, for the region was really controlled by Comanches, Lipan Apaches, Kiowas, Tonkawas, and Wichitas. The native people used the area as their hunting grounds and winter homes.

After Fort Mason was established in 1851, the era of Indian domination started to wane. With the U.S. Army offering some protection, German immigrants began moving north from Fredericksburg to the Llano River, establishing a line of scattered settlements that included Castell, Willow Creek, and the Saline Valley. A private agreement of friendship between the German Emigration Company and the Penateka Comanches in 1847 also helped keep the peace for a few years. From the southeastern states, descendants of old American families were drawn here as early as 1846 by the open grasslands with their ever-flowing springs, ravines, and creeks. This was ideal livestock country.

Fort Mason served as headquarters for the army's elite 2nd Cavalry and was temporarily home to Albert Sydney Johnston and John Bell Hood. The town of Mason grew up in the shadow of the military post. Robert E. Lee served as the fort's commanding officer for a few agonizing weeks in the early part of 1861, just before the nation broke apart.

The county of Mason was organized in 1858. Its population grew slowly during the first years for several reasons, most notably the outbreak of the Civil War in 1861. Another inhibiting factor was Indian raids. Once the Plains Indians discovered there were no military forces in the Hill Country during the war, horse-stealing raids resumed. This situation continued until the mid-1870s, when the U.S. Army returned to Texas.

The end of the Civil War also brought a large influx of newcomers, for Texas had an abundance of land for the taking. Moreover, it had relatively few laws or lawmen. All sorts of people arrived in the Hill Country—merchants, deserters from both armies, farmers, desperados, and carpetbaggers.

The vast supply of cattle provided a great temptation, and rustling became a means of support. As in many frontier communities, mob "justice" was carried out, which in turn led to revenge killings. For three terrible years in the mid-1870s, Mason County was torn apart by a bloody range feud known as the "Hoo Doo War." Based partly in ethnicity, this conflict pitted Germans against Anglos at a time when the raw wounds of the Civil War had not yet healed. The burning of the courthouse in 1877 destroyed most of the evidence.

Once peace finally settled in, Mason County enjoyed its first real progress. With a large number of cattle on hand and a ready market for beef in the northern states, the local cattle industry shifted into high gear. From the late 1860s until the close of the 1880s, over five million head of cattle were sent out of the county, both for consumption and for breeding stock. For decades, Mason County's cattlemen produced some of the nation's finest Hereford (and later Angus) cattle, winning numerous prizes and awards. Sheep, Angora goats, turkeys, and hogs were also raised in large numbers.

Mason County has been afflicted by periods of little or no rainfall, threatening the community's agricultural economy. Severe conditions arose in the 1880s due to the lack of windmills to bring underground water to the surface. Many cattle died during that time. The long drought of 1950–1956 also tested ranchers' stamina and resourcefulness.

Around the same time, a source of deep, abundant groundwater was discovered in the northern part of the county. Fields could be irrigated, and peanut farming rapidly increased. Mason County became one of the state's largest producers of peanuts.

Long before the first permanent settlers arrived, the nomadic Plains Indians were aware of the region's bounty as a wildlife habitat. Through the years, Mason County gained a reputation for excellent deer and turkey hunting. In addition, the pristine Llano River has always attracted fishermen and outdoors enthusiasts.

A Note about the Photographs

The turbulent early episodes of Mason County's past have been lost to visual history, except for a few studio portraits of the individuals involved. The first known picture of the town was taken in 1876 when McArthur Cullen Ragsdale, an itinerant photographer based at Fort Concho, set up his tent just south of where the Fritz Hoerster building now stands. They year 1876 was a significant turning point in Mason County's history. It marked not only the final year of the Hoo Doo War but also the end of three decades of violent conflicts in the region involving Native Americans, settlers, soldiers, Texas Rangers, outlaws, and vigilantes.

By coincidence, the advent of photography in Mason occurred at the beginning of an era when the county's inhabitants could finally stop shooting at their enemies and start enjoying themselves a little. Prosperity was on the rise. Dangers to life and property were quickly receding, as were the most severe hardships of frontier life. Rare photographs from the 1880s and 1890s show picnics on the Llano River and dances at Simonsville.

The first decade of the 20th century yielded many pictures of Mason's businesses and organizations. However, photography did not become a part of everyday family life until around 1912. By then, some individuals in Mason County had purchased Eastman Kodak's inexpensive Brownie cameras; others borrowed cameras from friends and relatives to document an outing to the river or a roundup on their ranch. In some of these early snapshots, "cut-ups" mugged for the camera, struck humorous poses, or even put on clothing of the opposite sex—a far cry from the stone-faced family portraits taken a few years earlier. During the 1920s, "kodaking" became a popular pastime among Mason's younger set.

Most of the photographs in this collection were taken on happy occasions. However, the "good old days," often viewed through the distorting lens of selective memory, were anything but carefree. Many of this county's families had to do without. Illnesses, accidents, and foreign wars claimed many young lives. Businesses went under as times changed. Churches brought people together but also divided them. Mason's schools, restaurants, barbershops, theaters, and cemeteries were segregated, and prejudice was widespread. The smiling faces in these photographs (*how could anyone smile while burning prickly pear?*) are a testament to courage and resilience rather than a reflection of a life of ease.

The Mason County Historical Commission sought out a variety of candid shots and action scenes that were representative of local experiences through the late 1950s. The photographs in each chapter are arranged in roughly chronological order. Some of them are informative; others are purely entertaining; several are surprising. Whatever your connection to Mason County may be, the Mason County Historical Commission wishes you a rewarding journey down memory lane.

One

Around the Square

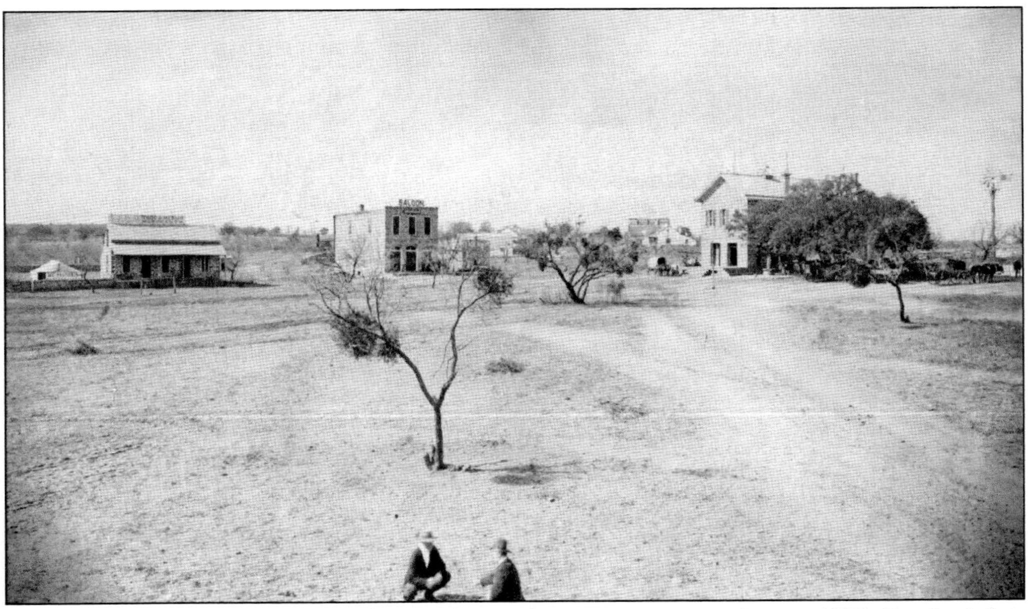

The earliest known photograph of Mason's courthouse square was taken in 1876. On the left is the Todd and Mebus general store, where the Fritz Hoerster building now stands. In the center is Martin Moran's saloon (now the site of the Commercial Bank), and the James Ranck building is on the right. Photographs required a long period of exposure at this time. The donkey beneath the mesquite tree in the background moved while the camera lens was open and appears ghostlike. (Photograph by M. C. Ragsdale; courtesy of MCHC.)

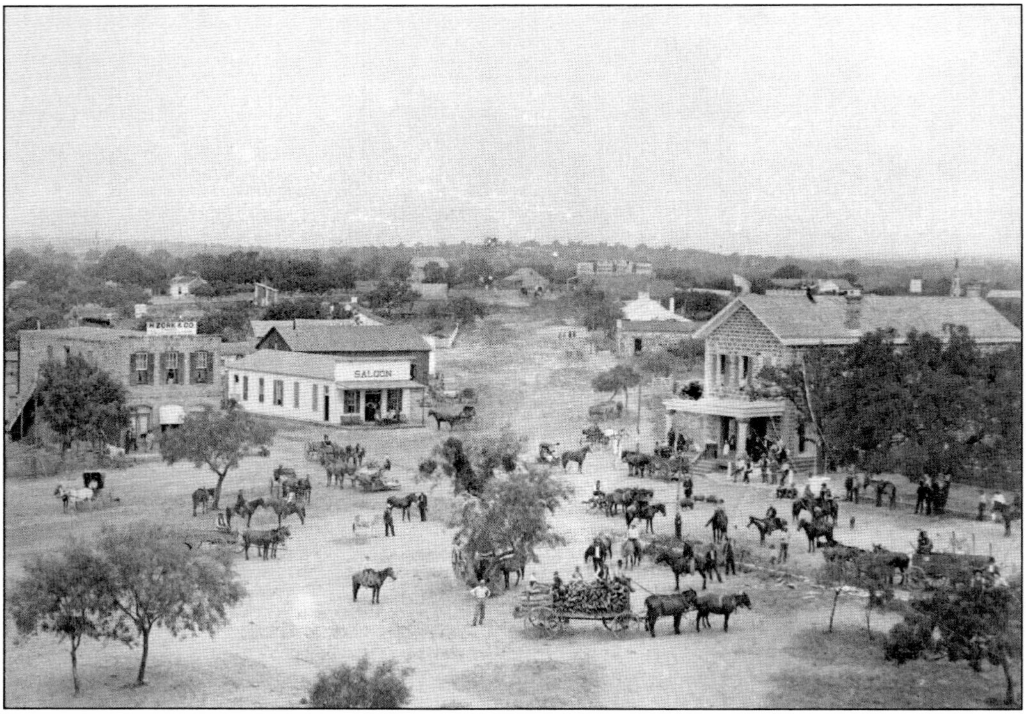

This view of Mason in the late 1880s shows a great increase in activity from the preceding photograph. By then, H. Zork and Company had moved into the Moran building (left). The single-storied saloon to the right of it was owned by Martin Moran and Theo Schmidt, and Harry Bierschwale's tin shop is visible behind it. James Ranck had added a porch to his building (right) and can be seen herding hogs on the street in front. (Courtesy of the Mason County Museum.)

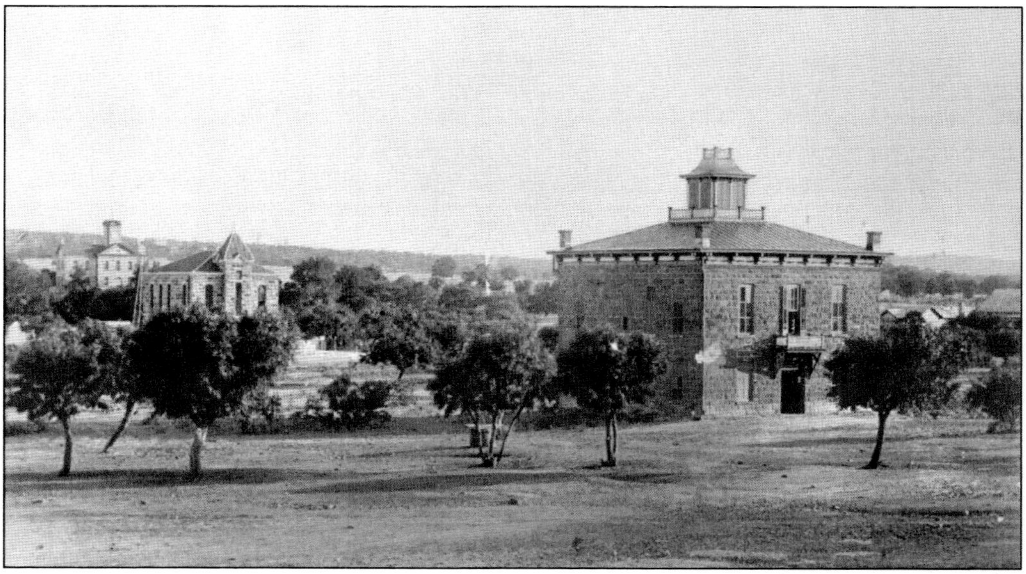

The second Mason County Courthouse (right) is pictured in 1894, while the jail (left) was still under construction. This courthouse, completed in 1878, replaced the one that burned in 1877. It was demolished and replaced in 1909 due to lack of space. Note the cupola on the school building (left background), which was later removed because of wind damage. (Courtesy of MCHC.)

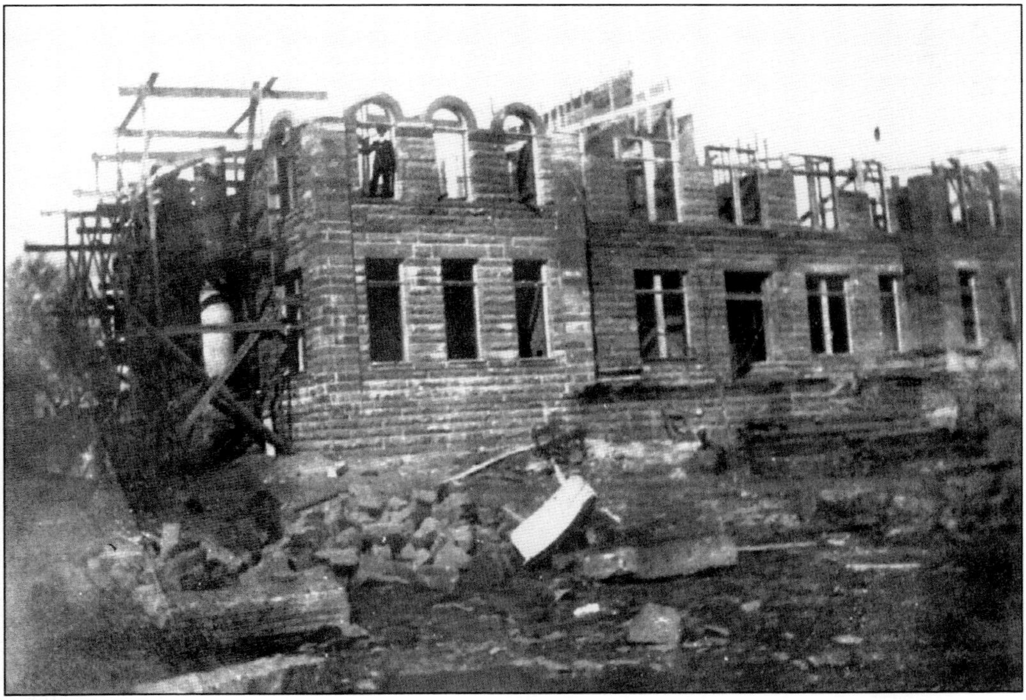

The construction of the third (and present) Mason County Courthouse began in 1909, and the building was completed in 1910 at a cost of $39,786. The above photograph shows the eastern side of the building before the pillars, steps, and porch were in place. The man seen in the second-floor window on the left may be the architect on an inspection trip from Dallas. The bottom photograph, taken at the same time, shows the construction crew on the south side. (Courtesy of Doug and Sherry Willmann.)

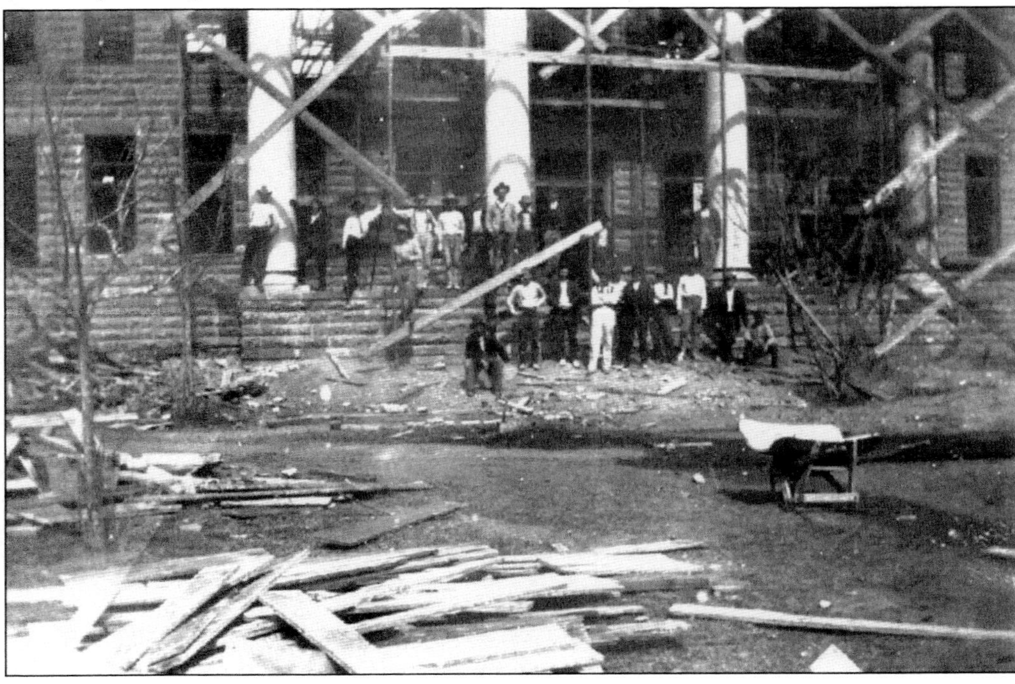

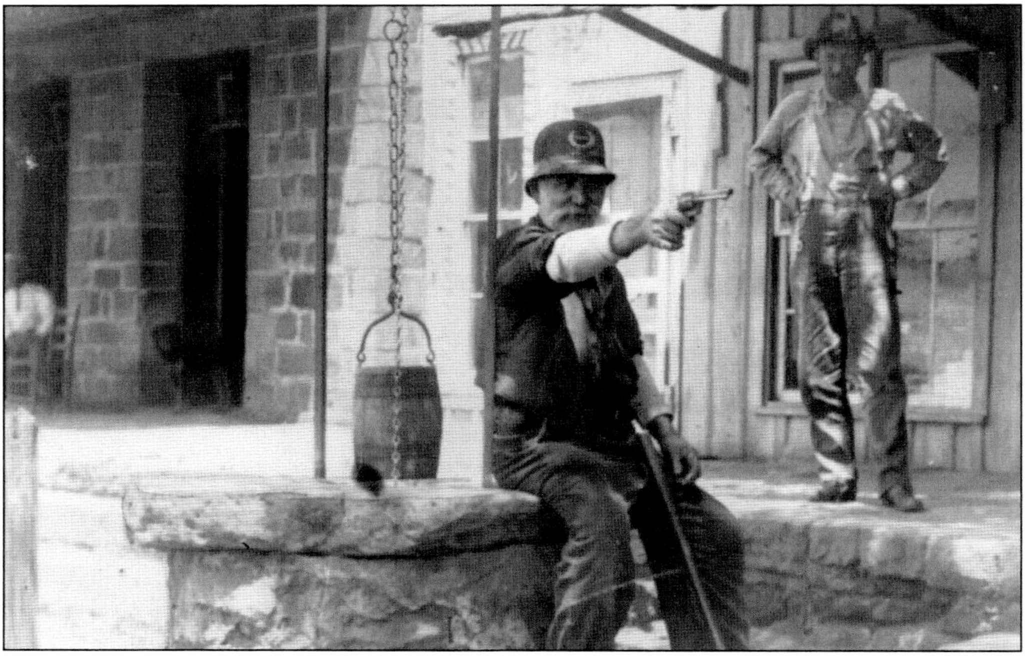

Charles Wartenbach (center) was an early lawman and Mason constable from 1892 until 1913. He shows off his Colt Single Action Army revolver to Charlie Hofmann (right), a painter and the "best and fastest" wallpaper hanger in Mason. Seated far left is Will Graff in front of the Graff Saloon on the north side of the square. (Courtesy of the Mason County Museum.)

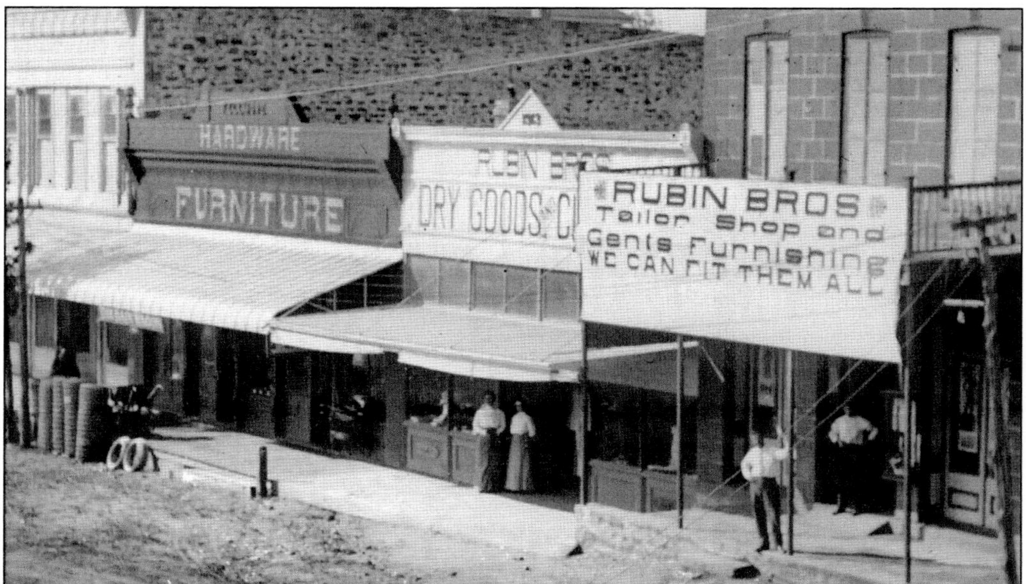

The west side of the square is shown in the mid-1910s. On the right is the Zork building (site of the present-day Commercial Bank). It was used as a tailor shop by Rubin Brothers, who also operated a dry goods store in the building next door, constructed in 1913. Their shop was adjacent to a hardware and equipment business that H. C. Fellmore started in the 1890s and W. H. Larimore and Charles Grote purchased in 1914. The building on the far left was erected by Fritz Hoerster in 1906. (Courtesy of Bobbie Baze.)

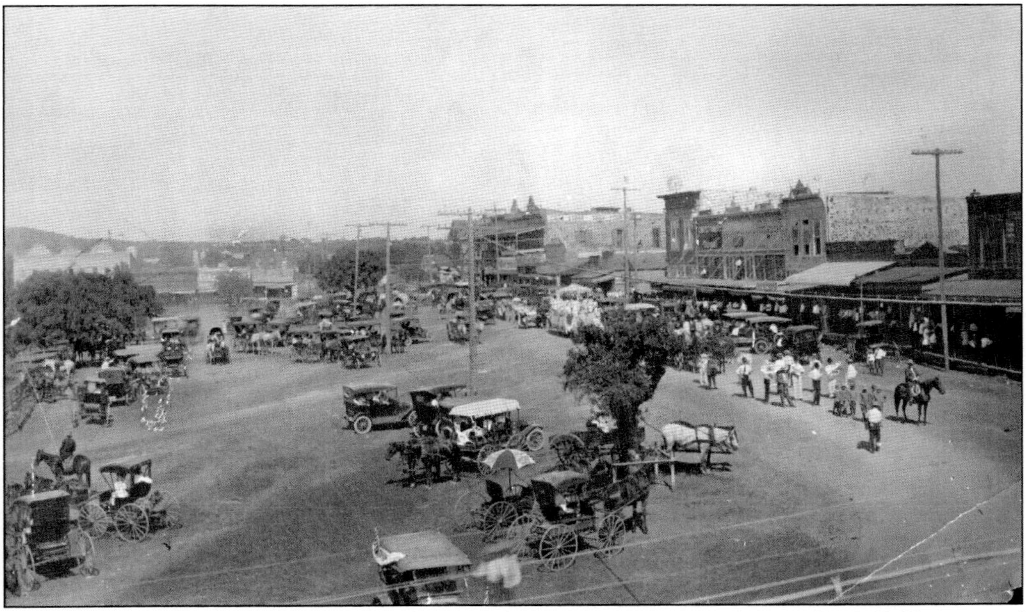

This Confederate's Day parade took place on the Mason square on August 5, 1915. Veterans of the Confederate Army and their families gathered at these annual reunions, which drew more than 10,000 people. Note the presence of electric lines and automobiles in the above photograph, although most people still used buggies. In the bottom photograph, Estella Hofmann (McDougall) (left) and Mary Lemburg (Doell) wear dresses of pink cheesecloth as they ride in the parade. The buggy, festooned with pink crepe paper, belonged to county judge Glen Smith, and the horse was Lee Eckert's. The girls were awarded first prize, a $5 gold piece. (Above photograph courtesy of the Mason County Museum; bottom photograph courtesy of June Brandenberger.)

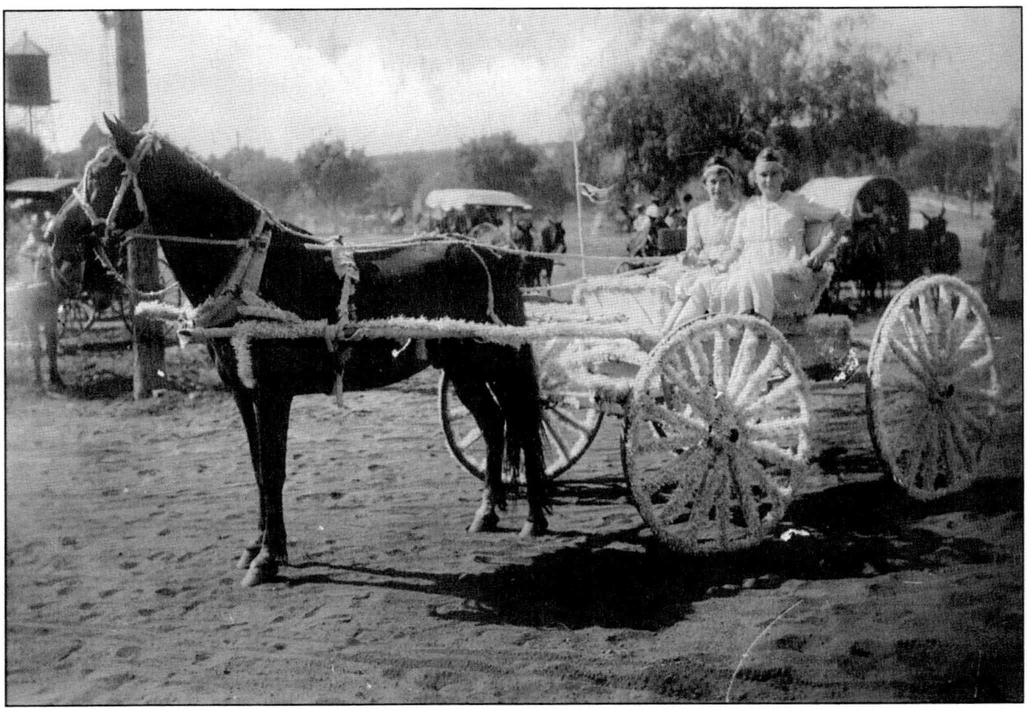

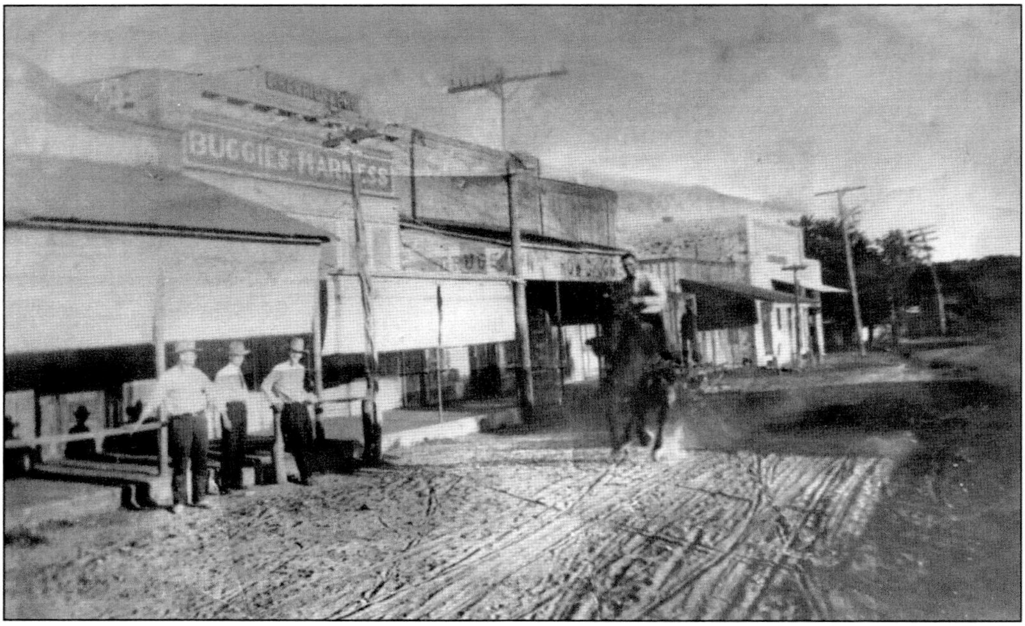

From left to right, Ed Henrich, Walter Henrich, and Ernest Henrich watch Ben King ride a horse along the east side of the square in 1916. The men are standing in front of the Henrich saddle shop. Ed established the business in 1894 and moved it to this location, known as the C&G building, in 1906. (Courtesy of Patsy Zesch.)

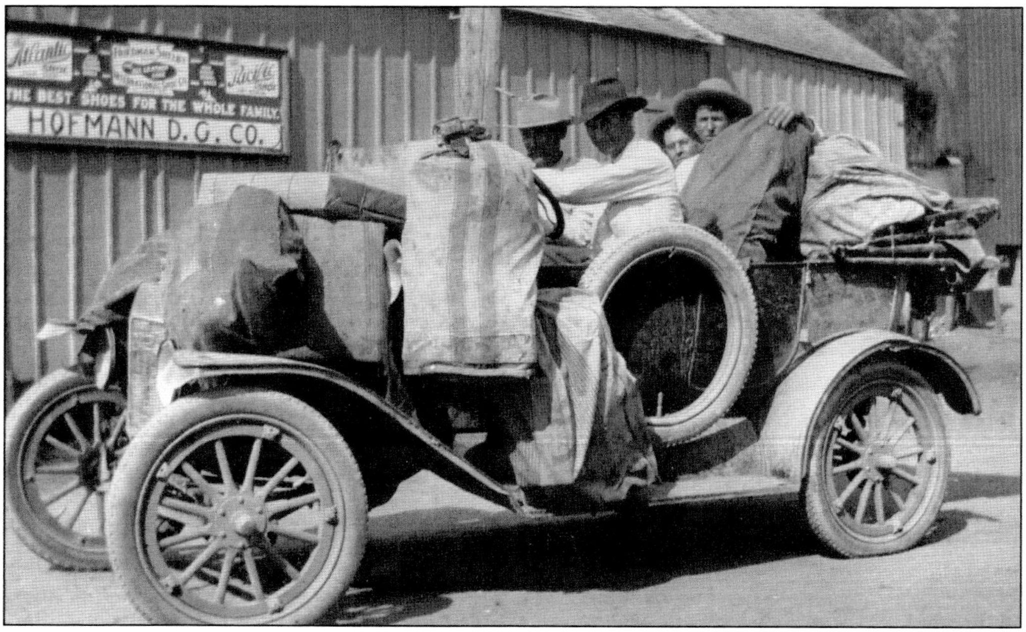

The mail car, loaded with passengers, mail sacks, and packages, pauses at the corner of Broad and Fort McKavitt Streets prior to 1918. The driver is Charlie Hofmann; William Willmann sits to his right. The sign advertising Hofmann's was on the east side of Leo Zesch's meat market. Mail arrived daily from the railroad terminal in Llano, originally by horse-drawn hacks and stagecoaches and later by automobile. Passengers commonly hitched a ride to some point on the mail car's route. (Courtesy of Wilburn Shearer.)

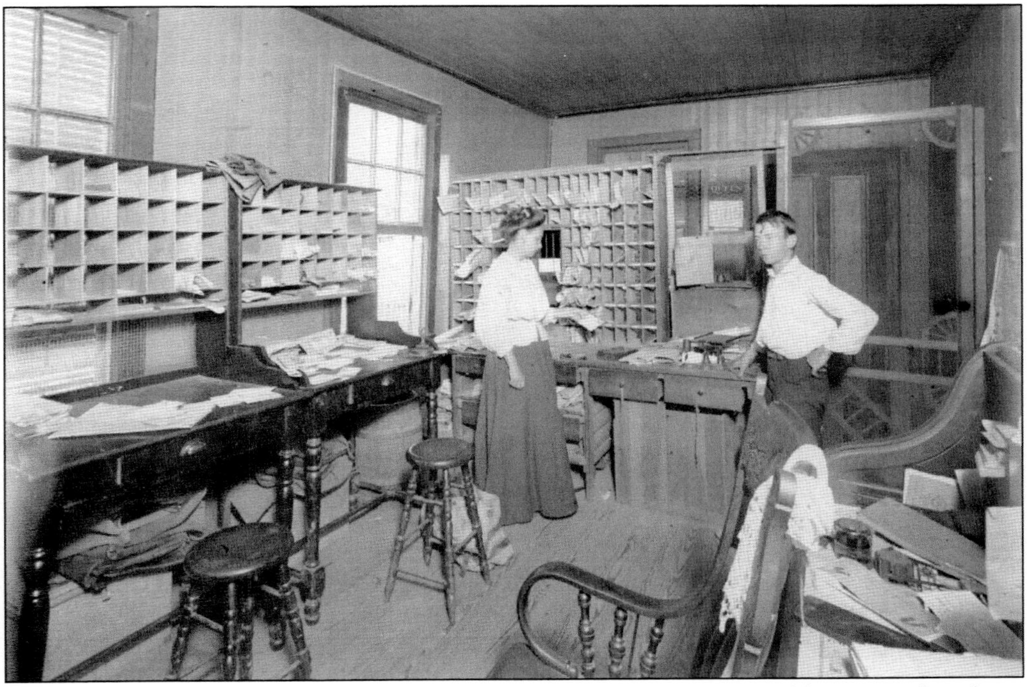

The woman on the left is postmistress Mary Virginia "Jennie" Reynolds, pictured with an unidentified assistant in June 1918. At that time, Mason's post office was located on Broad Street behind the Seaquist building. (Courtesy of MCHC.)

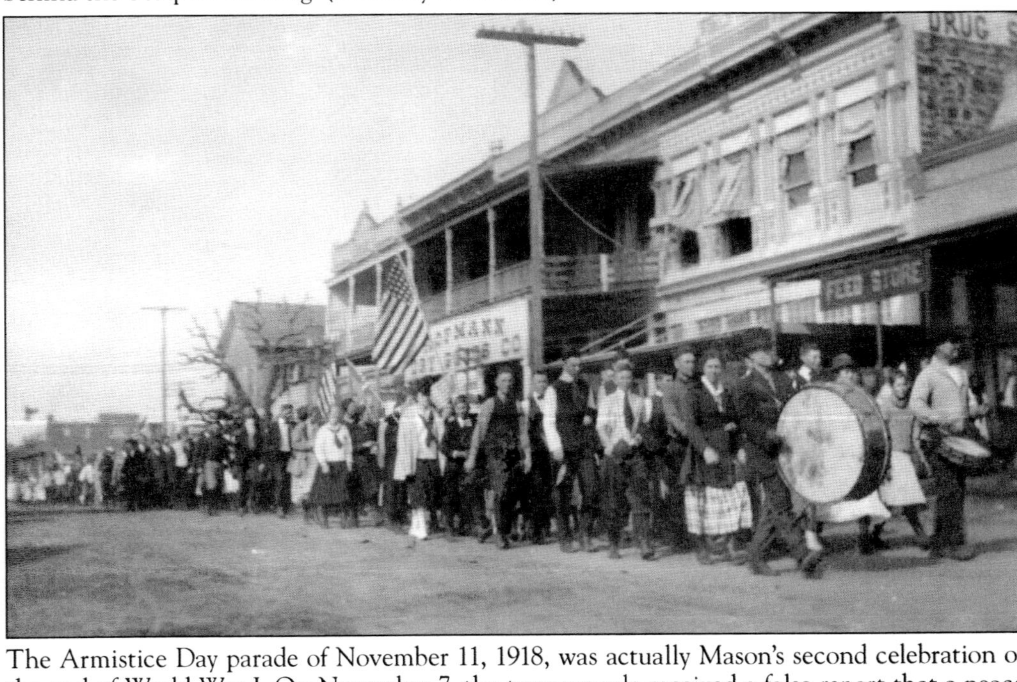

The Armistice Day parade of November 11, 1918, was actually Mason's second celebration of the end of World War I. On November 7, the townspeople received a false report that a peace agreement had been concluded and gathered in the streets to cheer and march with the flag hoisted high. They repeated the festivities four days later when official word reached town, setting off dynamite and firing guns until late into the night. (Courtesy of the Ischar family.)

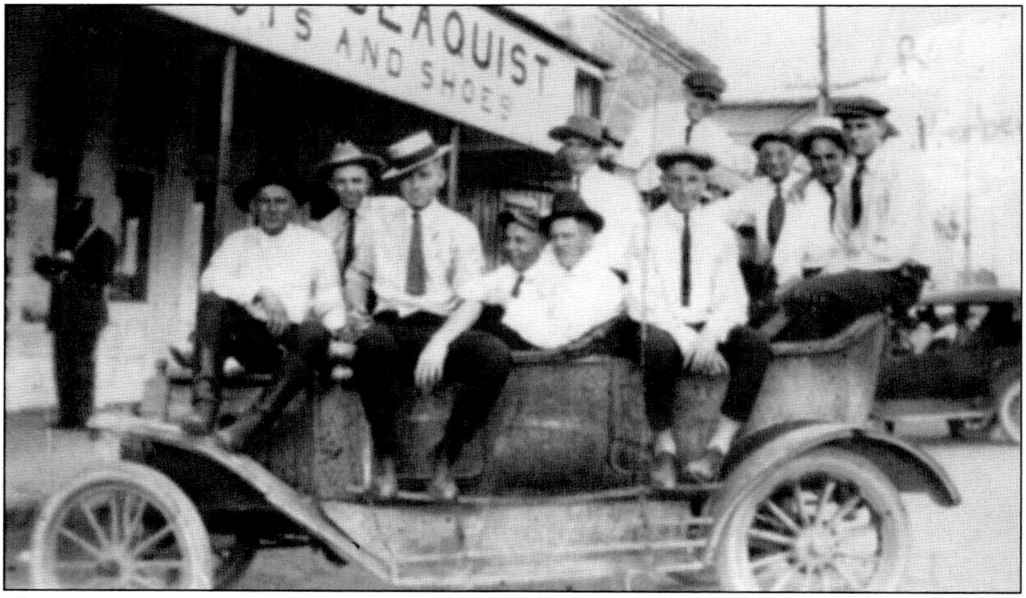

The 11 gentlemen captured in this early 1920s photograph may or may not have been customers of Oscar Seaquist, but it was said that "everybody who was anybody in Mason County" wore boots that he made to order. At that time, the boot shop was located on the northwest block of the square. Identified are Melchior "Mike" Beyer (second from the left), Herbert Splittgerber (far right), Roy Doell (third from the right), and Allan Doell (standing in the back). (Courtesy of Marilyn Mahon.)

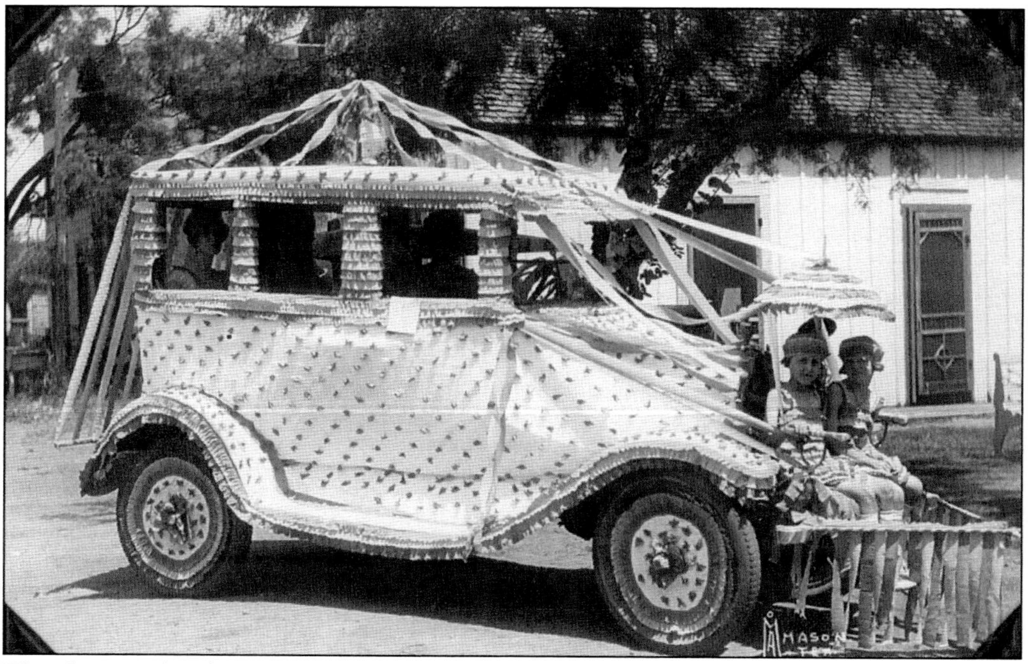

This photograph, taken on July 4, 1924, shows the winner in the parade category of "most artistically decorated car." Sitting on the front are Margaret Martin (Mueller) (left) and an unidentified girl. Ella Bierschwale Martin, Margaret's mother, is driving the car, and Elizabeth "Lizzie" Bierschwale Hensch, Margaret's aunt, can be seen sitting in the back seat. (Courtesy of Steven B. Kensing.)

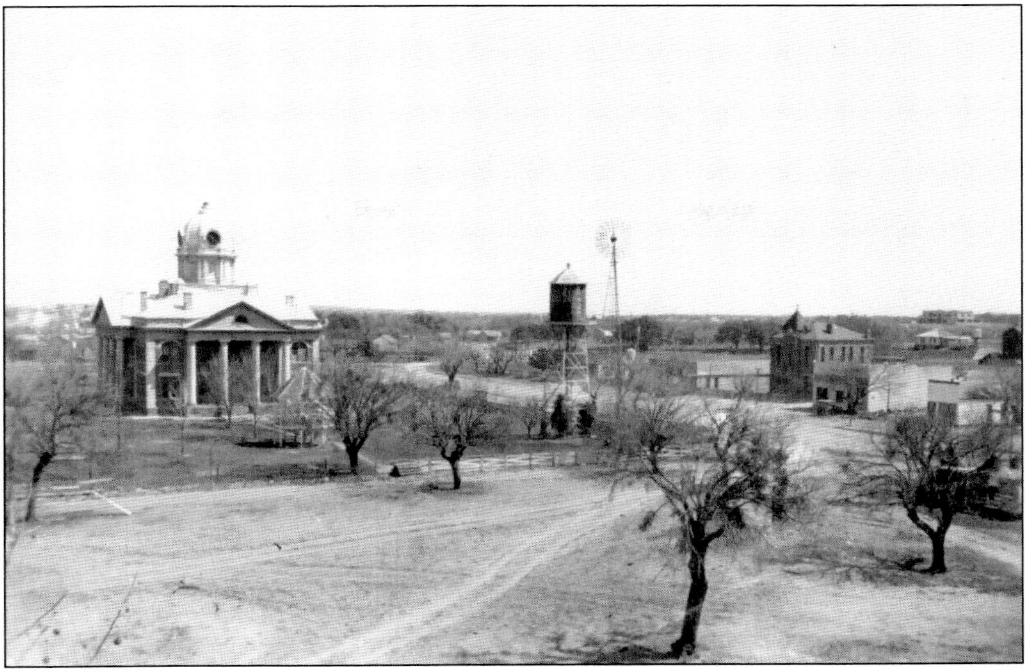

The west side of Mason's courthouse is shown in the mid-1920s, prior to the construction of the stone wall around the lawn in 1927–1928. Note the wood steps over the wire fence at the walkway. The well, windmill, and water tank were installed in 1910. (Courtesy of Wilburn Shearer.)

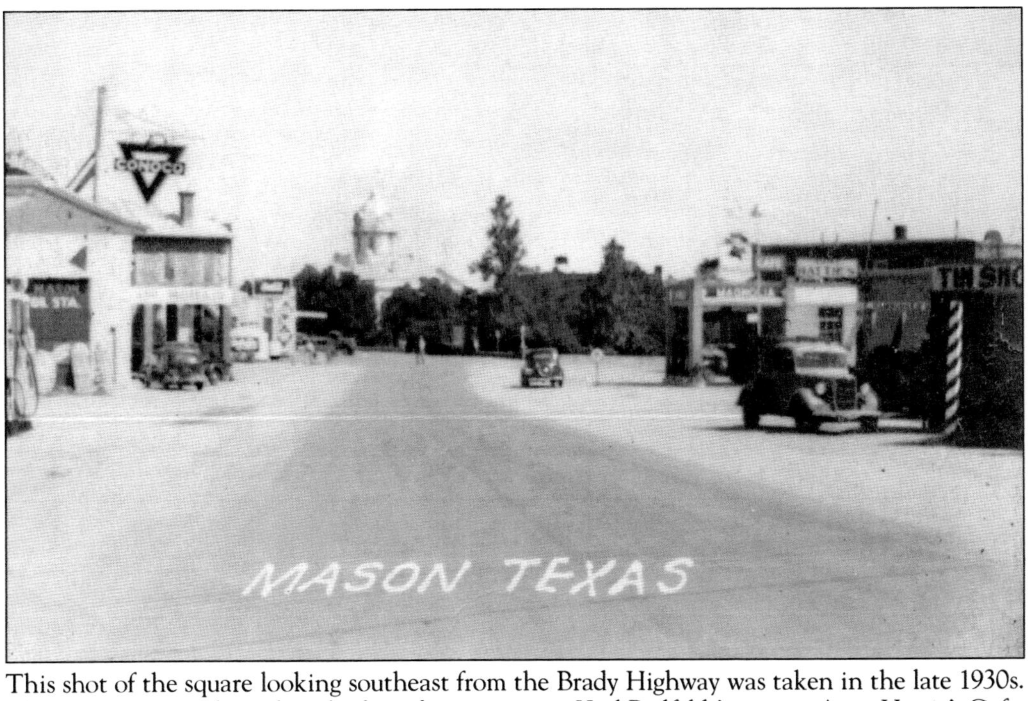

This shot of the square looking southeast from the Brady Highway was taken in the late 1930s. The businesses on the right side, from far to near, are Karl Bielfeldt's garage, Aunt Hattie's Cafe, and F. Lange's tin shop. On the left, Ray Walker's wool and mohair warehouse is visible behind the Conoco station. (Courtesy of Geneva Keller.)

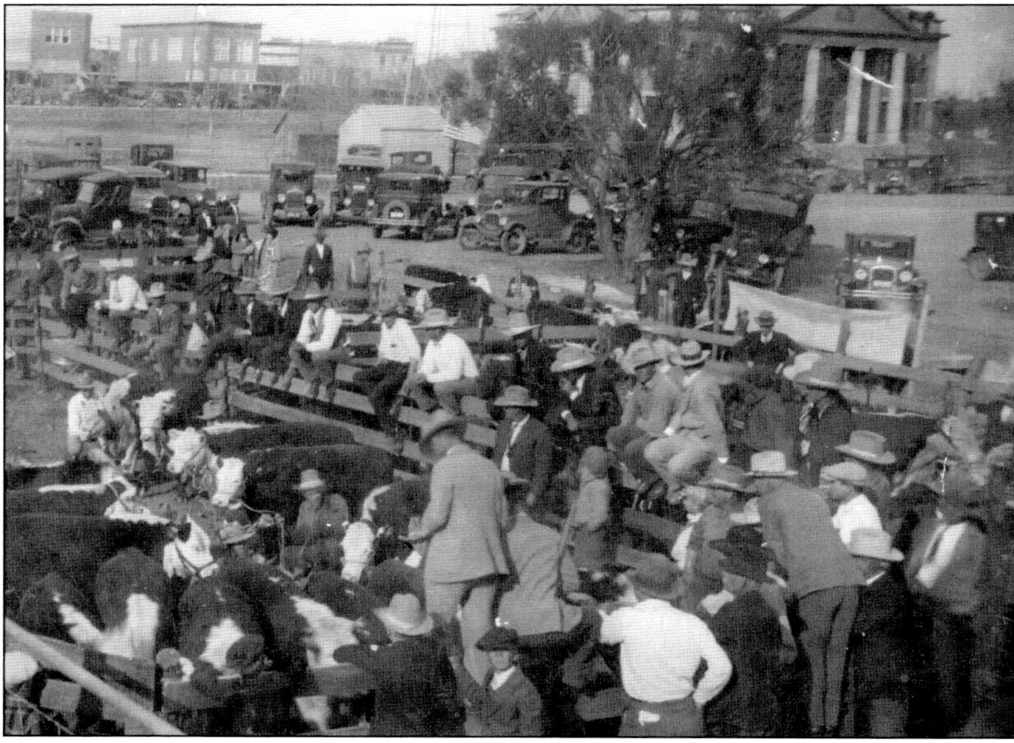

Mason County's livestock shows were held on the west side of the courthouse square in the 1920s and early 1930s, before the street was paved. Note how many of the men are well dressed in the above photograph. In the bottom photograph, Henry Hoerster Jr. shows Sam Hoerster's calf in 1929. (Above photograph courtesy of the Mason County Museum; bottom photograph courtesy of Sam and Maribelle Hoerster.)

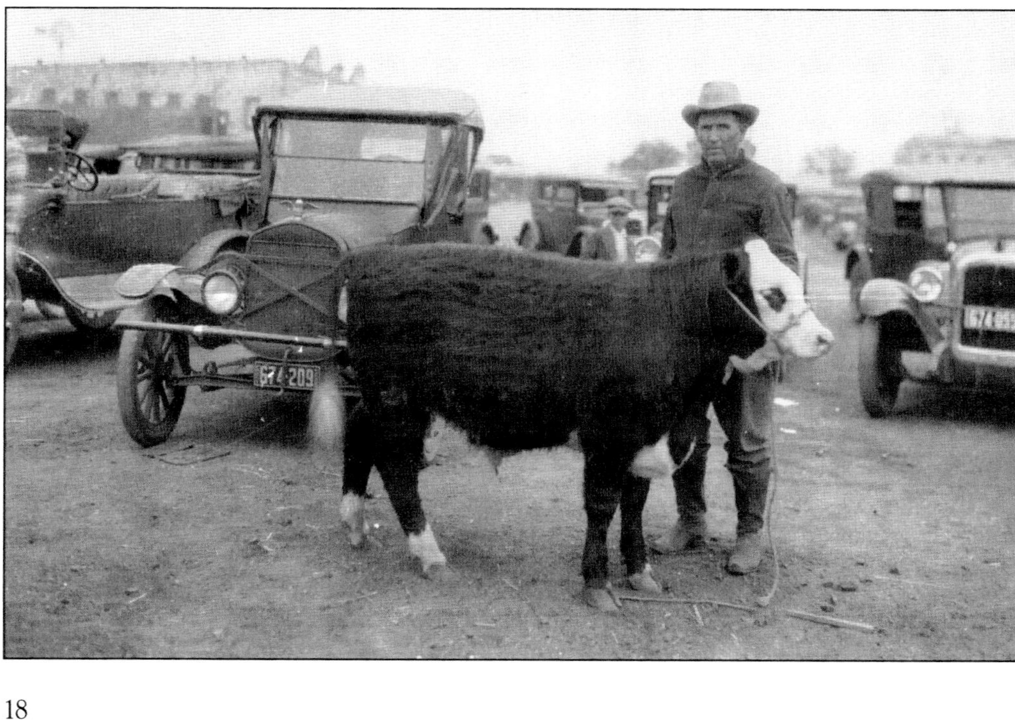

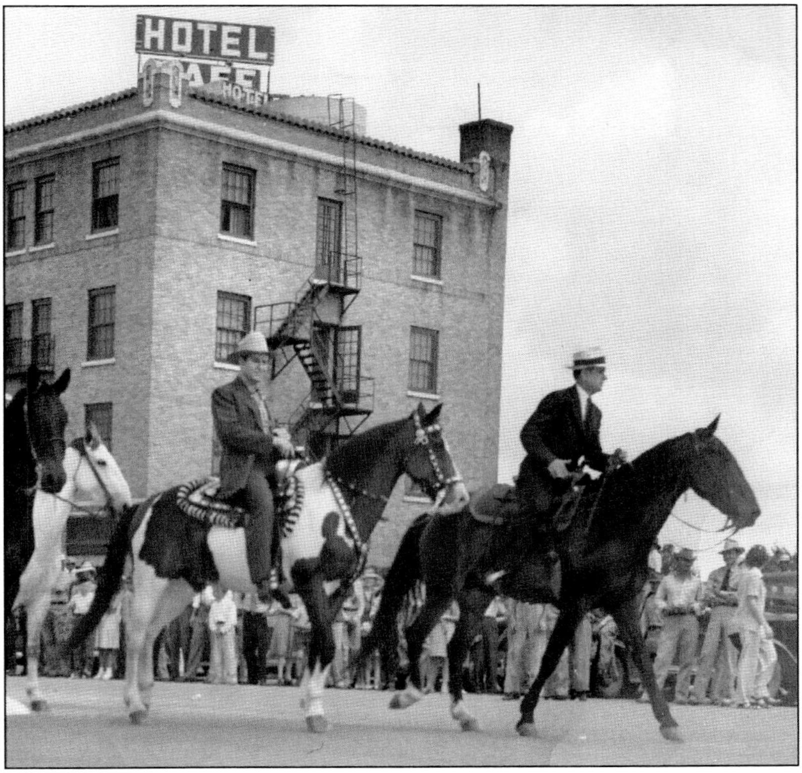

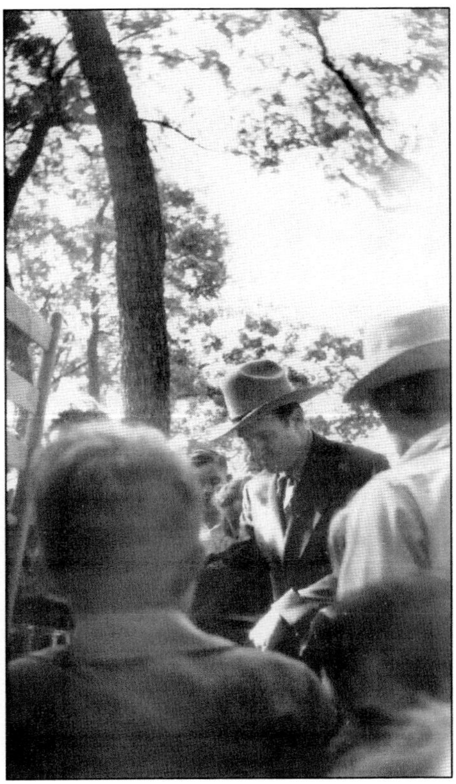

Gene Autry, the "Singing Cowboy" (left in the above photograph), rode Champion in a parade held in his honor on May 29, 1942. Autry came to Mason as the guest of W. A. Lee, who had recently assumed operation of the Fort Mason Hotel. Autry and Judge James Allred (right in the above photograph), a former Texas governor, led the parade that ended at the fairgrounds, where Autry gave an "impressive" talk (according to the *Mason County News*), sang several songs, ate barbecue, and visited with some of the estimated 6,000 to 7,000 fans present (left photograph). He then left for Austin to fly to Los Angeles to appear on his regular Sunday evening radio program. Accompanying Autry were 100 members of the Houston Good Will Boosters, who remained in Mason for the weekend and were treated to a squirrel dinner on Saturday and a fish fry on Sunday. (Above photograph courtesy of Peggy Laverty; left photograph courtesy of Linda Owen.)

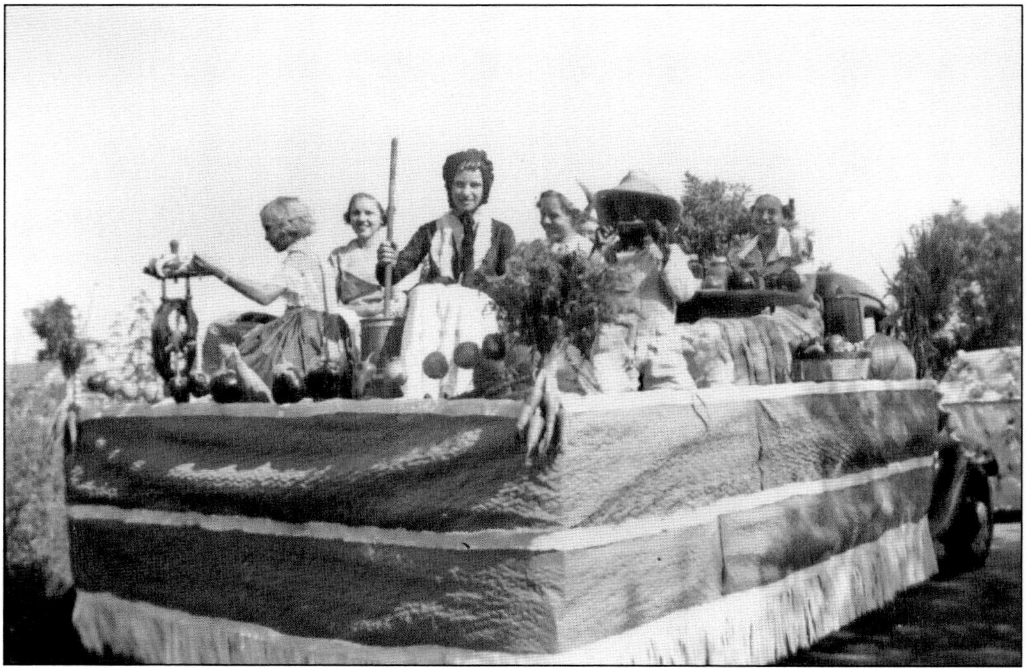

The Hilda community's 4-H float in the Mason rodeo parade, circa 1940, depicted their pioneer ancestors' way of life. Odessa Eckert (Kimbriel) is at the spinning wheel, and Myrtle Eckert (Geistweidt) is at the butter churn. (Courtesy of Kathryn Martin.)

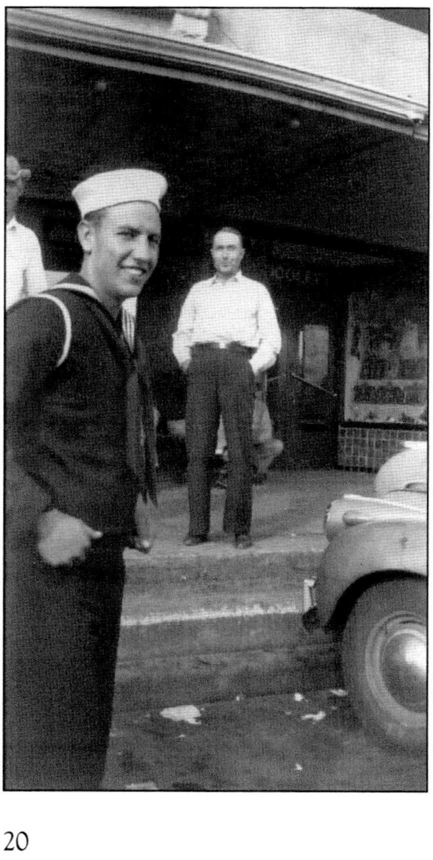

Travis Hofmann (left foreground) and Toddy Simpson, a barber in the Brown Barber Shop, are standing in front of Dooley's Variety Store on the northwest block of the square in 1944. Hoffman is waiting for a bus after being home on leave. He joined the U.S. Navy on September 28, 1943, and served in the Pacific. Mason County sent 598 of its citizens to serve in World War II, and 15 did not return. (Courtesy of Florene Hofmann.)

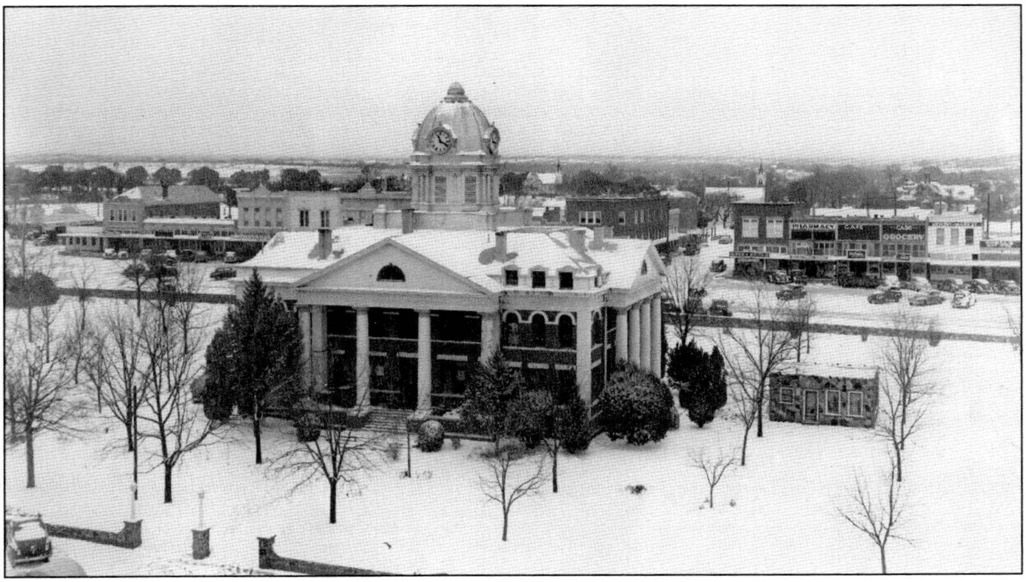

The snow that started falling on December 31, 1946, was the heaviest in many years, and an ice storm covered the area a few days later. This photograph, taken from the rooftop of the Fort Mason Hotel in early January 1947, shows the north side of the square much as it is today, with one exception: vehicles were allowed to park in the middle of Fort McKavitt Street. (Courtesy of Florene Hofmann.)

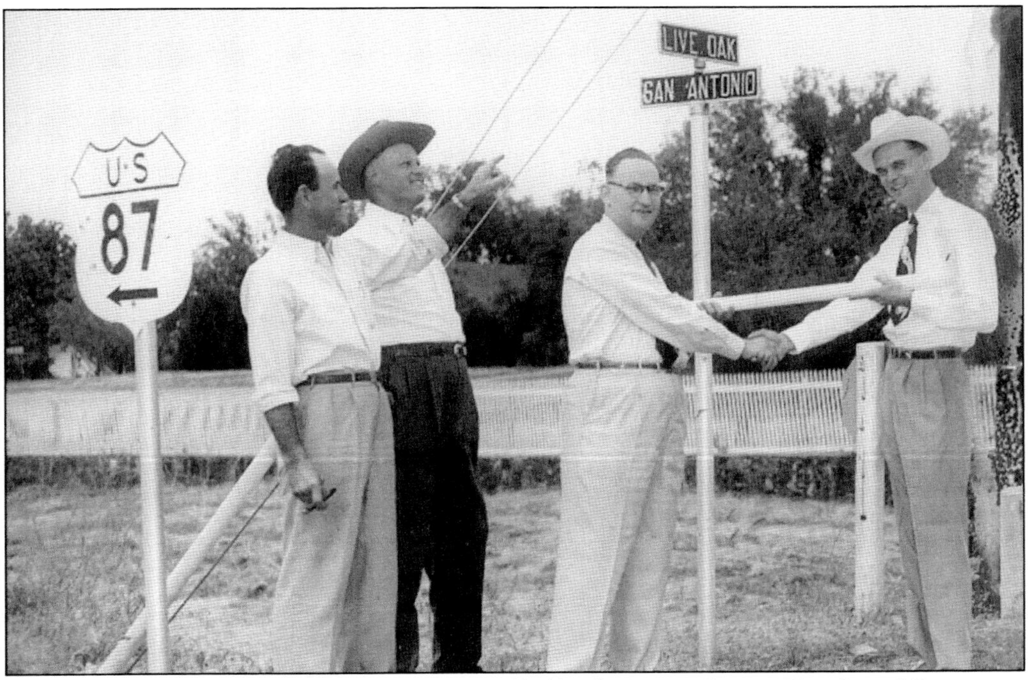

The first 500 street markers in Mason were installed by the Mason Junior Chamber of Commerce in the early 1950s, financed by voluntary contributions. From left to right, Ossie Chew, who initiated the program, and Bill Jordan, who had recently completed his term as Jaycee president, watch as Mason mayor Ray Hudson receives a map of the city from Jack Lee, the new Jaycee president. (Photograph by Clayton Schmidt; courtesy of Harold Hudson.)

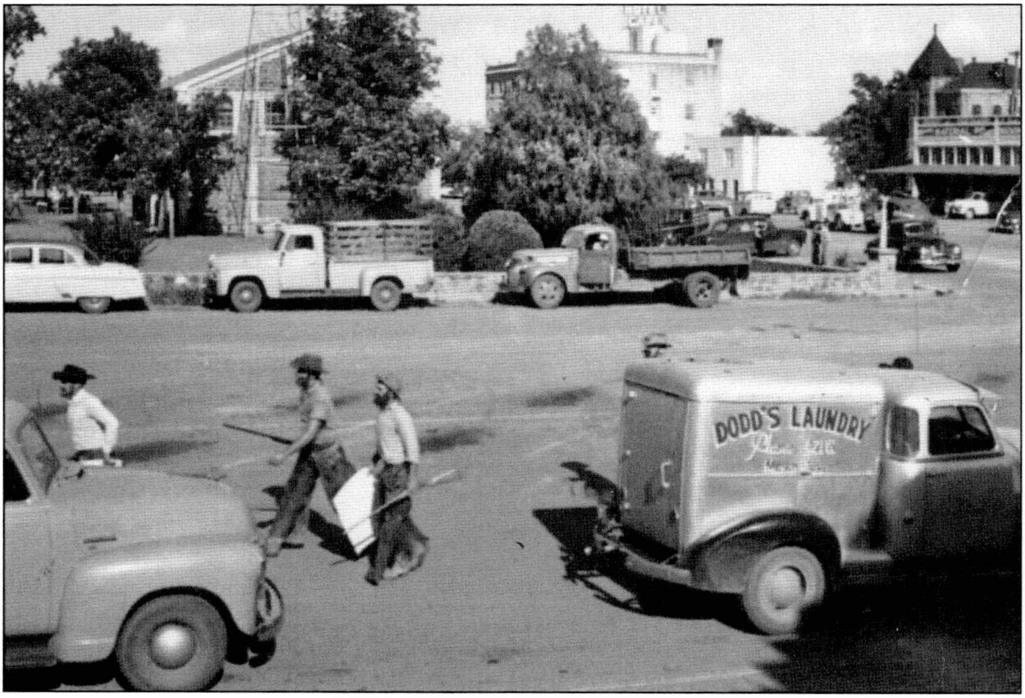

From left to right, Douglas Owen, George Keller, and Gene Zesch are dressed as outlaws, complete with rifles and fake beards, for a 1954 parade. Their gang circled the square in a Ford Model T. The delivery truck in the foreground belonged to Dodd's Laundry, which was located at the corner of Bryant and Pecan Streets near the Boy Scout hut. (Courtesy of Peggy Laverty.)

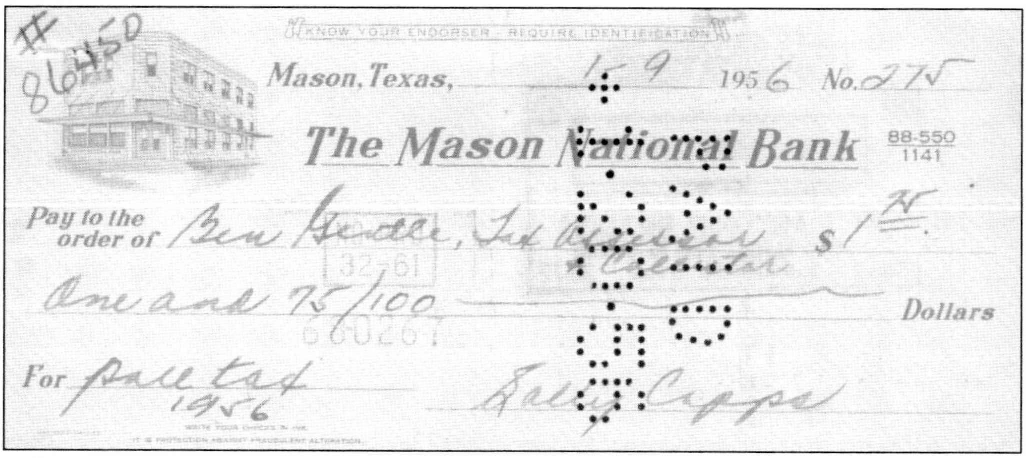
KNOW YOUR ENDORSER - REQUIRE IDENTIFICATION

Mason, Texas, 1-9 1956 No. 275

The Mason National Bank 88-550 / 1141

Pay to the order of Ben Hodge, Tax Assessor & Collector $1 75/

One and 75/100 Dollars

For Poll tax 1956 Sally Capps

Sally Capps saved this check dated January 9, 1956, because she believes it was the last time she paid poll tax. In 1964, the 24th Amendment to the U.S. Constitution barred the poll tax in federal elections. The U.S. Supreme Court finally abolished it as a qualification for voting in any election in 1966. (Courtesy of Sally Capps.)

Mason author Fred Gipson's *Old Yeller* (1956) became an icon of American popular culture and sold more copies than any other book written by a Texan. The 1957 film adaptation also became one of Walt Disney's highest-grossing successes. In 1963, Disney's film version of the sequel, *Savage Sam*, premiered at Mason's Odeon Theater. Born in Mason County in 1908, Gipson heard firsthand the tales of old-timers who had lived through Mason's frontier days in the 1860s. At right, Gipson is pictured with a canine friend. The bottom photograph, taken during the centennial parade in 1958, features the main characters in Gipson's most famous story. From left to right are Ronnie Johnson as "Travis," Patsy Zesch as "Mama," Jerry Kothmann's yellow Labrador, Sala, as "Old Yeller," and unidentified "Little Arliss." (Right photograph courtesy of the M. Beven Eckert Memorial Library; bottom photograph courtesy of Patsy Zesch.)

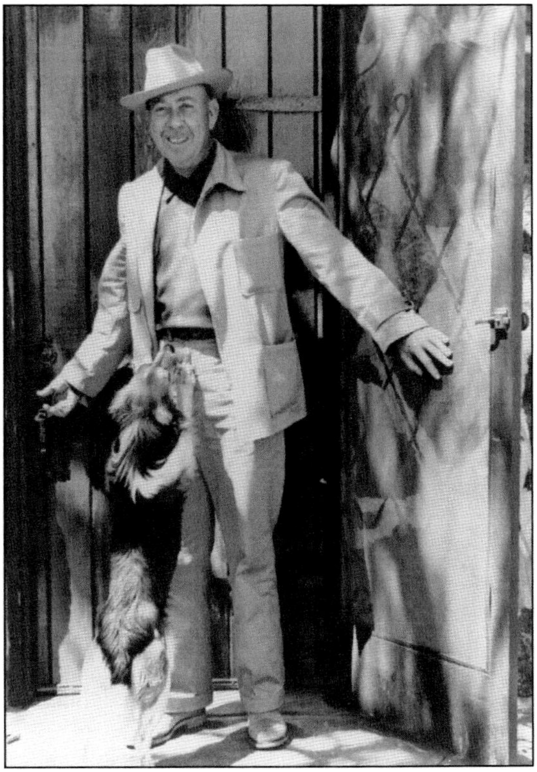

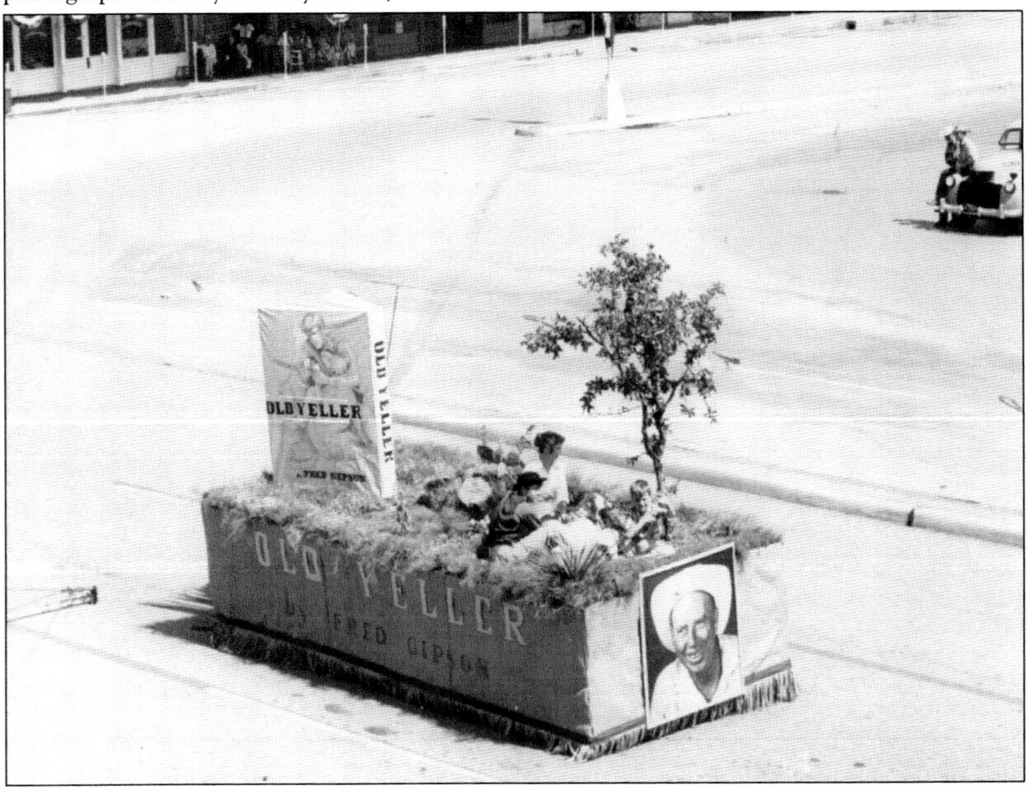

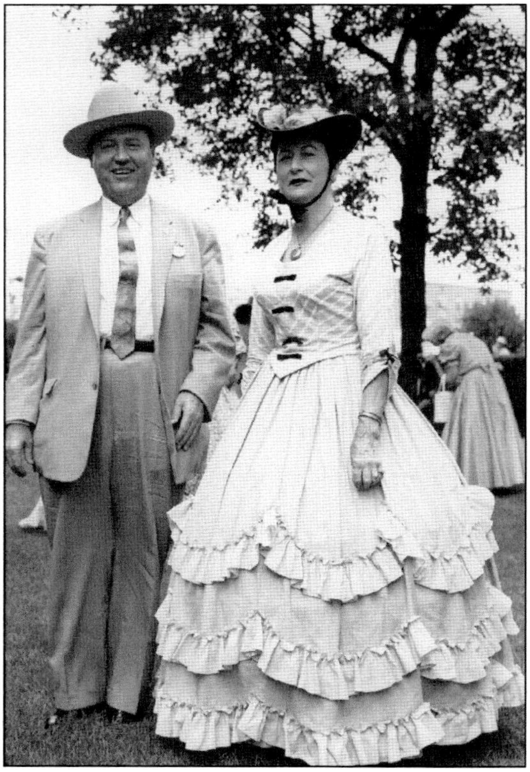

At left, U.S. senator Ralph Yarborough is pictured with Jessie Gamel Lindsay at Mason's centennial celebration in 1958. The senator spoke on the courthouse lawn on June 21, 1958, introduced by Congressman O. C. Fisher. A pageant at the fairgrounds featured a cast of over 300 actors and 50 head of livestock. About 8,000 people attended the festivities. The people of Mason County went all out for the centennial. Men grew beards and mutton chops, and women donned bonnets and long dresses. In the bottom photograph, Kenneth Loeffler (left) and Ron Birk compare the status of their centennial beards. (Left photograph courtesy of MCHC; bottom photograph courtesy of Carolyn Loeffler.)

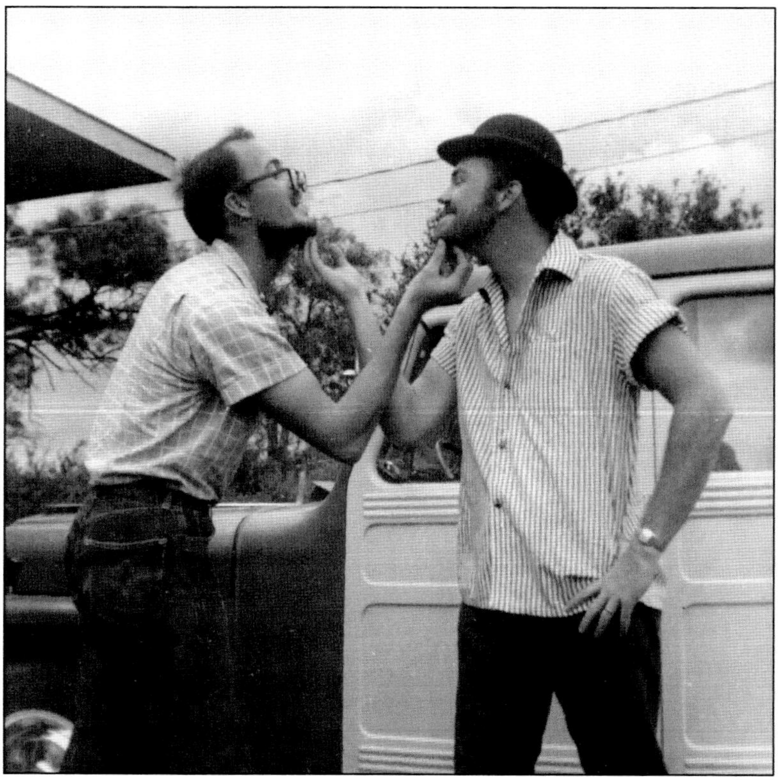

Two

BUSINESSES

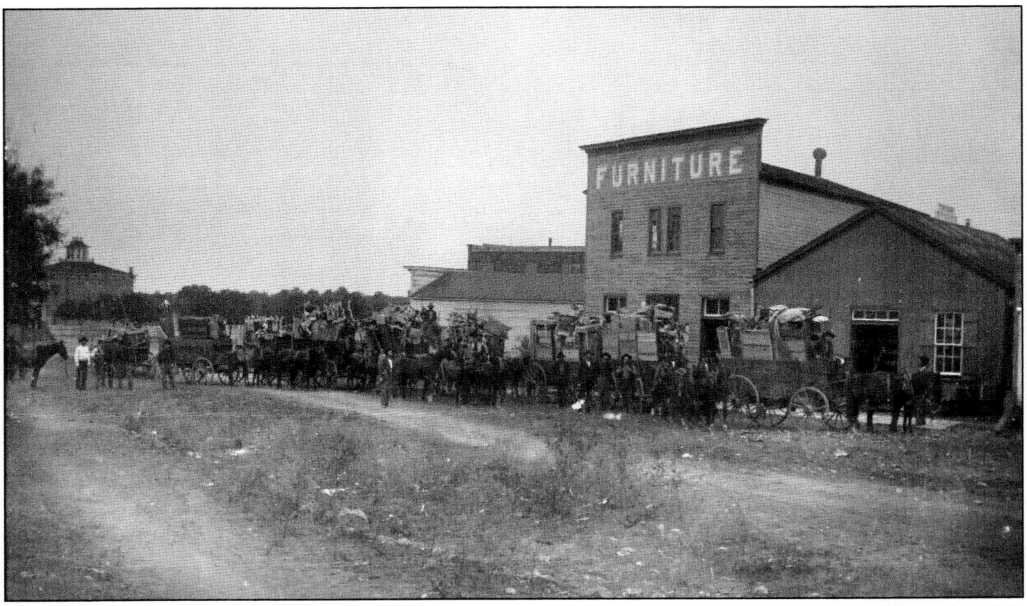

This 1897 photograph shows a large wagon train of furniture in front of Harry Bierschwale's furniture store. The low, light-colored building to the left was a saloon (now the site of Nu-Way Grocery), and the taller rock building behind it was the Zork building (present-day Commercial Bank). The second Mason County Courthouse can be seen in the left background. In the early 1900s, Harry Bierschwale organized Mason's first fire department, and the firemen traveled to fires in his delivery truck. (Courtesy of MCHC.)

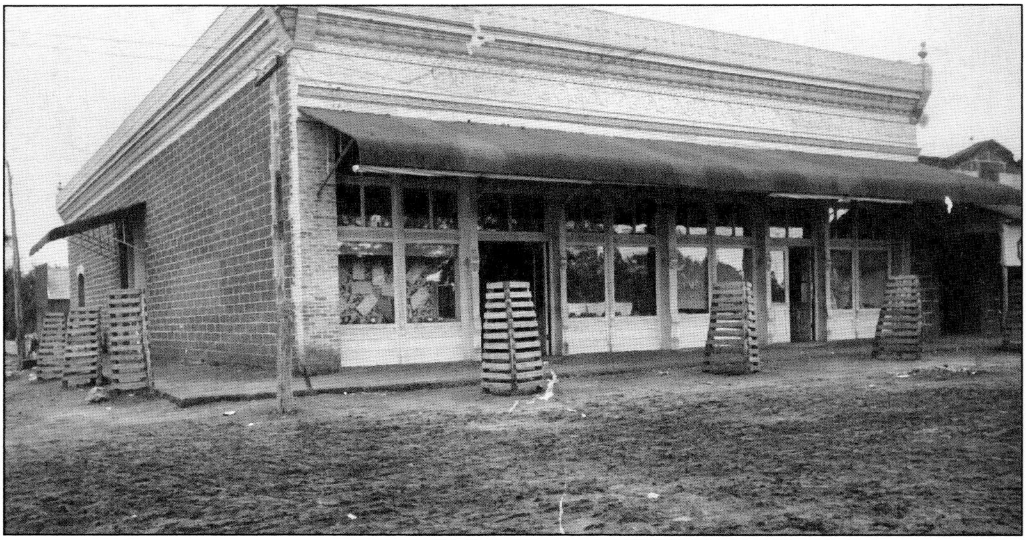

The above photograph shows Ernest J. Lemburg's store on the northeast corner of the square after the concrete sidewalk was poured in 1923. Ernest clerked in a grocery store for over eight years until 1893, when he went into the mercantile business with Benno Schmidt. He and his brother John formed the E. Lemburg and Brother Dry Goods and Grocery in 1895, with Ernest handling the general merchandise and John the groceries. The bottom photograph shows Ernest (left) with his store clerks (from left to right) John Moneyhon, Ernest Willmann, and Kate Hey around 1900, modeling the latest floppy sombrero headwear. "Mr. Ernest," as he was called, operated his dry goods store until his death in 1961. (Above photograph courtesy of Charles Banta; bottom photograph courtesy of the Mason County Museum.)

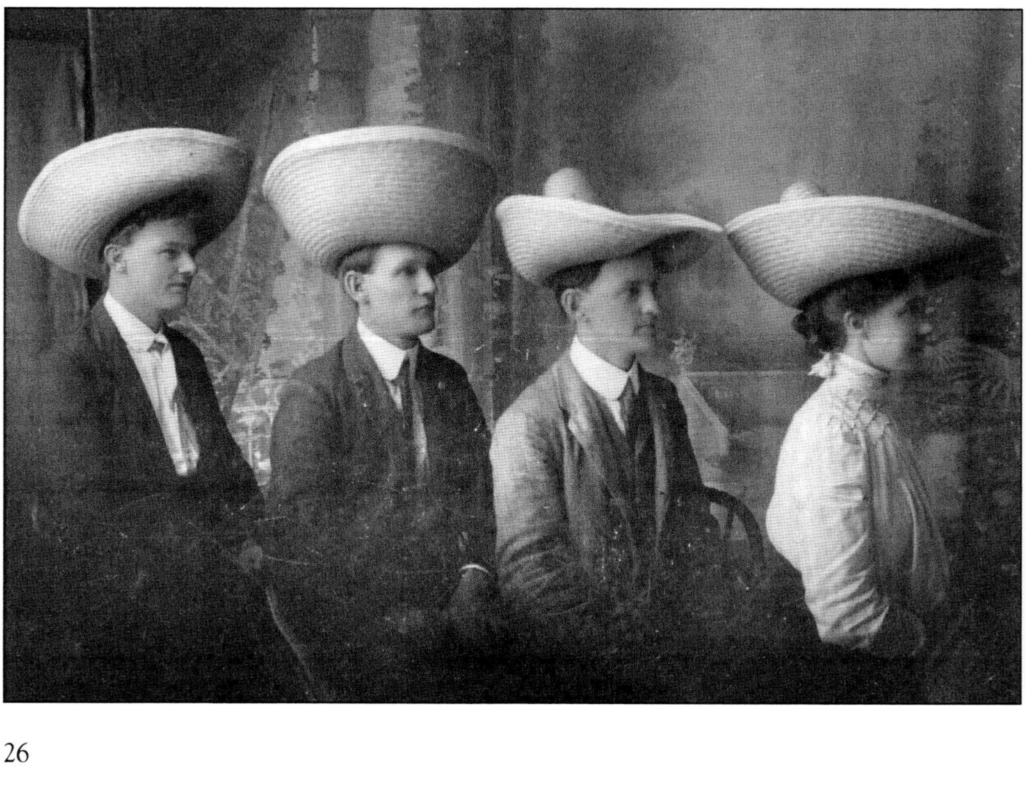

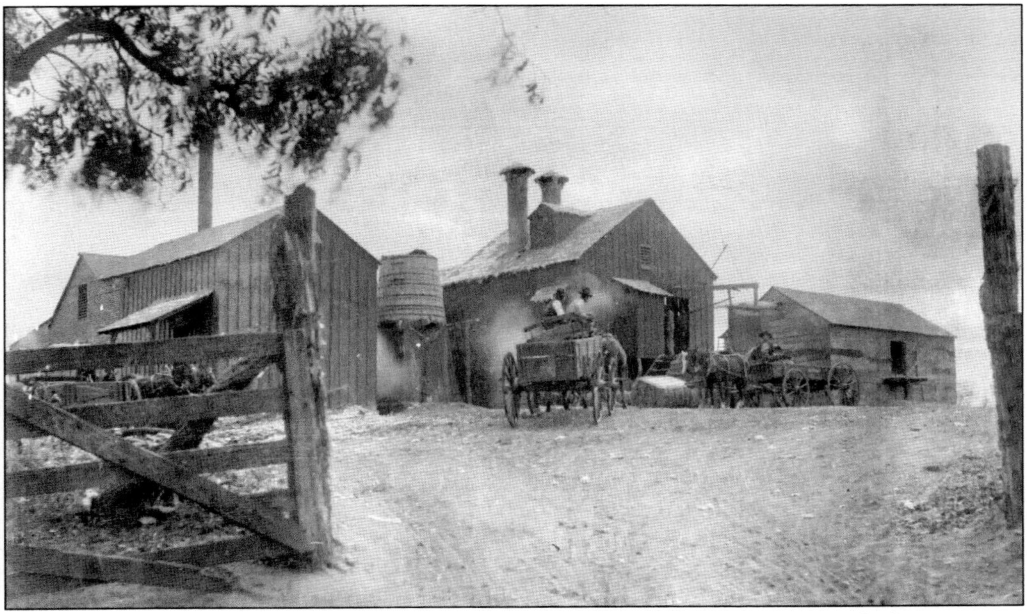

Around 1900, Will Ellebracht opened this cotton gin and seed house on the site of a former steam mill, located diagonally across Post Hill Street from the present-day library. The above photograph, taken in 1905, shows the gristmill on the left, the rear of the cotton gin in the middle, and the seed house on the right. The business was sold in 1915 to Fred C. Beyer, shown wearing overalls and standing on the far left in the bottom photograph. Mason County produced over 5,000 bales of cotton in 1914, and a large number of its African American men worked in the cotton industry. The site of the gin was later occupied by the Mason Power and Light Company and then by an icehouse and meatpacking plant. (Above photograph courtesy of MCHC; bottom photograph courtesy of Gene and Patsy Zesch and Spider Johnson.)

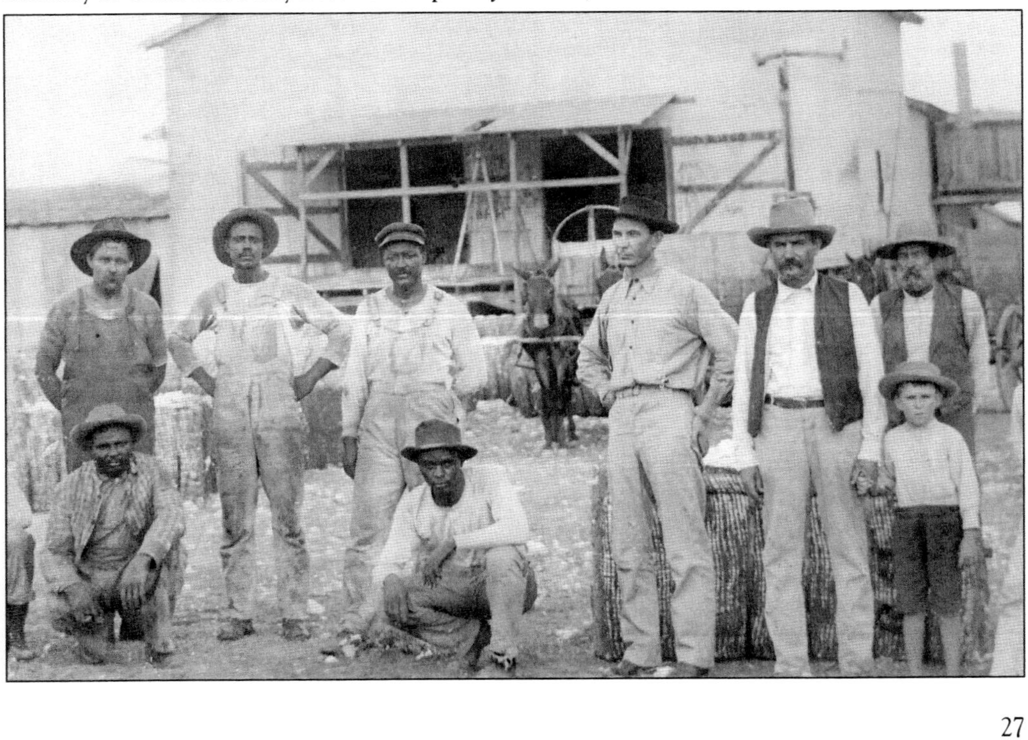

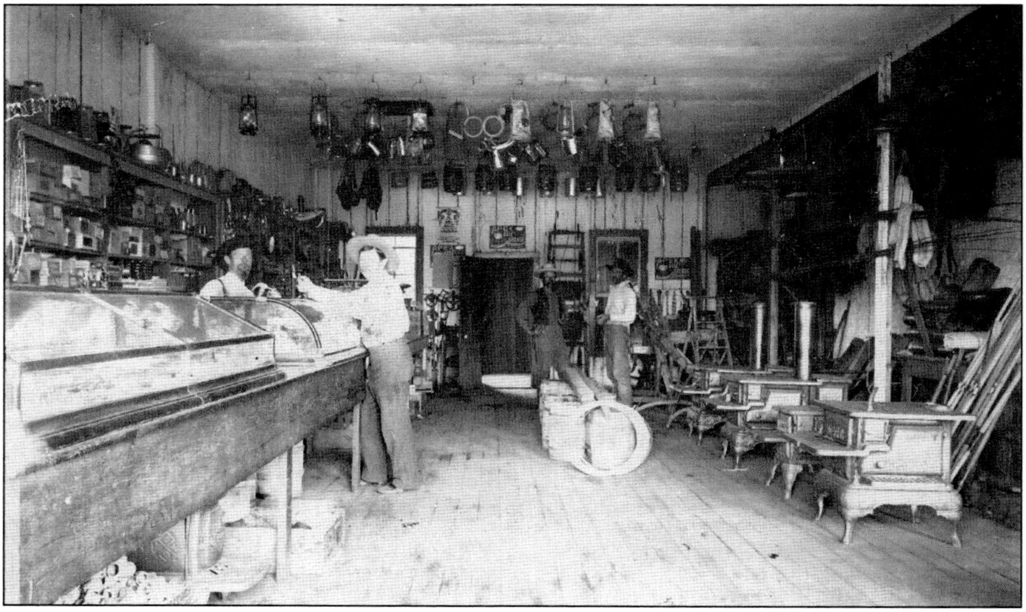

These two photographs, taken around 1906, show different sections of the building that Louis Schmidt constructed on the northeast block of the square in 1904 (the Willow Creek Café since 1996). In the above photograph, Louis Schmidt is standing behind the counter in his hardware store, which also sold wagons, buggies, and agricultural implements. The man across the counter from him is Sheriff Will Taylor of Junction. In the bottom photograph, Theo Schmidt (in the dark jacket) is behind the bar in his saloon, and his brother Louis (wearing suspenders) stands in front. Theo, in an 1886 advertisement, declared himself the agent for a "Celebrated Bohemian Export, a Beer for family use, guaranteed to be first class." Through the years, Mason County has shown a fickle attitude regarding liquor sales. From 1877 until 1900, four local option elections were held, with the law changing each time. (Above photograph courtesy of Bobbie Baze; bottom photograph courtesy of Wilburn Shearer.)

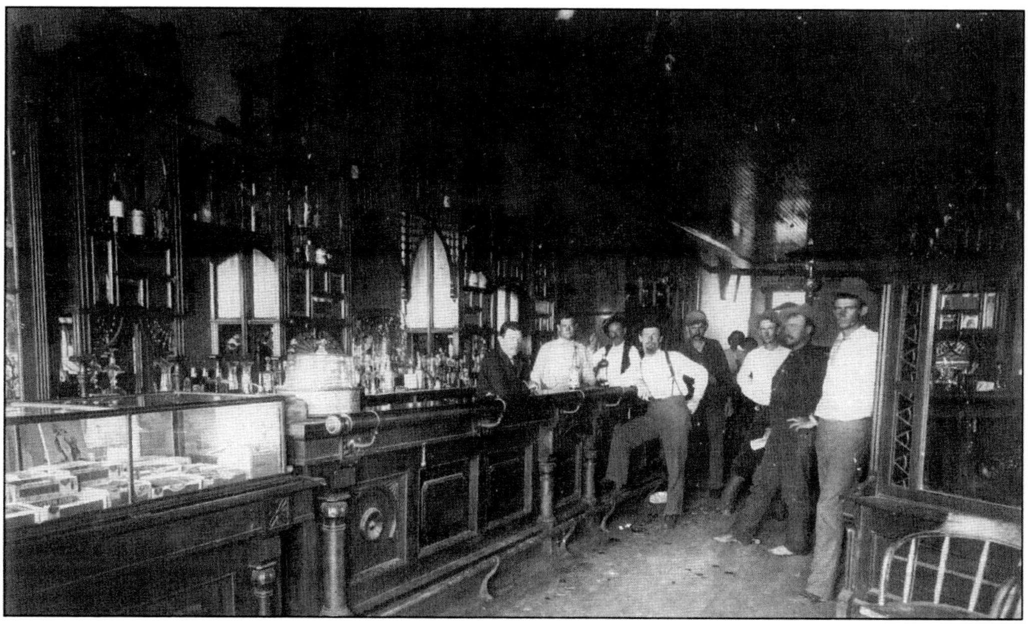

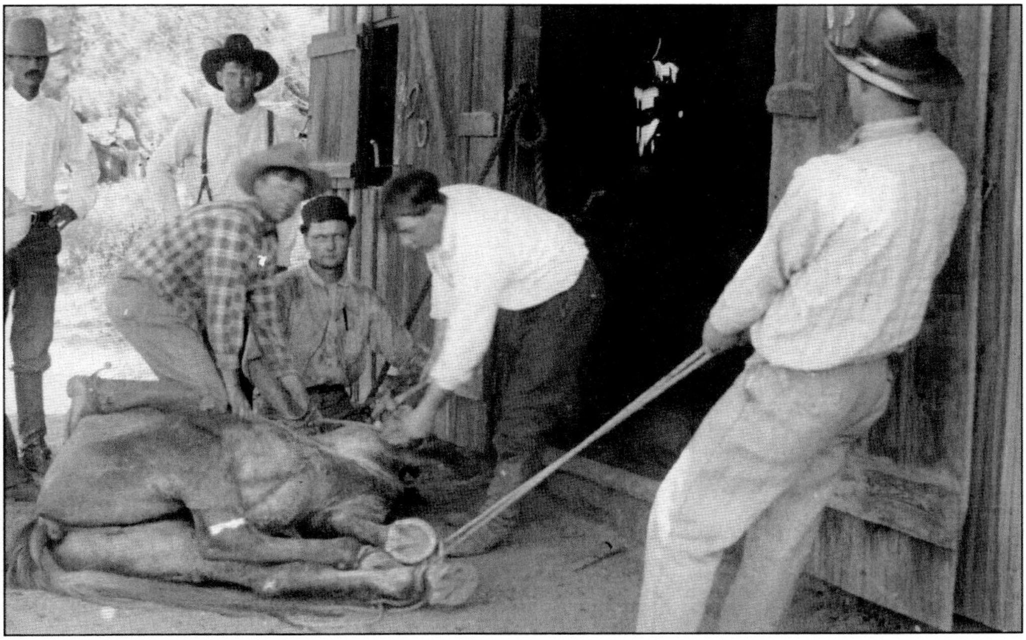

Hugo Reichenau's blacksmith shop, shown in these two photographs from 1910, was located across Spring Street from the Ranck building. In the above photograph, Jim Searcy's horse was being shod and got caught in a board in the doorway. After it stood up, it kicked Hugo in the leg, leaving a black hoofprint for a long time. Hugo is seen kneeling in the center. In the bottom photograph, Hugo (left) and Herman Schmidt are examining wagon wheels outside the shop. (Courtesy of Charles Reichenau.)

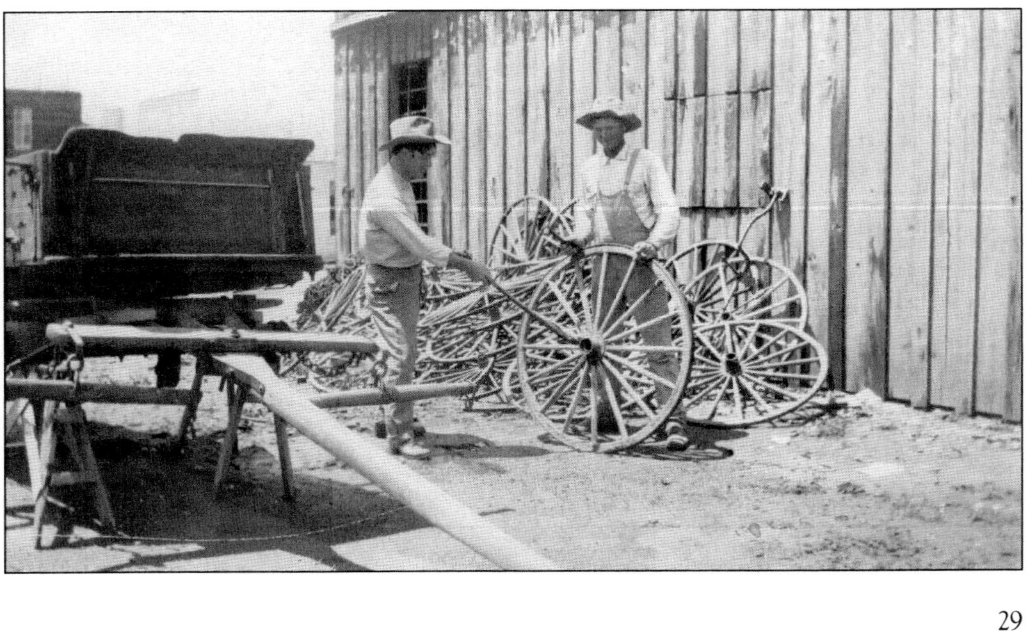

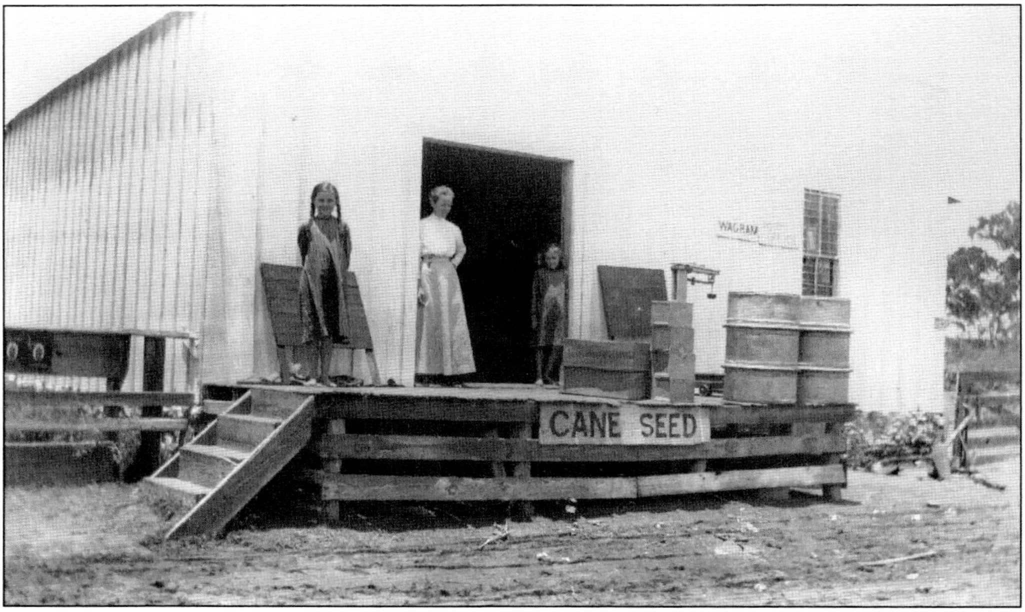

Pictured is the Wagram General Store owned by Ruff Kuhn "Cap" Bellows, who was also the postmaster from 1906 until 1912. Standing left to right are Edith Bellows (Grote), unidentified, and Averill Bellows. Wagram was located about 3 miles west of Fredonia and once had a school, gin, and millinery shop. (Courtesy of MCHC.)

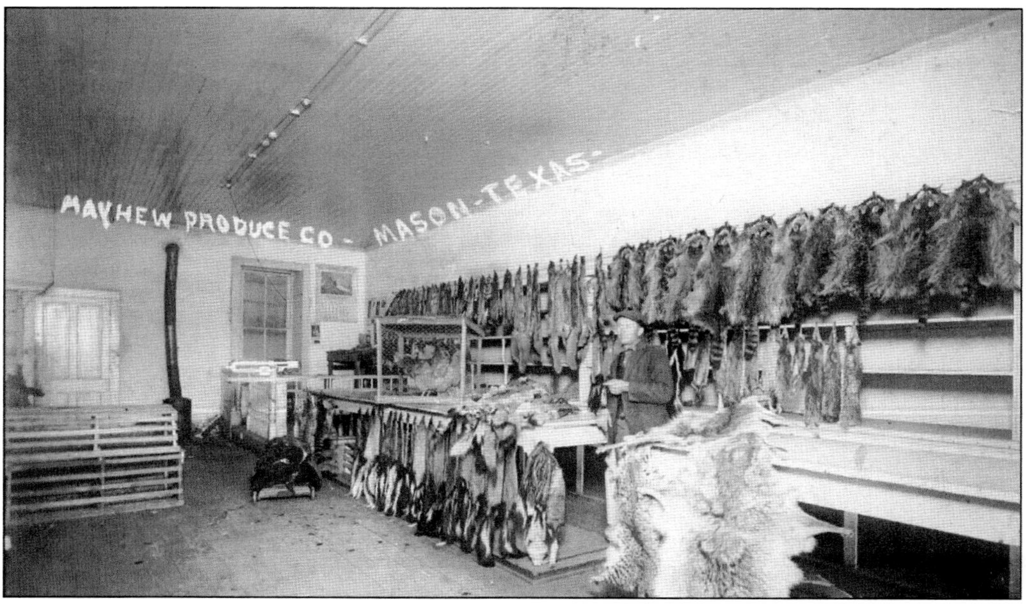

The Mayhew Produce Company, located in the Smith and Hofmann building on the northeast block of the square, bought an extensive variety of farm and ranch produce. Charles Christian Willmann, who managed the business until 1919, is pictured with the hides of raccoons, opossums, coyotes, foxes, bobcats, wolves, skunks, civet cats, and cows, in addition to live chickens. The store must have had a distinct aroma! In 1939, it was sold to the T. O. Reardon Grain Company. (Courtesy of Wilburn Shearer.)

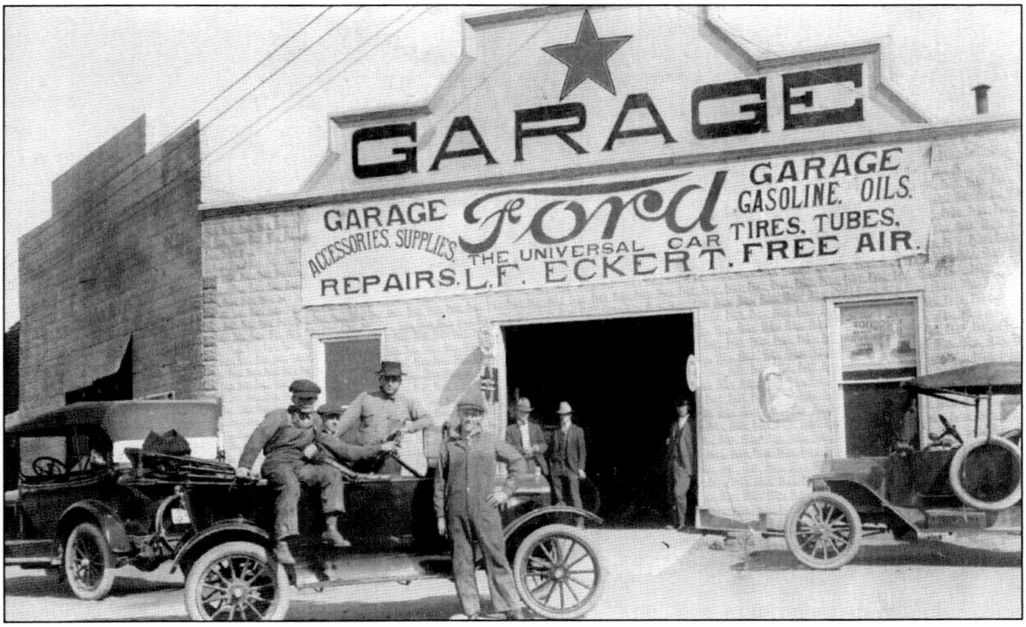

Lee F. Eckert's Star Garage serviced Ford Model T automobiles at this location from about 1917 until 1923, when the Mayo Garage acquired the property and the Ford dealership was relocated. The building, with its distinctive facade, also served as a movie theater and can still be seen on the northwest corner of the square where Spring Street meets Fort McKavitt Street. (Courtesy of Wilburn Shearer.)

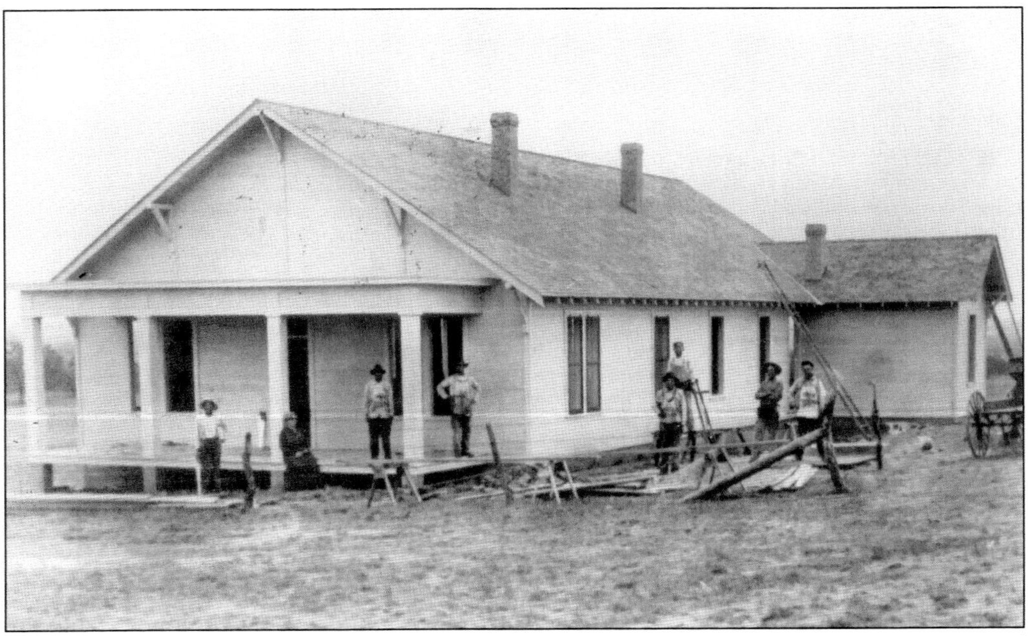

These workers and one woman overseer (possibly Mary Hey) pause during the construction of Mason's first hospital, located on the corner of Rainey and Live Oak Streets. Mary Hey was the owner and manager of the Mason Sanitarium, in which Drs. P. A. Baze, C. L. McCollum, and Oscar Huff attended patients. In 1921, the hospital was sold to Dr. Baze. It burned in 1937. (Courtesy of MCHC.)

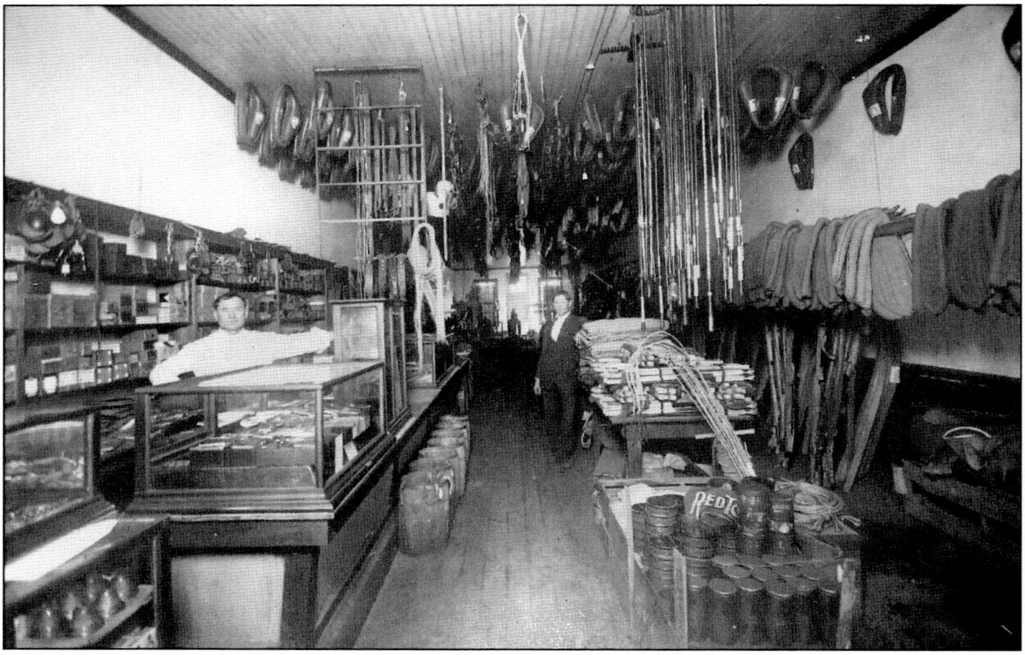

In 1906, Ed and Robert Henrich purchased the C&G building, located on the east side of the square, for $1,600. Ed moved his saddle business there, and his son Stanford continued to operate it until the mid-1980s. This 1920s photograph reveals a store well stocked with plain and fancy saddles, bullwhips, quirts, chaps, bridles, horse collars, holsters, saddle bags, saddle blankets, spurs, and stirrups. Ed Henrich is seen behind the counter, and his brother Walter is in the aisle. (Courtesy of Patsy Zesch.)

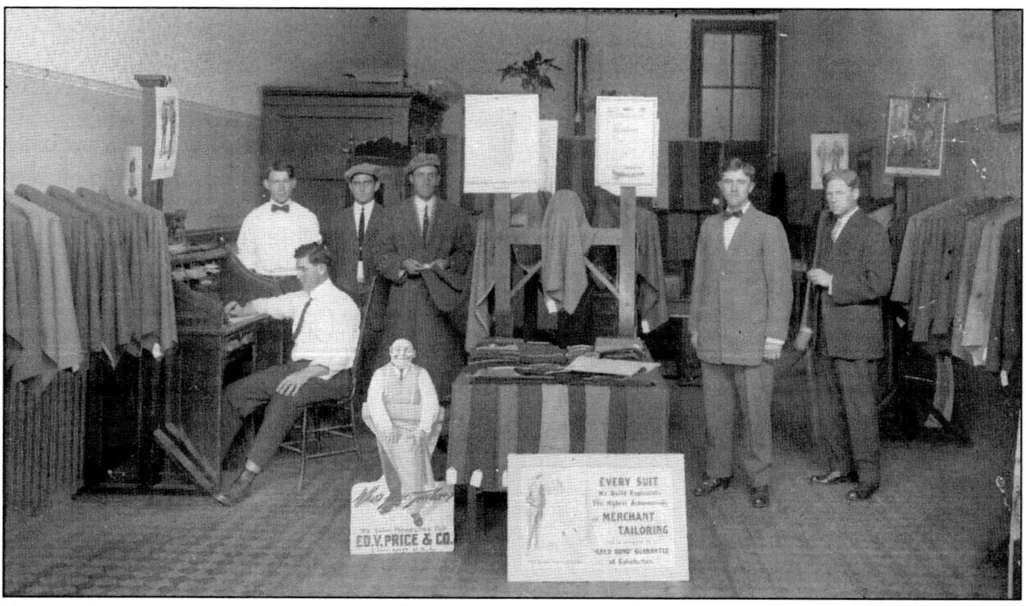

This 1920s Mason tailor shop seems highly confident of its services. The center advertisement boasts: "Every suit we build represents the Highest achievements in Merchant Tailoring and is protected by a Gold Bond Guarantee of satisfaction. We invite your criticism." The two young men wearing caps may be Roy Doell and Smith Louis. (Courtesy of MCHC.)

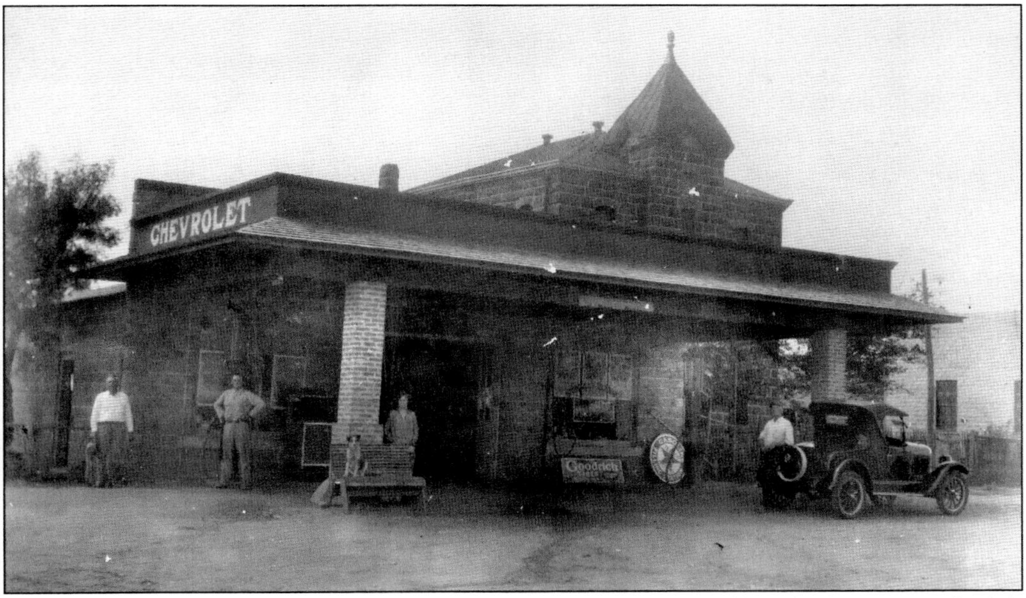

The second Mason Auto Company, a Chevrolet dealership, was owned by Charles Kensing (right). His daughter Bessie (Ischar) (second from the right) worked in the office. Son-in-law Emil Ischar (far left) also worked there. The original Mason Auto Company sold Cadillacs and Studebakers and also housed the city fire truck. It burned down around 1925, along with the fire truck. The building pictured also burned down and was replaced by Frank Polk's two-story boot shop in 1947. (Courtesy of Steven B. Kensing.)

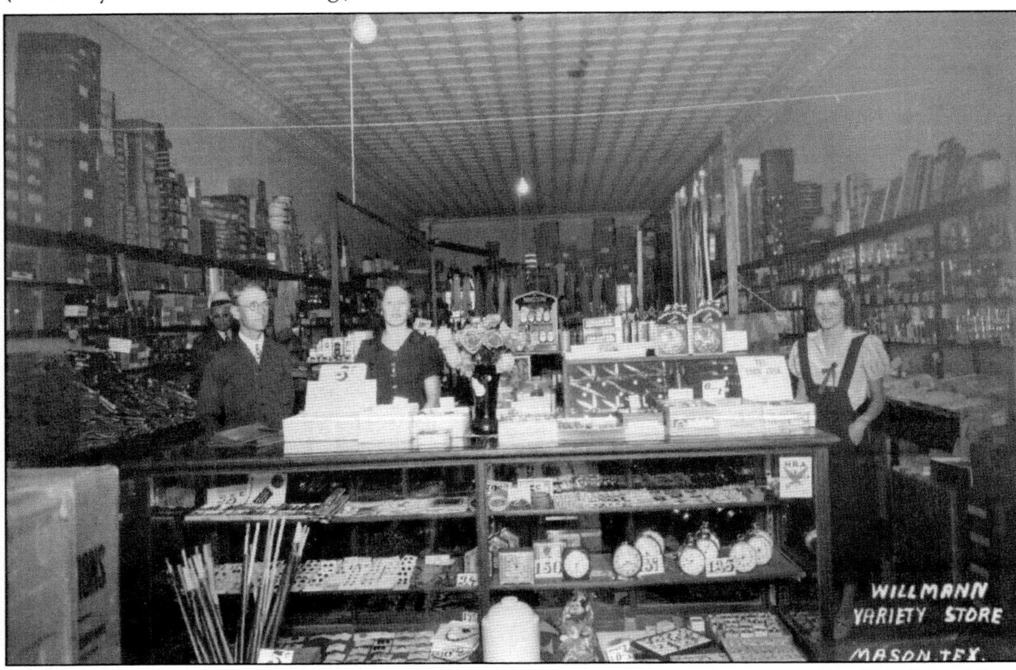

Mason's first modern variety store, the Willmann Variety Store, was located in the Ranck building. Owner Ernest Willmann is standing on the left in this 1932 photograph, and a Mr. Miller, who sold blue jeans, can be seen behind him in the background. Sales clerks Violet Durst (Strackbein) (center) and Esther Vater (Grimsley) are also present. (Courtesy of Charles Reichenau.)

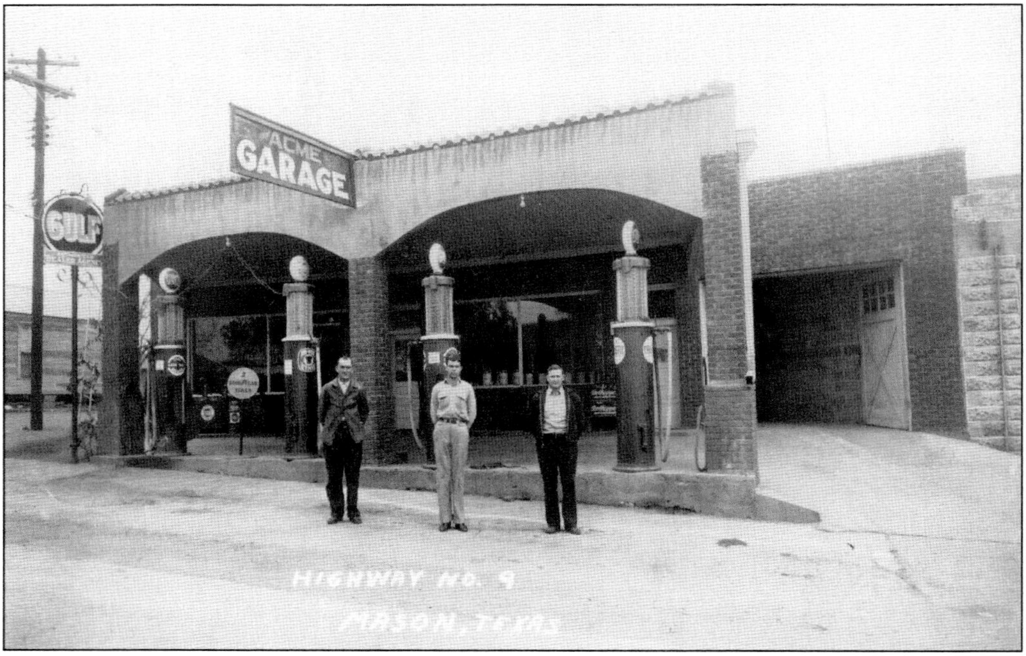

The Acme Garage is shown in February 1934. Pictured are the owners, Oran Tinsley (left) and Herbert Splittgerber (far right), and their employee Percy Metzger. The garage was in business for several decades on Highway 9 (now Highway 87) at the location presently occupied by the Mason Community Thrift Store. (Courtesy of Marilyn Mahon.)

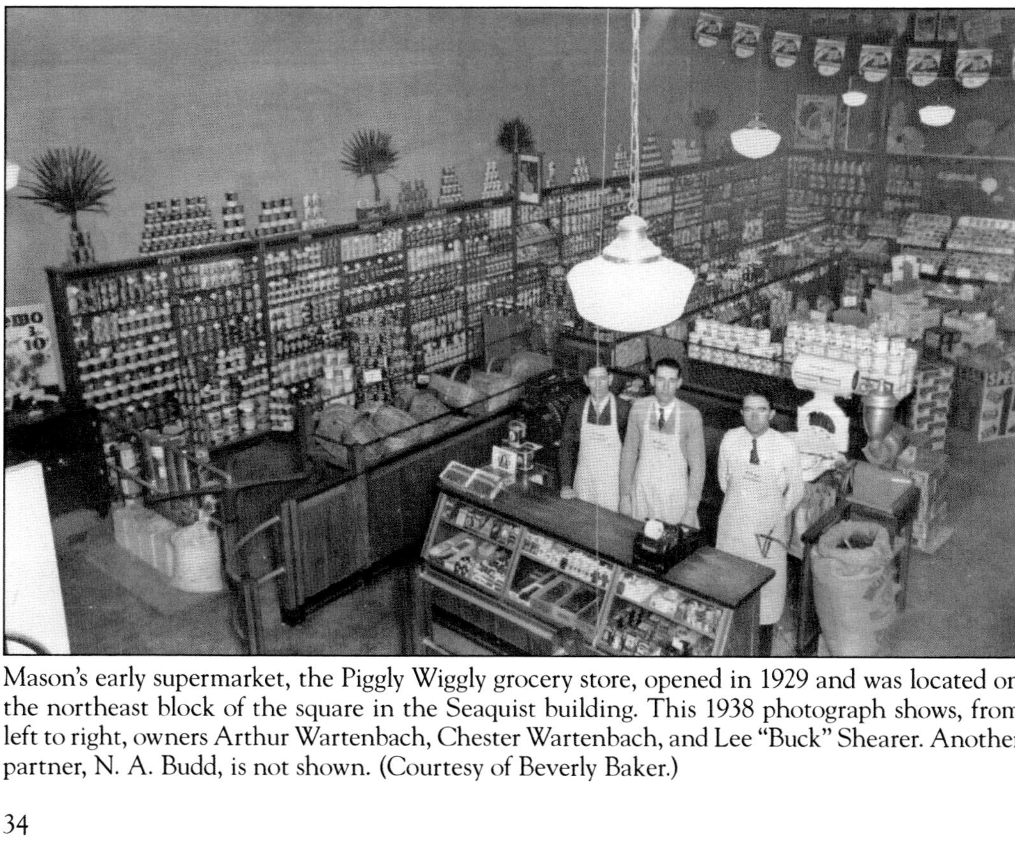

Mason's early supermarket, the Piggly Wiggly grocery store, opened in 1929 and was located on the northeast block of the square in the Seaquist building. This 1938 photograph shows, from left to right, owners Arthur Wartenbach, Chester Wartenbach, and Lee "Buck" Shearer. Another partner, N. A. Budd, is not shown. (Courtesy of Beverly Baker.)

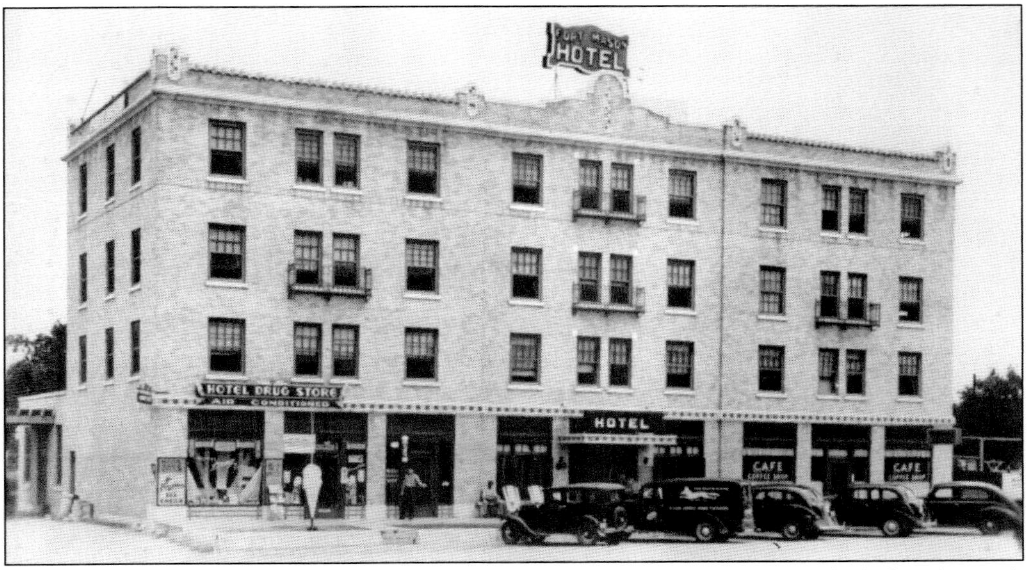

E. O. Kothmann and Carl Runge's Fort Mason Hotel opened in 1929, a few months before the stock market crash. This photograph was taken around 1940, about two years before the Hotel Drug Store (owned by Rocky Davenport and Roy Bratton) moved to the northeast block of the square and became Davenport Pharmacy. With its 54 guest rooms, ballroom, restaurant, barbershop, and drugstore, the establishment was touted as the "largest and most modern hotel between San Angelo and San Antonio." The business struggled financially, and the owners finally sold the property to the Mason National Bank in 1966. (Courtesy of the Mason County Museum.)

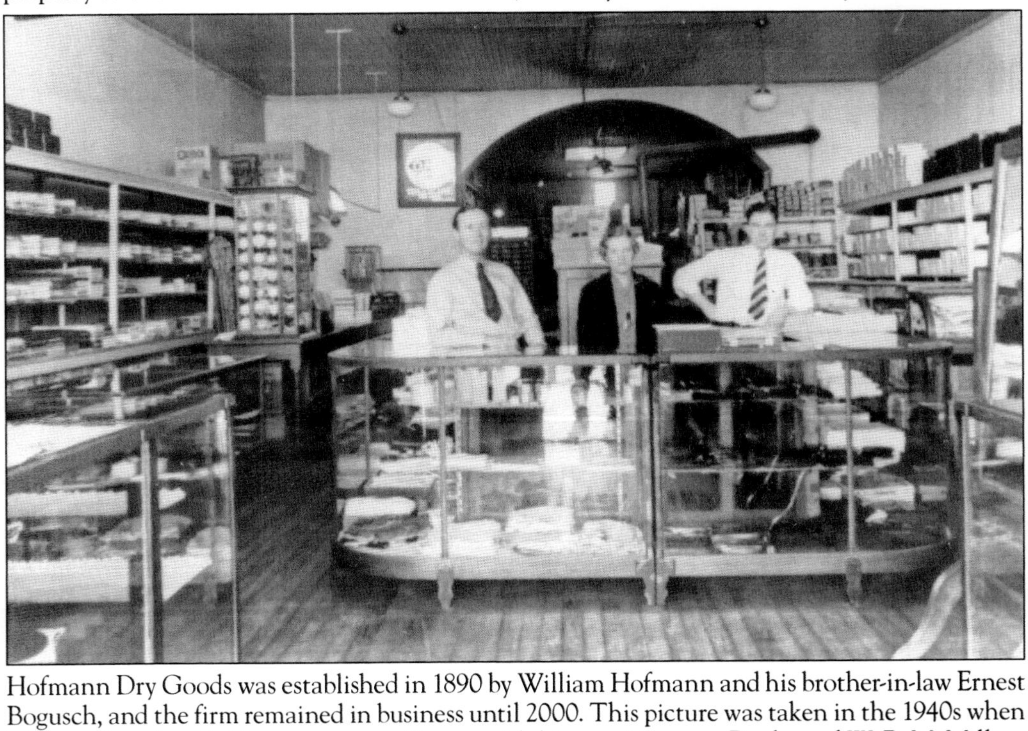

Hofmann Dry Goods was established in 1890 by William Hofmann and his brother-in-law Ernest Bogusch, and the firm remained in business until 2000. This picture was taken in the 1940s when Thomas Reardon (left) was manager. Shown with him are Margaret Banks and W. B. McMillan. (Courtesy of Florene Hofmann.)

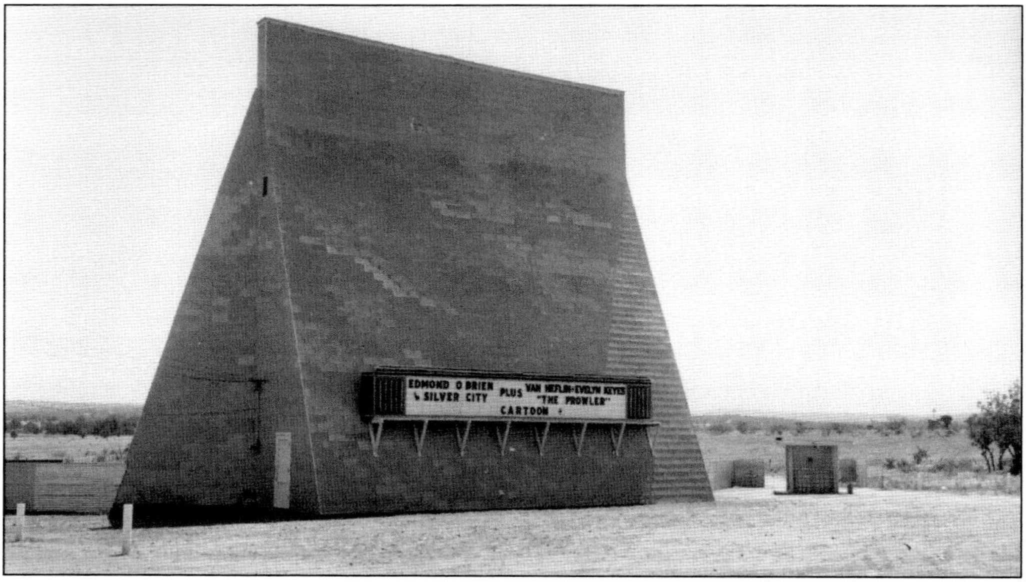

In July 1952, R. L. "Buck" Whitehead, Ossie Chew, and B. F. Grimsley opened the Roundup Drive-in Theater about half a mile southeast of Mason on Highway 87. The movies advertised in the above photograph were both released in 1951 and were likely the first features shown there. The bottom photograph shows the building housing the projection room (right side) and concession stand. The property, which covered 7.25 acres on the southwest side of the highway, could accommodate 200 cars—and even an occasional airplane! The two-seater Monocoupe 110 Special, a 200-mile-per-hour sport racer of the 1940s, landed on Highway 87 and taxied to the projection building. It carried a technician who was there to ensure that the projectors performed properly for the opening. The theater closed in late 1966. (Photographs by Clayton Schmidt; courtesy of Lila Jo Polk.)

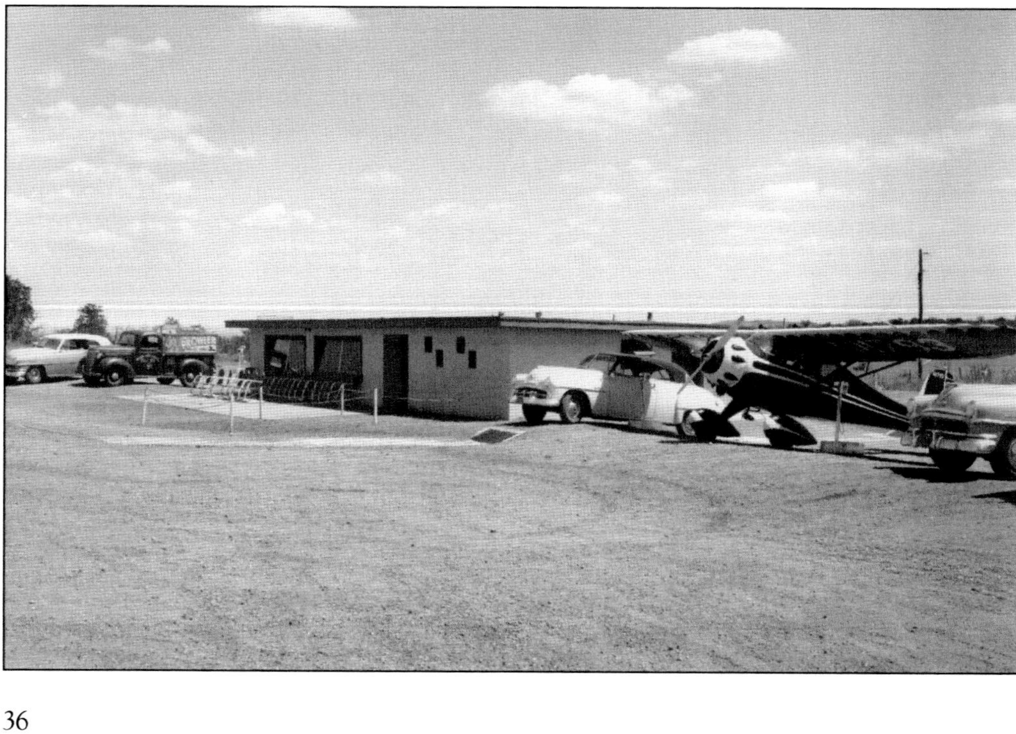

Jean Roberts Lehmberg (left) and Lou Schwanke Lehmberg stand in front of the grocery store that their husbands, Roy and Rae, leased and operated in 1950. The store, located just north of the Llano River Bridge about 10 miles southeast of Mason, was built by C. A. Donop in the 1930s. Border patrol agents often questioned Hispanics who stopped there for soda water and bologna and sent many back to Mexico. In 1951, J. W. "Pee Wee" Johnson took over the lease and purchased the inventory for $4,000. (Courtesy of Judy Lehmberg.)

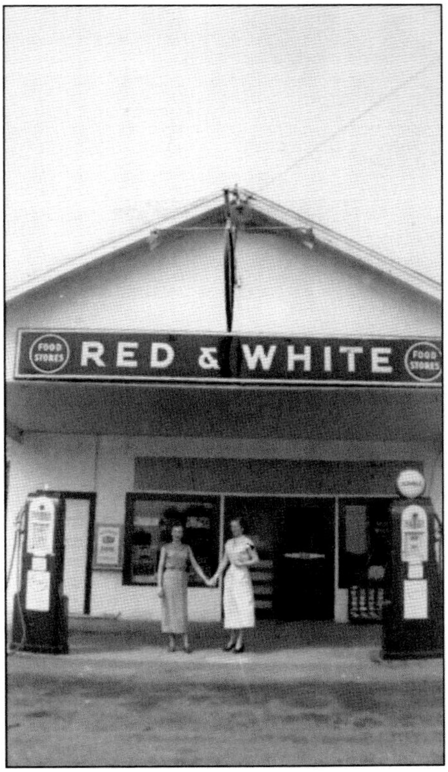

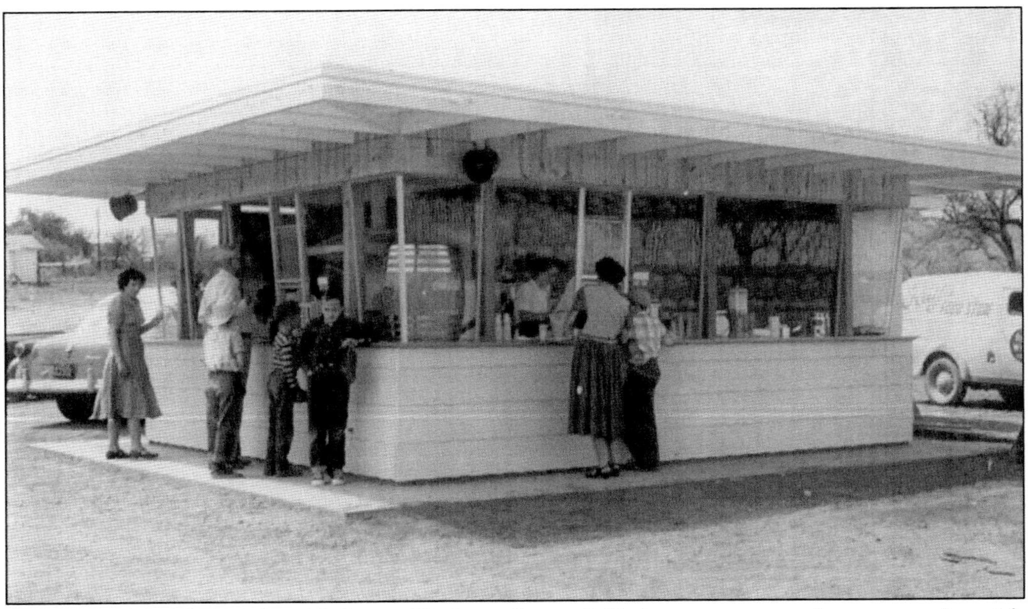

The Kreme Kup, located on Highway 87 where Cooper's Barbeque now stands, was popular with high school students from the time it opened in 1952, when this picture was taken. It featured "someburgers," frozen custards, malts, hot dogs, and root beer. Velma Gibbs is standing on the left, and the young man facing the camera is Daymond Brandenberger. Leo Hudson's 1952 Ford can be seen (left), with Ray Hudson's 1947 Thames English Ford behind it. (Courtesy of Harold Hudson.)

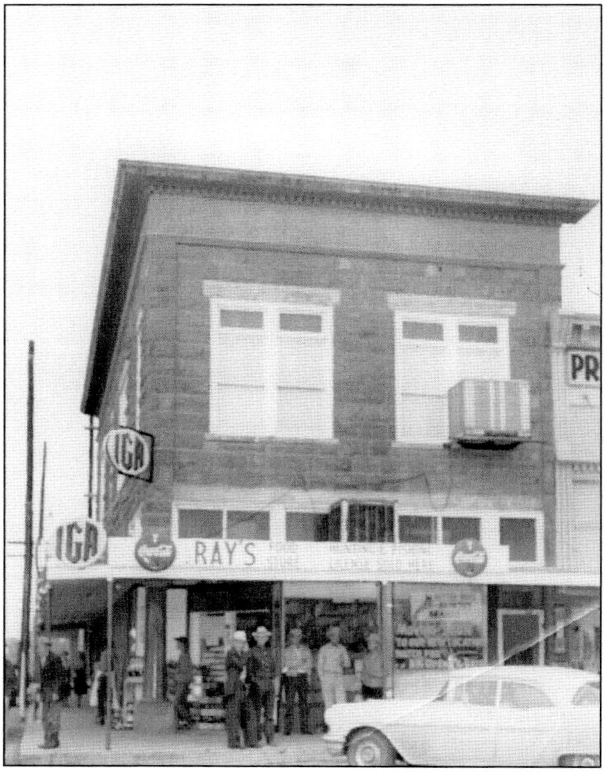

Ray Hudson's downtown grocery store occupied the Seaquist building at the corner of Fort McKavitt and Broad Streets at the time this photograph was taken around 1957. It moved down the block to the Louis Schmidt building shortly afterward. (Courtesy of Harold Hudson.)

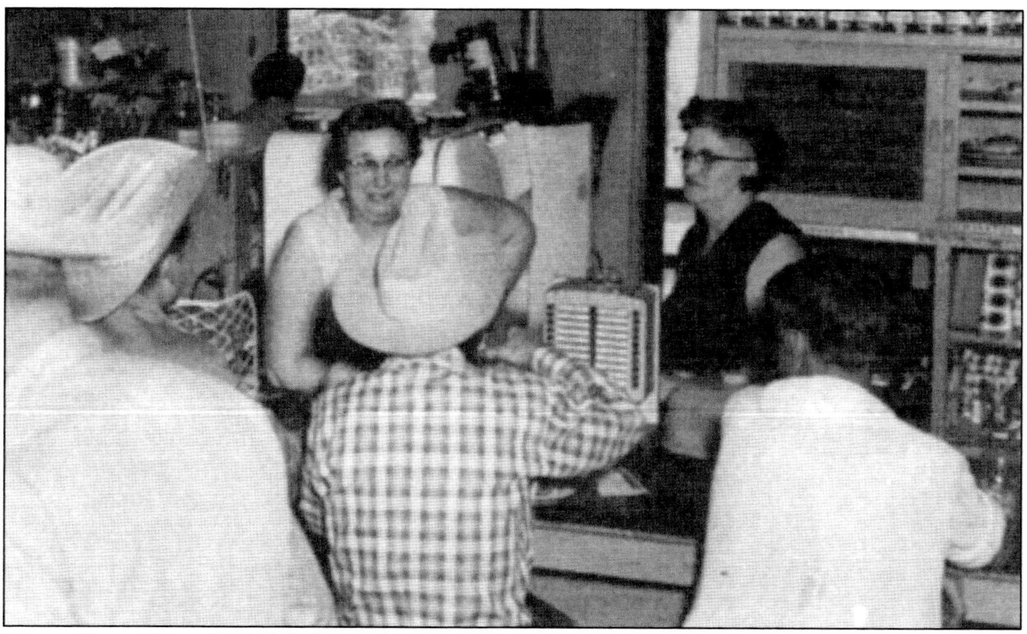

"Aunt Hattie" Lively, left behind the counter, shoots the breeze with her customers in 1958. Hattie's Café, located just behind the present-day Nu-Way Grocery, was renowned for its delicious home-style food. Aunt Hattie also enjoyed playing pranks on her favorite customers, such as serving them dinner rolls filled with cotton or cake "sweetened" with salt. (Photograph from the *Branding Iron*.)

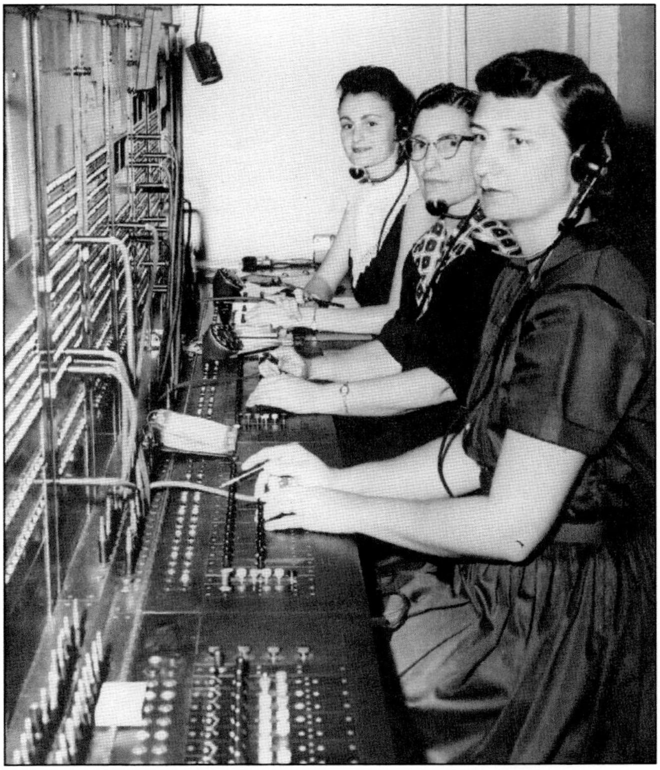

From left to right, Patty Moss, Grace Schroeder, and Mary Lou Lange are working the telephone switchboard in 1958, located above the old Mason National Bank on Broad Street. Some callers did not know the numbers of the people they were trying to reach and would simply say something like "Get me Aunt Bertha." In the days before rotary dialing, a switchboard operator not only connected Mason residents with the world but could also tell them where the fire had broken out when the alarm went off or whether someone's baby had been born. (Courtesy of Fae Danz.)

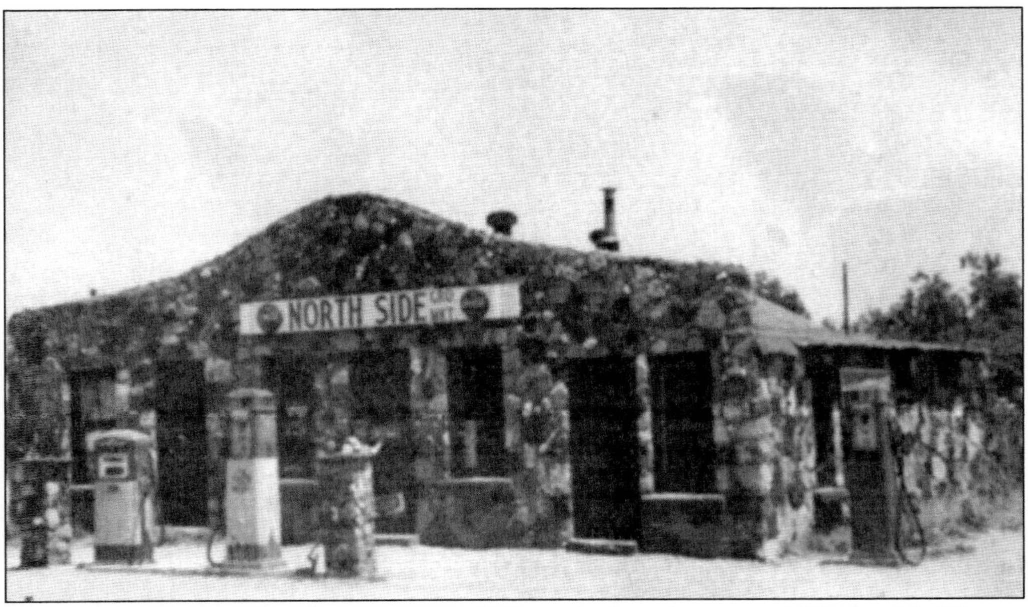

North Side Grocery and Market, pictured in 1958, was built in the spring of 1934 by a Mr. Werner, its first proprietor. Stonemason W. D. "Dee" Kelso placed a whimsical rock "face" with marble eyes left of the door. Subsequent owners included Ross Kothmann, Glen Farmer Sr., and Eli Leifeste Sr. Eli's son J. D. Leifeste and his wife, Vera, purchased the business in 1951 and enlarged it in 1961. J. D., who had helped dig the foundation at age 15, ran the store until 2004. It became a café in 2007. (Photograph from the *Branding Iron*.)

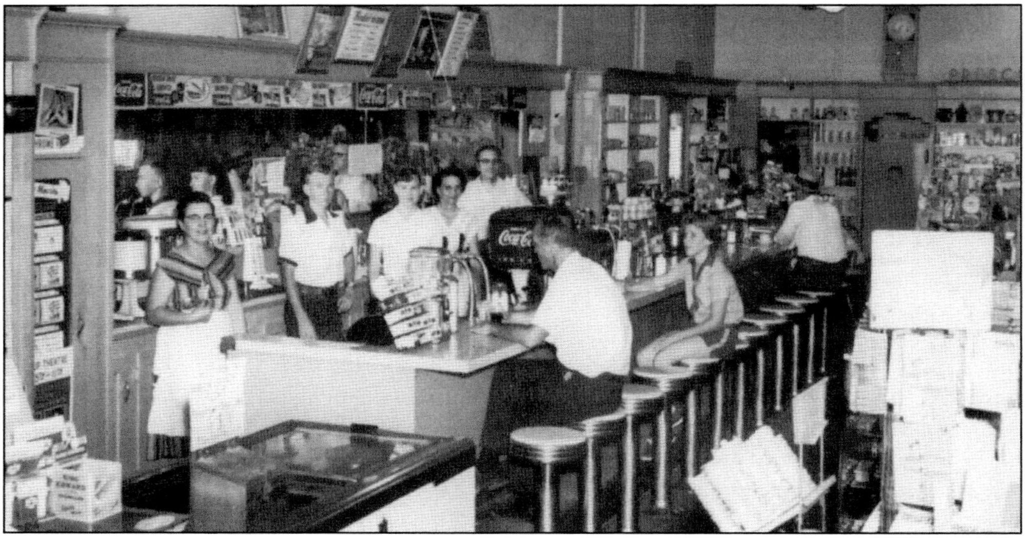

The Mason Drug Company on the northwest block of the square is shown in the late 1950s. From left to right behind the counter are employees Vivian Langerhans, Reuben Ake, Eva Coates (Lang), Ruby Johnson, and Fritz Stengel (co-owner). Mason's high school students enjoyed eating lunch there and especially liked driving up to the store in the evening, when they could honk their car horns and get curb service for fountain drinks. For decades, election night returns were posted at the drugstore, which served as a social center. (Photograph from the *Branding Iron*.)

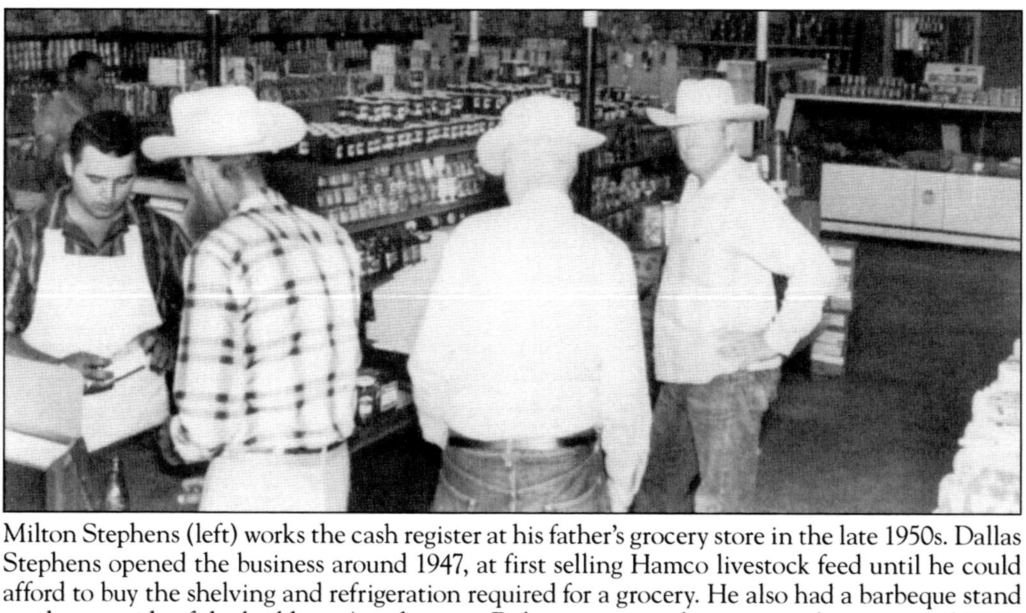

Milton Stephens (left) works the cash register at his father's grocery store in the late 1950s. Dallas Stephens opened the business around 1947, at first selling Hamco livestock feed until he could afford to buy the shelving and refrigeration required for a grocery. He also had a barbeque stand on the east side of the building. Another son, Dalton, continued to operate the store until 2003. (Photograph from the *Branding Iron*.)

Three

Schools and Organizations

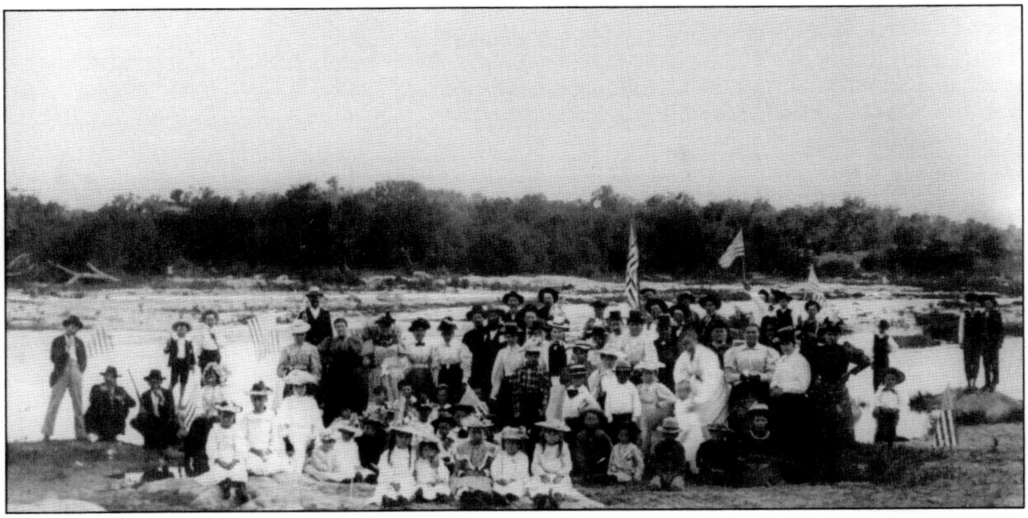

Anna Martin, founder of the Commercial Bank, started a one-room school at Hedwig's Hill in 1894, and it remained open until 1908. It did not lack for students, as shown by this photograph of a school picnic on the Llano River on May 30, 1887. In 1868, May 30 became known as "Decoration Day" in honor of all Civil War dead. The term "Memorial Day" came into use in 1882 to honor the dead from all wars, especially after World War I. (Courtesy of MCHC.)

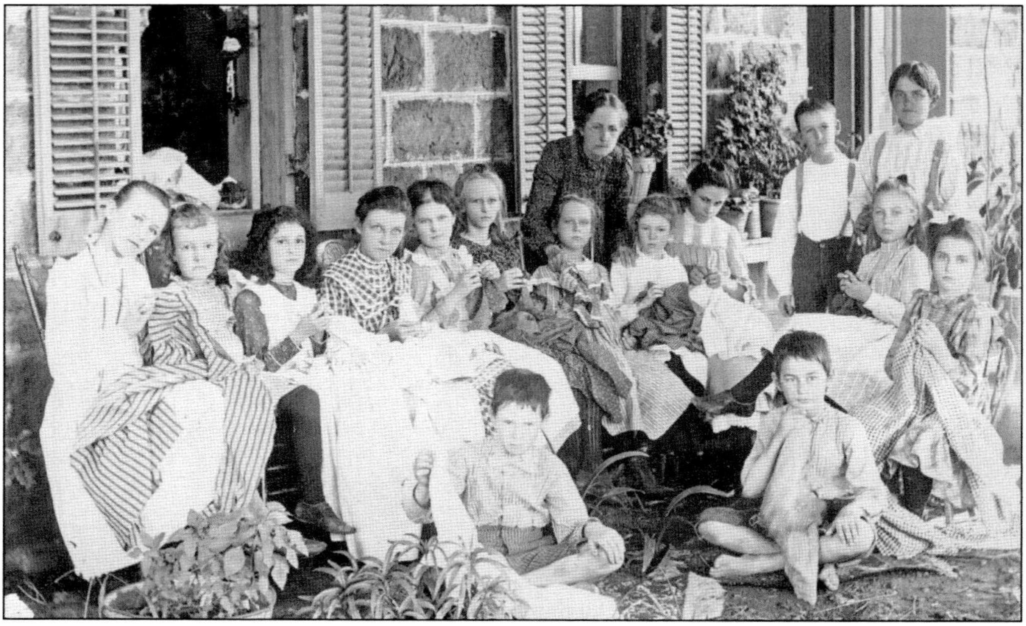

This sewing class in the late 1890s included a few boys. The teacher and most of the students have not been identified, although Benellen Reynolds (Jordan) and Ruth Reeder (Runge) are among them. Having sewing skills in those days was something that came in handy whether you were male or female—although the boys do not look too happy about having their picture taken. (Courtesy of the Mason County Museum.)

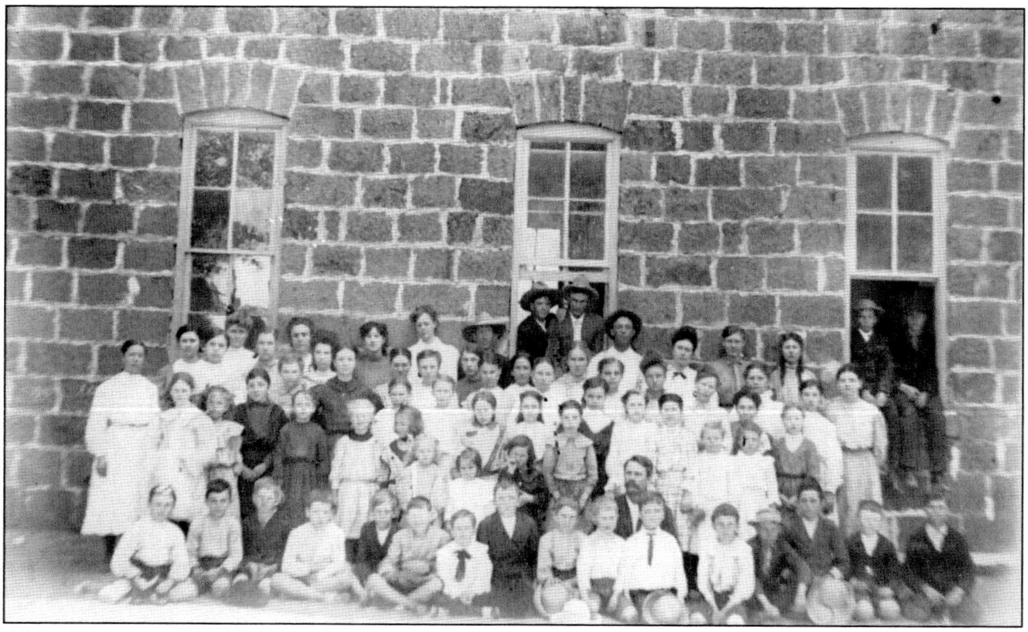

The Pontotoc School, originally the San Fernando Academy, is pictured with students and teachers around 1900. The academy was built in 1882 and housed as many as 200 pupils. Because it could not meet its debts, it was sold to the Willis brothers. In 1898, their heirs sold it to the Pontotoc School Trustees, and it was used as a public school until 1927. Today only the walls remain. (Courtesy of MCHC.)

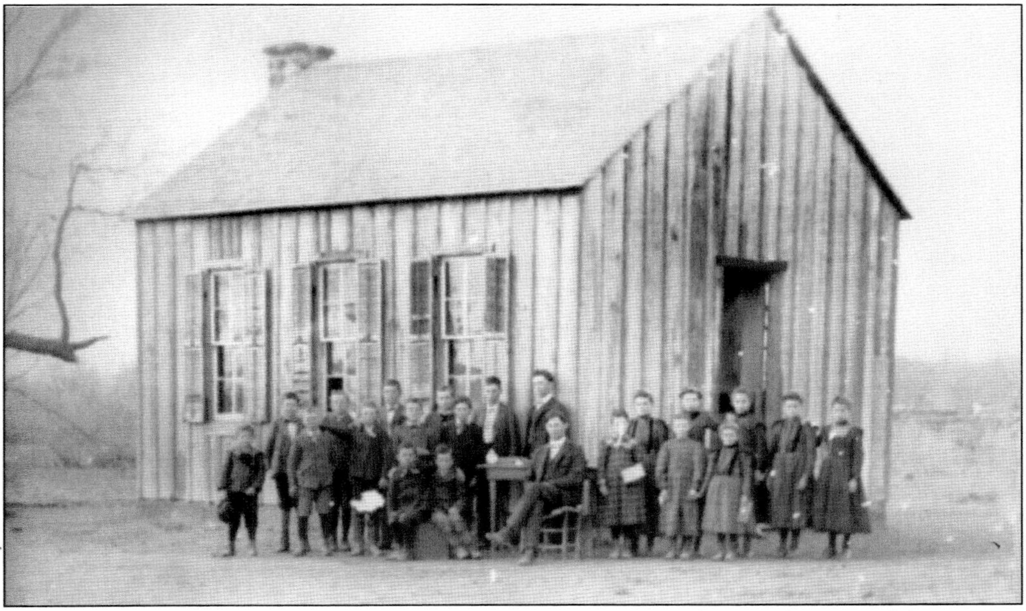

The Bauerville School, pictured in 1900, was located approximately 3.5 miles west of the present-day town of Castell and operated from 1869 until 1920. From left to right are (first row) Ben Tatsch, Robert Kothmann, Ben Bode (teacher), Dora Kothmann, Melinda Leifeste, and Hulda Bauer; (second row, order uncertain) Wesley Bauer, Sam Leifeste, Elo Kothmann, Walter Ottens, Frank Bauer, Emma Bauer, Cora Bauer, Olga Tatsch, Olga Bauer, and one unidentified; (third row) Max Ottens, Wilkes Kothmann, Damon Kothmann, Max Schuessler, Albert Bauer, and Alonzo Leifeste. (Courtesy of MCHC.)

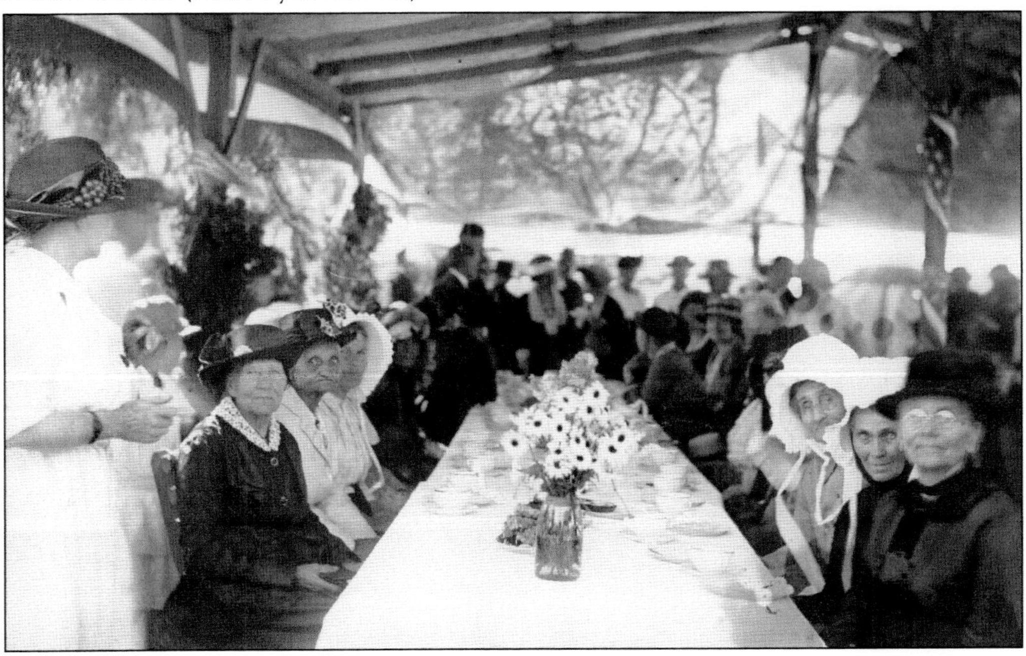

Although not much is known about this picture, it certainly has some memorable faces. The event is possibly a meeting of the Woman's Foreign Missionary Society (begun in 1869 in the Methodist Episcopal Church) or a Confederate reunion. (Courtesy of the Mason County Museum.)

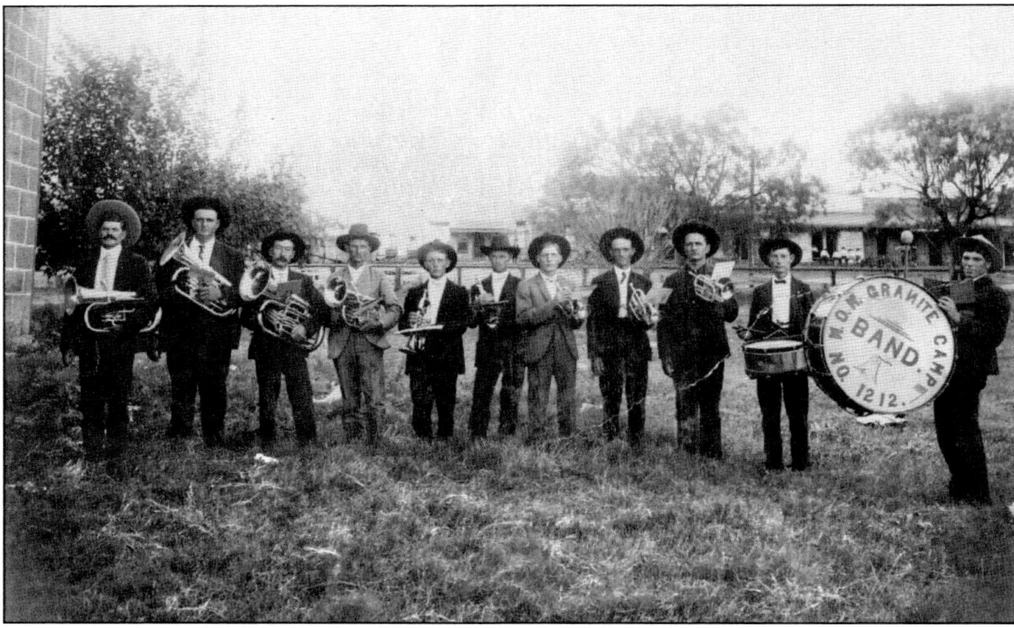

The WOW (Woodsmen of the World) Granite Camp Band No. 1212 entertained folks throughout the county. The musicians who have been identified in this photograph are Eugene Jordan (second from the left), Edward Jordan (fourth from the left), Hubert Jordan (eighth from the left), and Felix Jordan (ninth from the left). The Woodsmen of the World was one of the first fraternal benefit societies in the United States, begun in 1890 in Nebraska. (Courtesy of Florene Hofmann.)

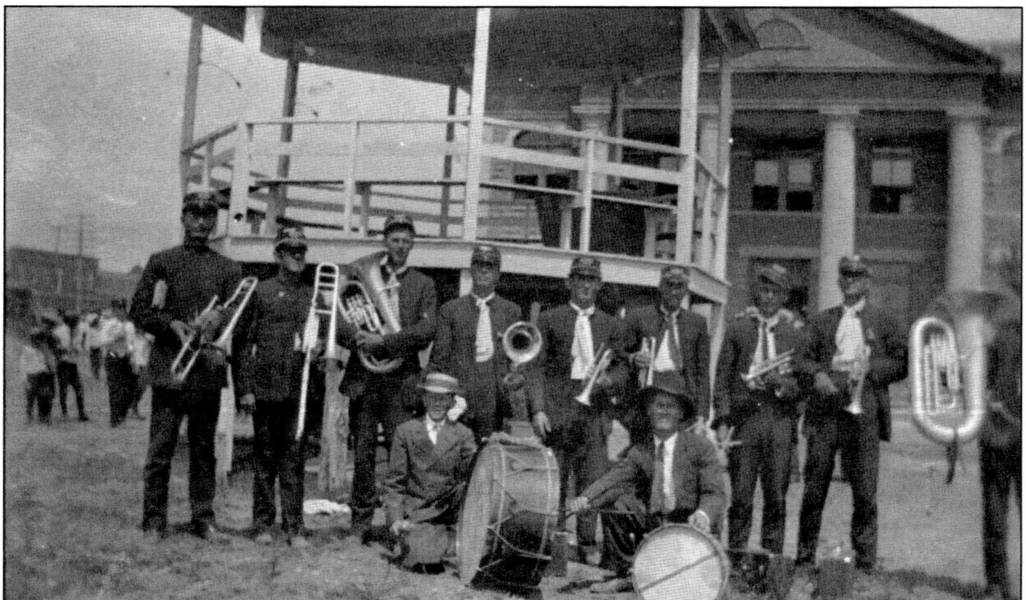

Pictured is the Charlie Hofmann Post Hill Band on the west side of the courthouse lawn in the early 1910s. Those identified are Arch Reichenau on the bass drum, John Johnson on the snare drum, and Herbert Zesch and Max Reichenau on the slide trombones. Ernest Beckmann, Ed Gross, Charlie Hofmann, and Max Metzger are also in the group. The band provided entertainment for town celebrations, parades, and other events. (Courtesy of the Mason County Museum.)

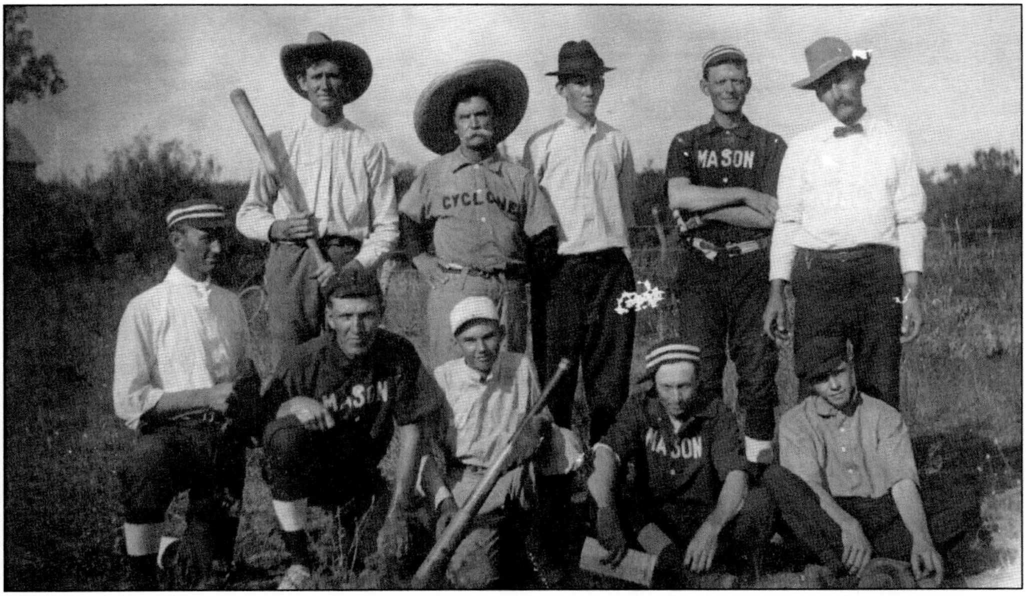

These photographs show two baseball teams, the Leans and the Fats, in 1908. The Leans are, from left to right in the above photograph, (first row) Charles Willmann, Oscar Hensch, "Piggy" Lange, Jim Miller, and Martin "Bug" Loring; (second row) John Teague, Theodore Splittgerber, ? Kidd, Will Jordan, and Christian Leifeste. In the bottom photograph, the Fats are, from left to right, (first row) Jim Brown, Roscoe Runge, Bob Hofmann, and Willard Baker; (second row) A. N. Moursand (manager), Dr. James M. Thompson, Dee Gibbs, Bob Motley, Charlie Hofmann, Arthur Carter, and Ben Hey. Many communities nationwide boasted of their Fats and Leans baseball teams during the first decades of the 20th century. The teams were usually composed of men who enjoyed baseball but did not relish playing strictly by the rules. According to some accounts, the players wore costumes that were "undescribable." (Courtesy of the Mason County Museum.)

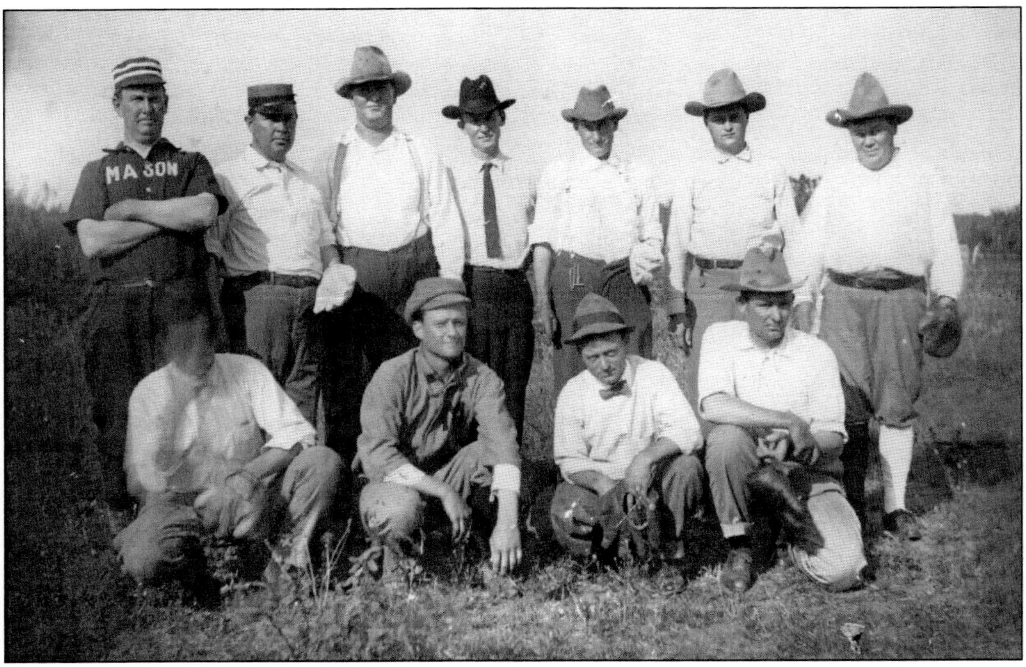

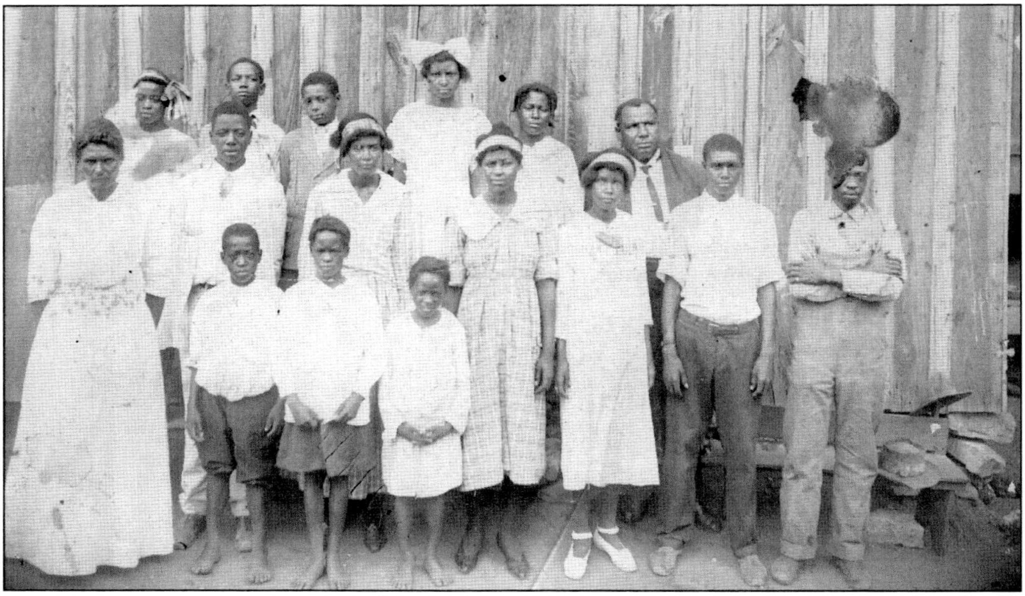

The schoolhouse for African Americans, located south of Gamel Creek and between present-day Elm and Pecan Streets, is pictured around 1912. It was built in the early 1900s and served as a school Monday through Friday and as a church on Sunday. Professor Wilson taught from "hand-me-down" books from the white school and demanded punctuality and good behavior. From left to right are (first row) Julie Peters, Tom Mason, Evelyn Mason, and Fannie Jackson; (second row) Erv Gipson, Sophia Peters, Viola Mason, Irene Peters, Dave Peters, and unidentified; (third row) Louise Gipson, Alonzo Gipson, Sam Peters, Nell Peters, Beulah "Mae" Mason, and Professor Wilson. (Courtesy of Sandy Miller.)

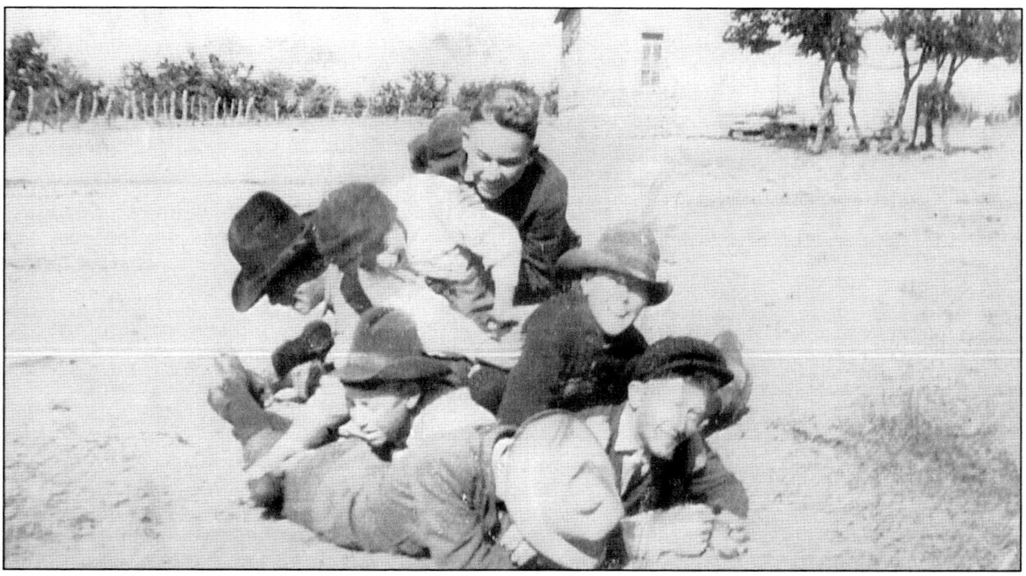

The boys at Ranch Branch School "pile on" about 1920. From left to right are (bottom) Hilmar Eckert and (possibly) Harold Schmidt; (middle) Alvin Harper and Sammy Harper; (top) Calvin Coffey, Hugo Ficker, and Hugh Soules. The school was erected in 1909 to educate the children of 20 families in the area. The building was later used for church services and community activities until it collapsed during a storm in 2005. (Courtesy of Charles Eckert.)

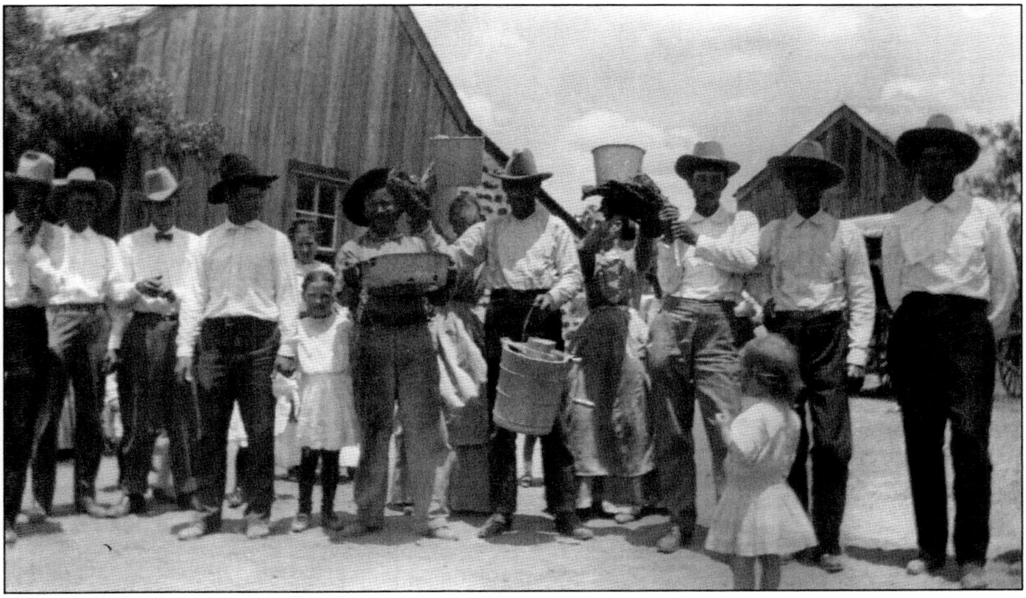

These photographs capture residents of the Wagram community as they prepare for an ice cream social and a baseball game. Originally known as Blue Stretch, possibly because of blue-stemmed grasses growing in the area, Wagram was located about 12.5 miles northeast of Mason. The community school had 60 students in 1914, but began to decline in 1934 when fire destroyed the general store. The gentleman in the center of the above photograph holds an ice cream freezer in his left hand and has a baseball mitt on his right hand. Several of the children on the front row of the bottom photograph hold bowls, cups, and spoons in readiness for the ice cream. (Courtesy of MCHC.)

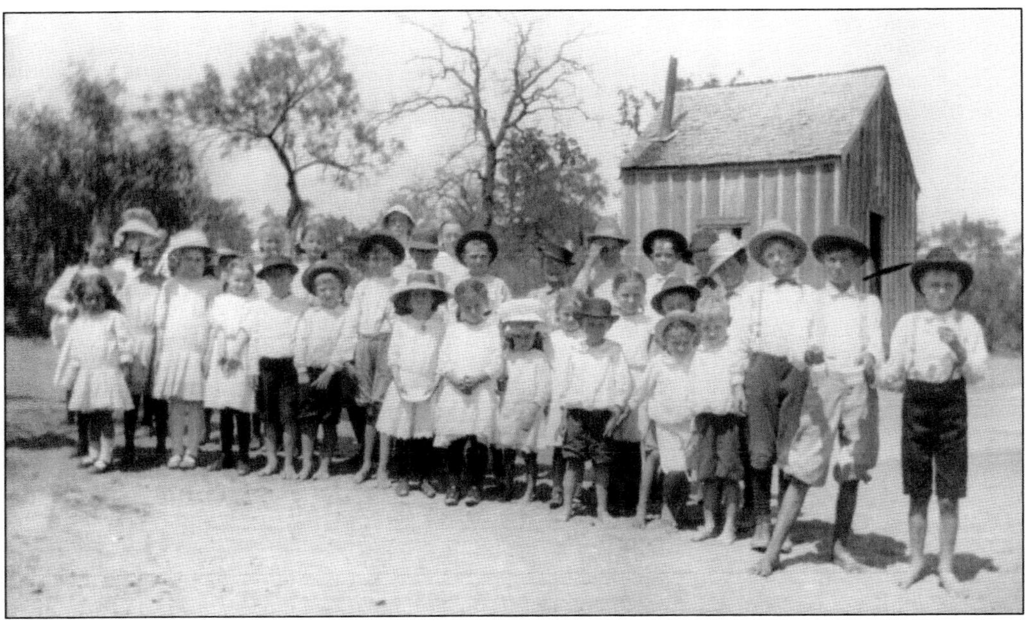

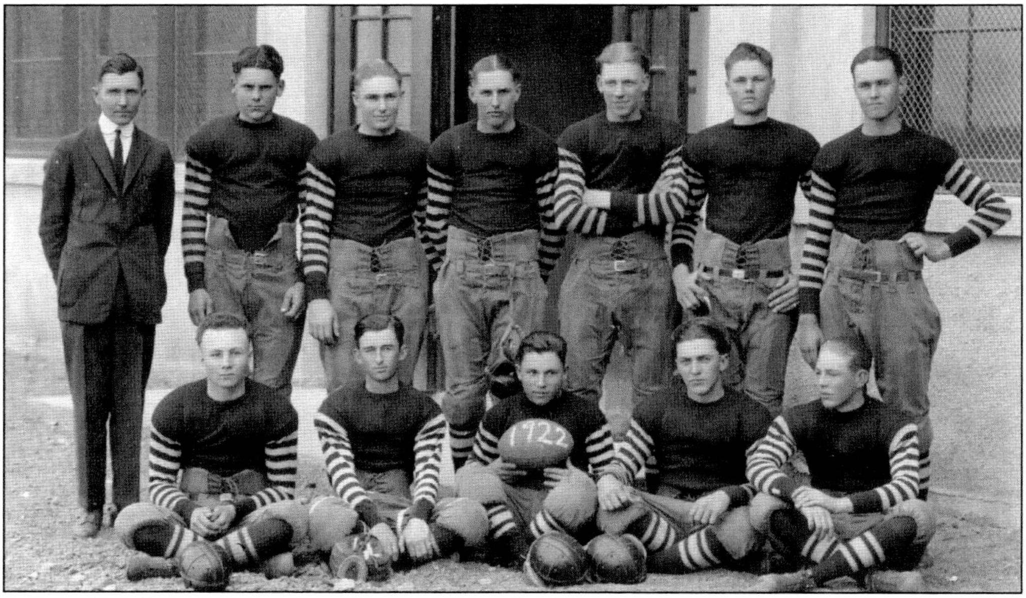

Pictured in this photograph is the Mason High School football team of 1922, which had no name at that time. The members are, from left to right, (first row) Milton Loeffler, Roy Bratton, King Charles Smith, Walter "Pinkie" Willmann, and Henry "Slick" McDougall; (second row) L. W. Dumas (coach), Walter Doell, Milton Zesch, Alton Clark, William "Koockie" Koock, Alvin Zesch, and Sam Leifeste. A female classmate, in her diary, described various team members as "downright handsome," "a determined hugger and kisser," and "a young Fortinbras" (from *Hamlet*). (Courtesy of Carolyn Loeffler.)

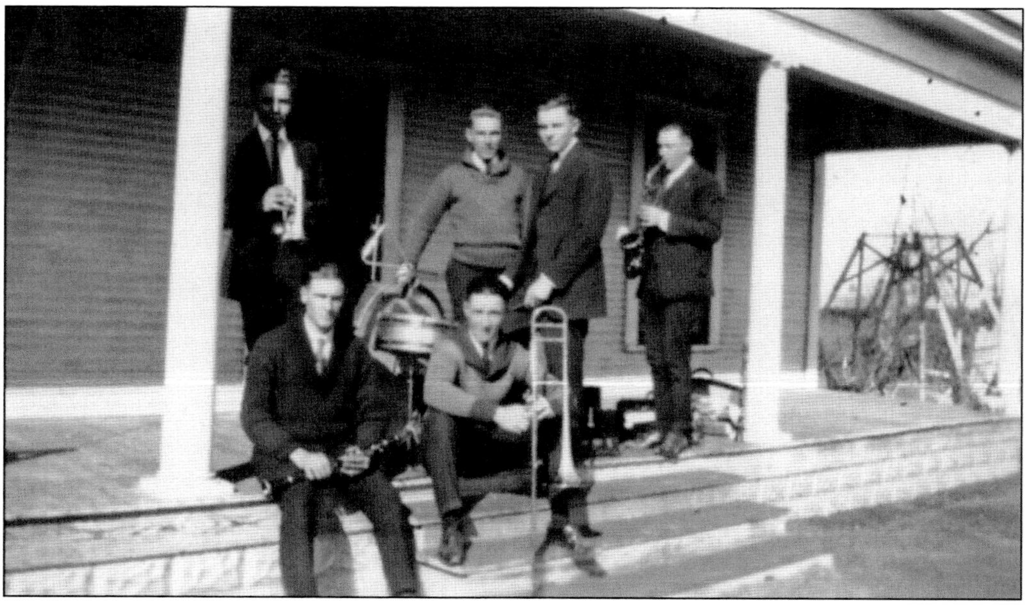

A Mason jazz band is pictured in 1922 at the Rudolph and Jennie Doell house on Fort McKavitt Street (opposite the present-day Short Stop). Seated are Herbert Splittgerber (left) and Allen Doell. Standing are, from left to right, two unidentified, Bill Donop, and Roy Doell. The Splittgerbers were a musical family. Herbert's father, Julius, was a founder of a quartet in Fredericksburg that became the basis of the town's choral society. (Courtesy of Marilyn Mahon.)

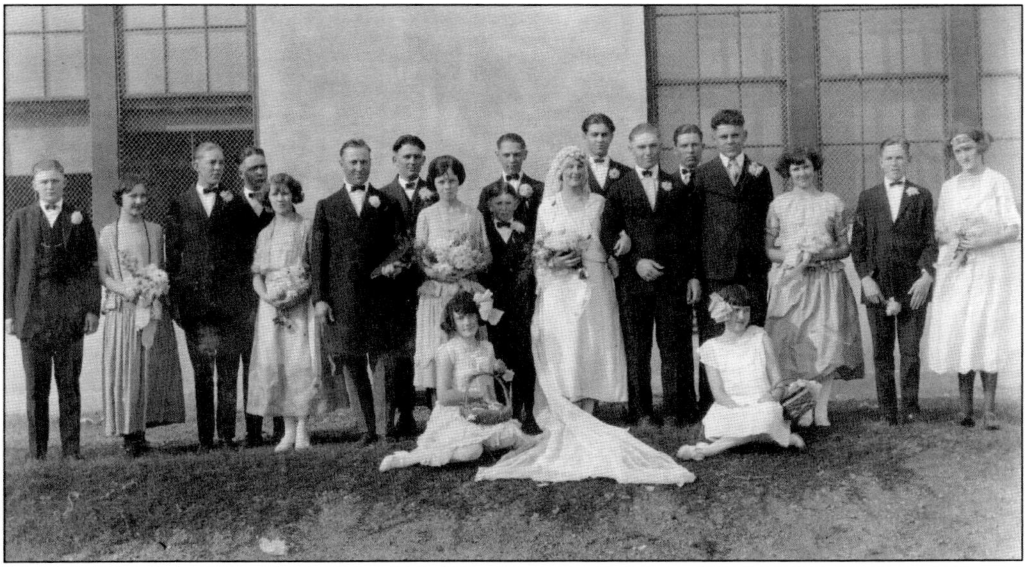

A mock wedding at the Mason High School auditorium on November 21, 1923, drew a full house. Senior Dixie Fae Hey recorded in her diary that her younger sister, Benellen, portrayed a flower girl but "looked more like a chorus girl, as her dress was a low necked affair without sleeves, and extremely short at both ends. … Benny's arms and legs were well advertised." Benellen Hey (Zesch) is seated on the left. (Courtesy of Peggy Laverty.)

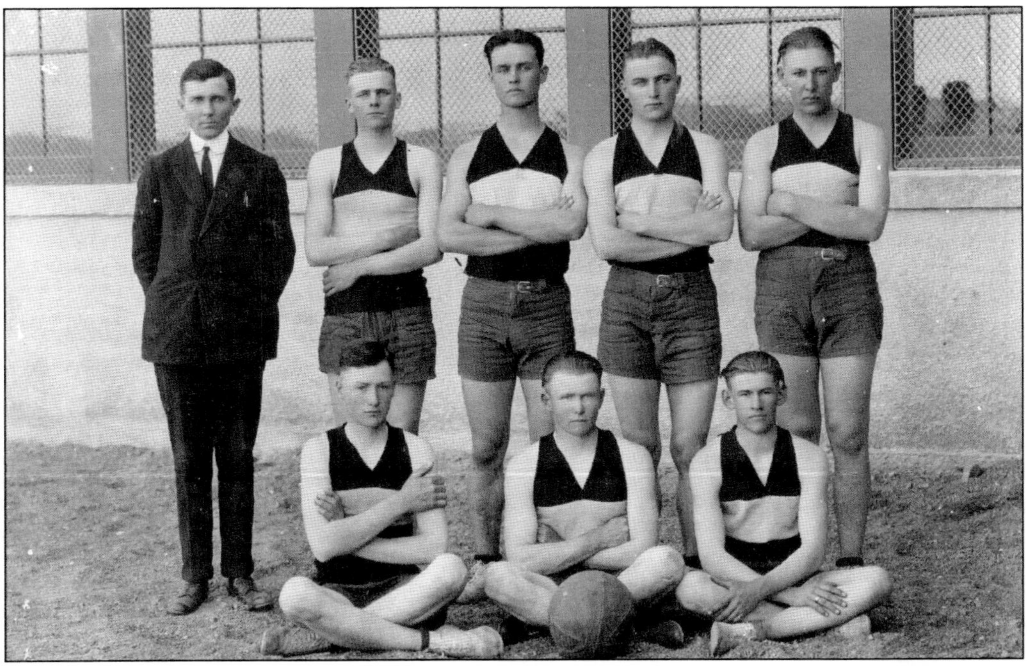

This photograph shows members of a Mason High School basketball team from the 1920s. From left to right are (first row) Ben Loeffler, Marley Fussel, and Garland Brewer; (second row) L. W. Dumas (coach), unidentified, Walter Doell, Arthur Geistweidt, and Henry Keller. Dumas taught several subjects and coached both football and basketball. Some of his female students were heartbroken when a rumor circulated in 1924 that he had gotten married. It turned out to be false. (Courtesy of the Arthur Geistweidt family.)

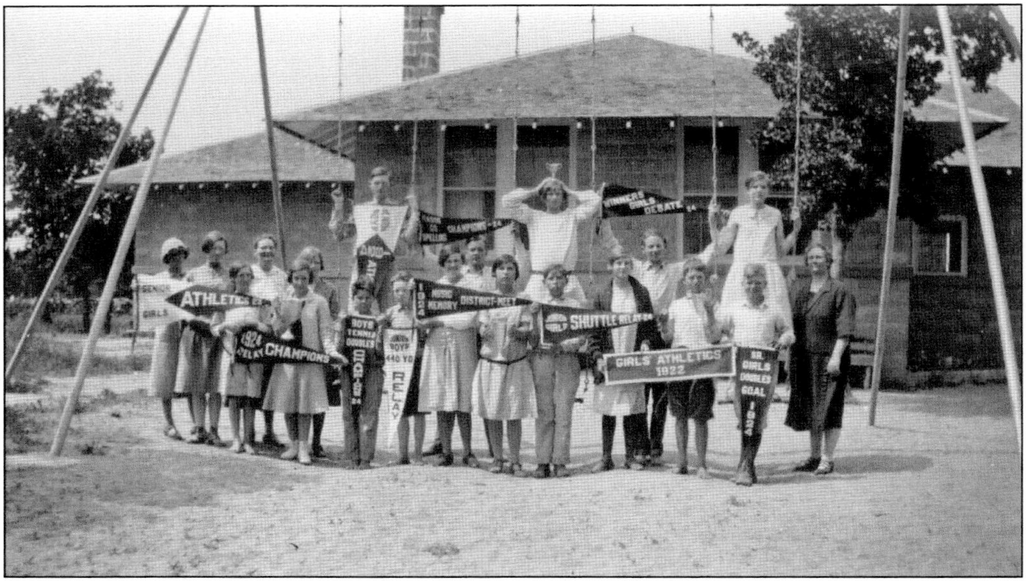

Students at Peters Prairie School, around 1927, are displaying pennants and banners in the above photograph, signifying their successes in academic and athletic competitions between 1922 and 1924. On the right is Sadie Westbrook, their advisor, teacher, and principal. The school, which had three teachers and 10 grades, produced champion debaters and tennis players. In the bottom photograph, the school's students are assembled in 1929 with their right hands over their hearts as the older students raise a flag with 48 stars. Those without hats appear to be saluting, but they are actually shielding their eyes from the sun. Rural schools in Mason County held a flag ceremony each Monday morning. (Courtesy of Dick Hahn and B. H. and Julie Nobles.)

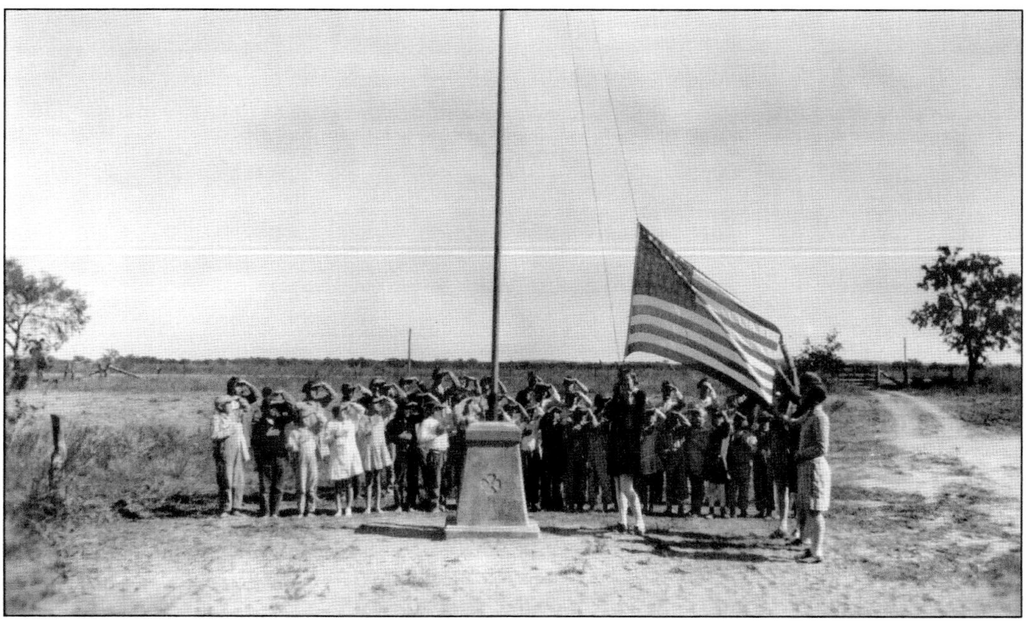

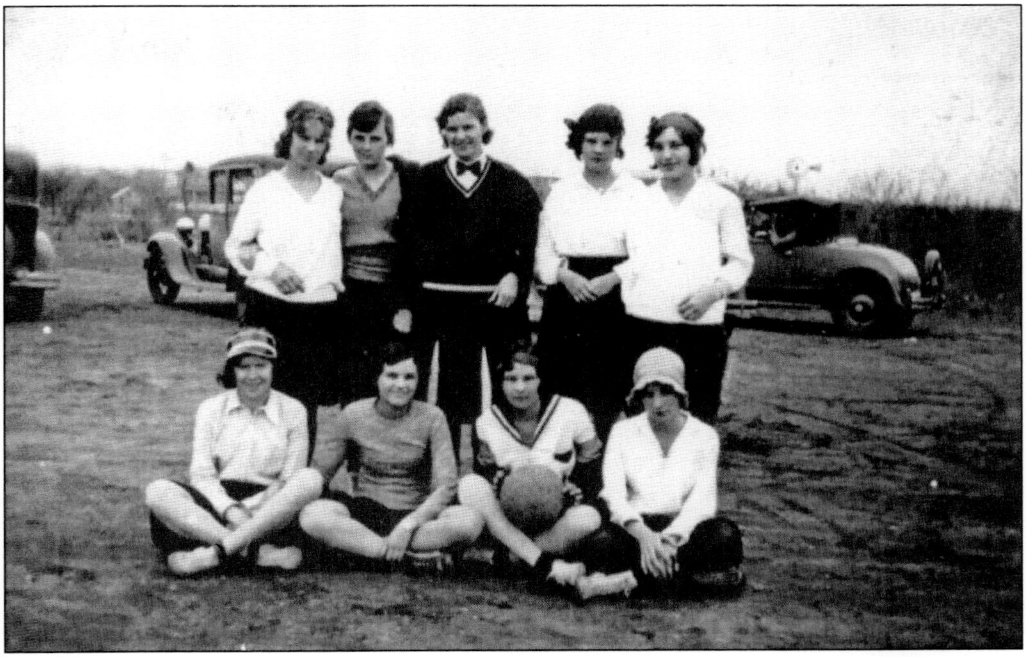

These gals were members of Mason High School's 1929–1930 basketball team. From left to right are (seated) Evelyn Wiedemann (Stinson), Opal Rolston, Elfrieda Loeffler (Durst), and Lanita Dillingham; (standing) Irene Dillingham, Grace McMillan, Coach Randerson, Alice Loeffler (Kothmann), and Florine Loeffler (Magee). (Courtesy of Jan Appleby.)

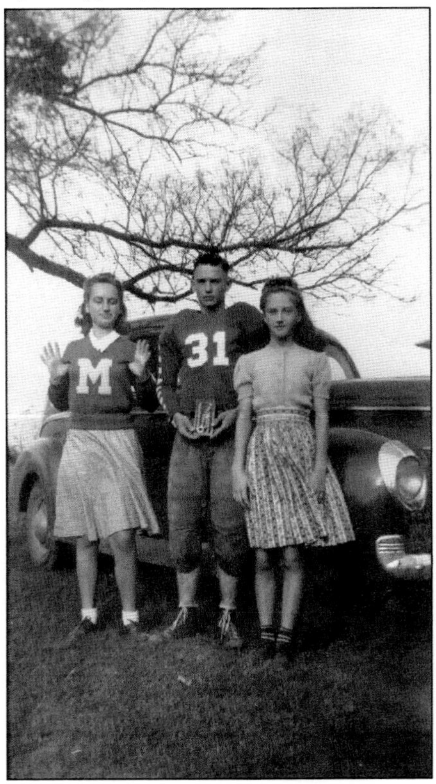

These three children of Walter and Meta Eckert are ready for the next Mason High School game around 1941. Ervin looks plenty tough in his football gear, but his sister Myrtle Eckert (Geistweidt) (left), who played the cymbals in the drum corps, is not taking the moment too seriously. Their younger sister Violet Eckert (Itz) stands proudly beside Ervin in front of what appears to be a 1938 Chevrolet coupe. (Courtesy of the Homer Geistweidt family.)

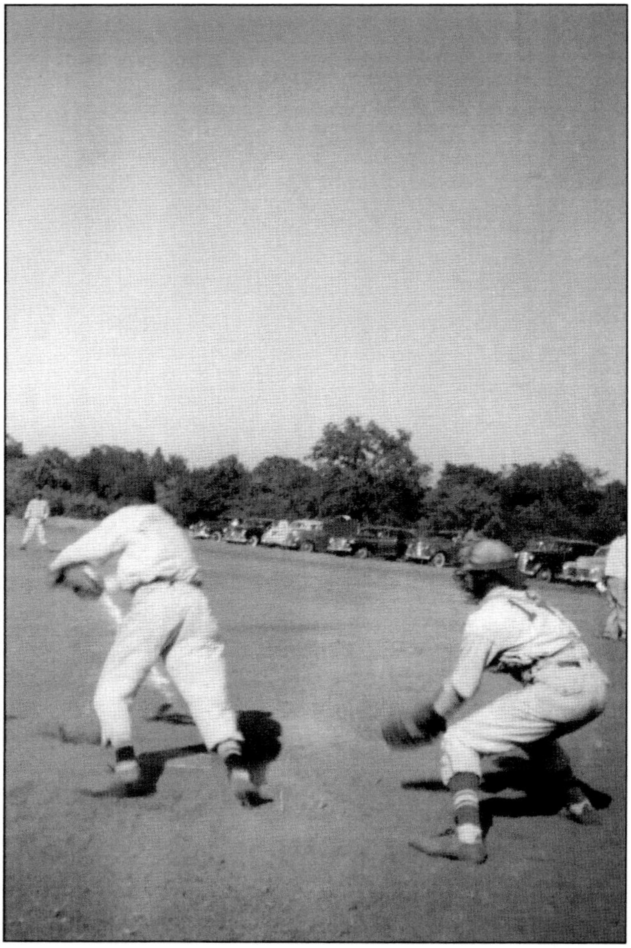

A black baseball team, the Mason All Stars, was organized in the 1930s and competed with teams from surrounding towns until the 1950s. The baseball field came to be located near Comanche Creek, not far from the present-day North Side Café. White players also participated, and everyone wore white uniforms with red letters. The catcher in the left photograph from the 1940s is possibly Albert Pen. In the bottom photograph, members of the Mason family are gathered at the baseball field in the 1930s. From left to right are (first row) Shirley Mason (Revada), Nell Marie Mason, and Violet "Sandy" Mason (Miller); (second row) Lizzie Mason and her brother Frank Mason Sr., one of the original All Stars. (Courtesy of Sandy Miller.)

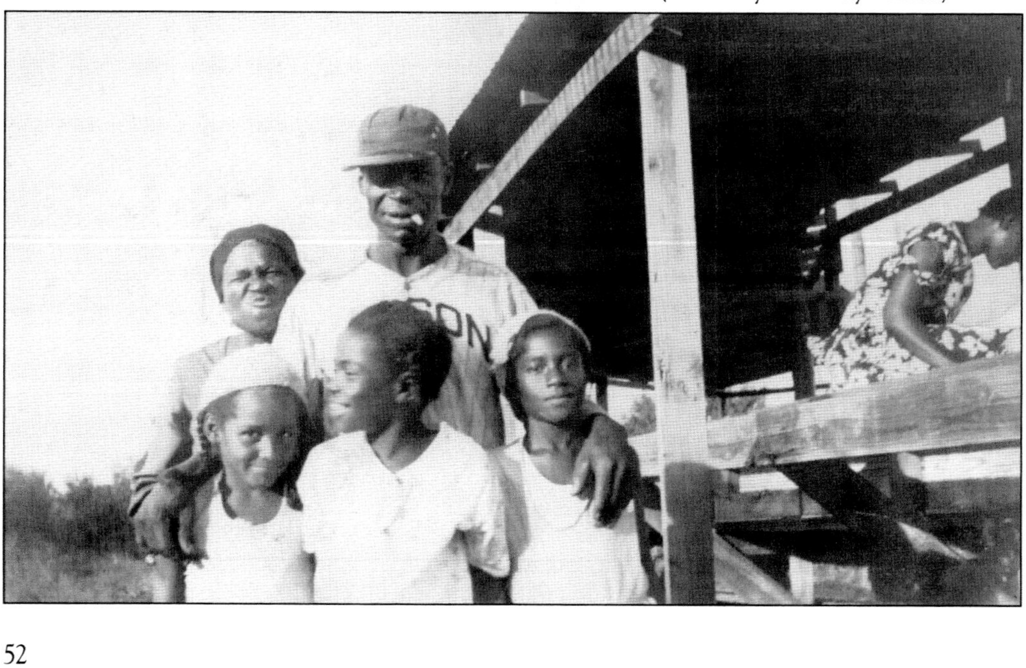

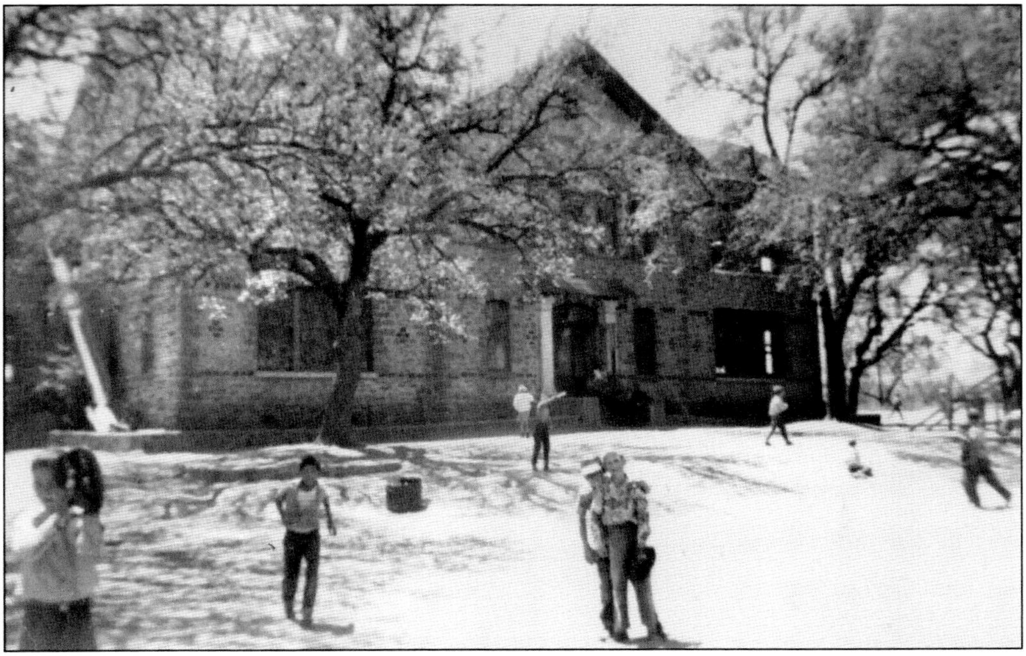

Thoughts of baseball arrive each spring in the minds of boys. This game is being played on the grounds of Mason Elementary School in 1951. The school moved to its present location on College Street during the 1952–1953 school year, and the old facility became known as the Historical Building. (Courtesy of the Arthur Geistweidt family.)

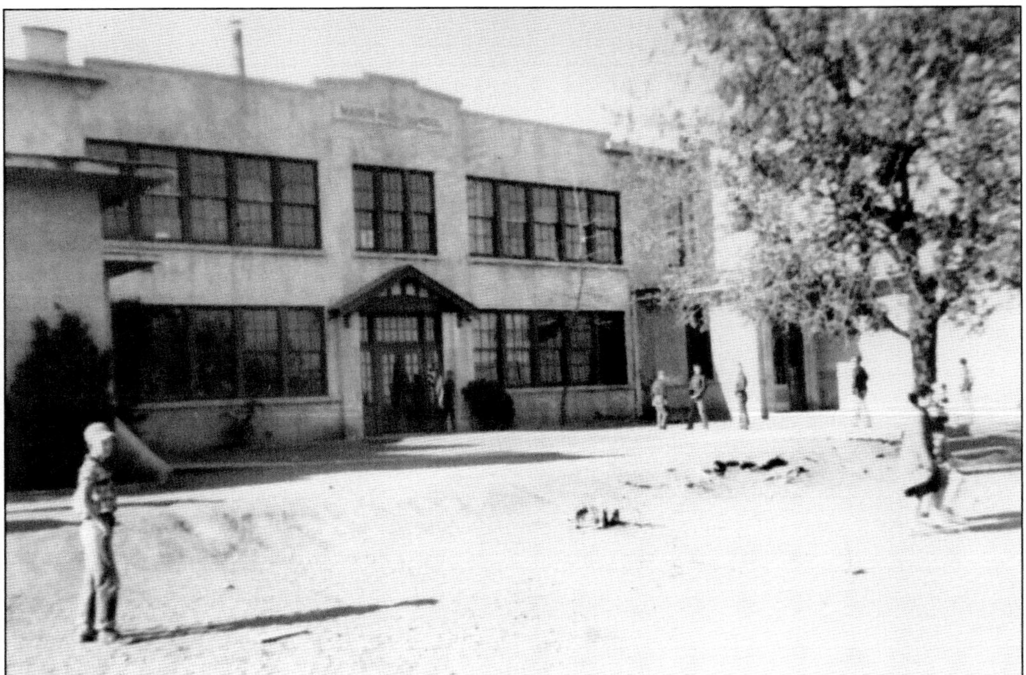

This photograph shows the campus of Mason High School in 1951. The facility was built in 1921 at a cost of $75,000, and it served as the county's high school until 1976. (Courtesy of the Arthur Geistweidt family.)

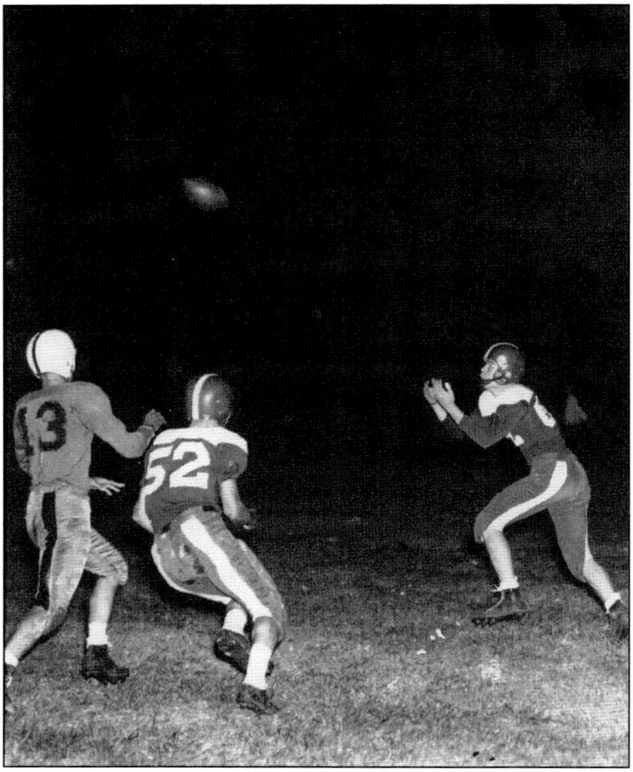

Mason County residents have always loved football and have been proud of their Cowpunchers or "Punchers," the high school football team. In this photograph, Ron Birk is just about to catch a touchdown pass in a game against Goldthwaite in the fall of 1951. No. 52 is Buddy Eckert, getting ready to block Goldthwaite player No. 43. (Photograph by Clayton Schmidt; courtesy of Ron Birk.)

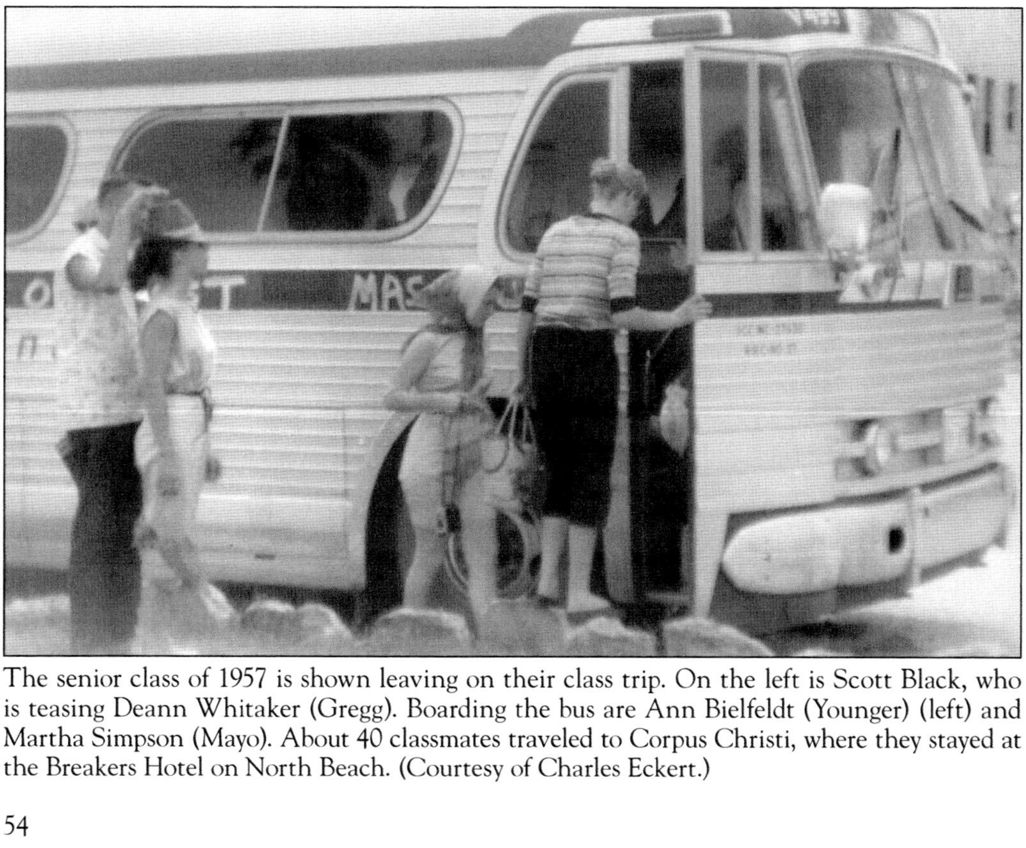

The senior class of 1957 is shown leaving on their class trip. On the left is Scott Black, who is teasing Deann Whitaker (Gregg). Boarding the bus are Ann Bielfeldt (Younger) (left) and Martha Simpson (Mayo). About 40 classmates traveled to Corpus Christi, where they stayed at the Breakers Hotel on North Beach. (Courtesy of Charles Eckert.)

Four

CHURCHES

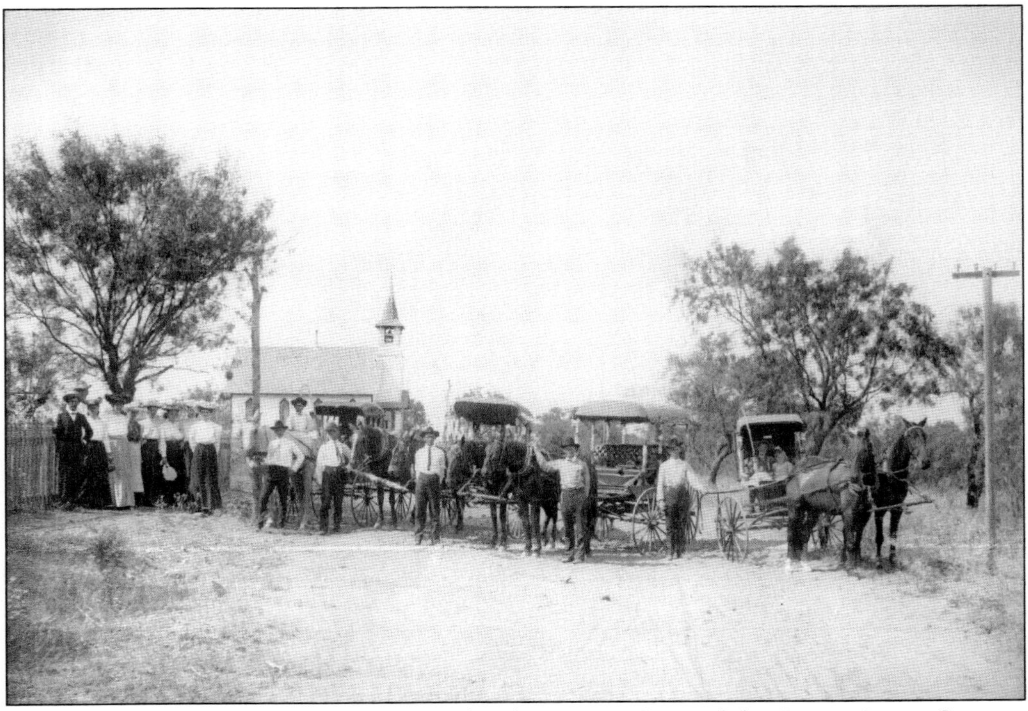

These Sunday worshipers are visiting under the trees in front of the Spring Street German Methodist Episcopal Church, North, built in 1892. The "North" designation resulted from a split in the church over slavery that first occurred nationally in 1844 and eventually divided the German Methodists of postwar Texas in 1869, pitting Unionists against Confederates. The utility poles reflect either telephone or electrical service. Mason was connected to nearby towns by telephone in 1887, and some buildings had electric lights by 1902. (Courtesy of the Mason County Museum.)

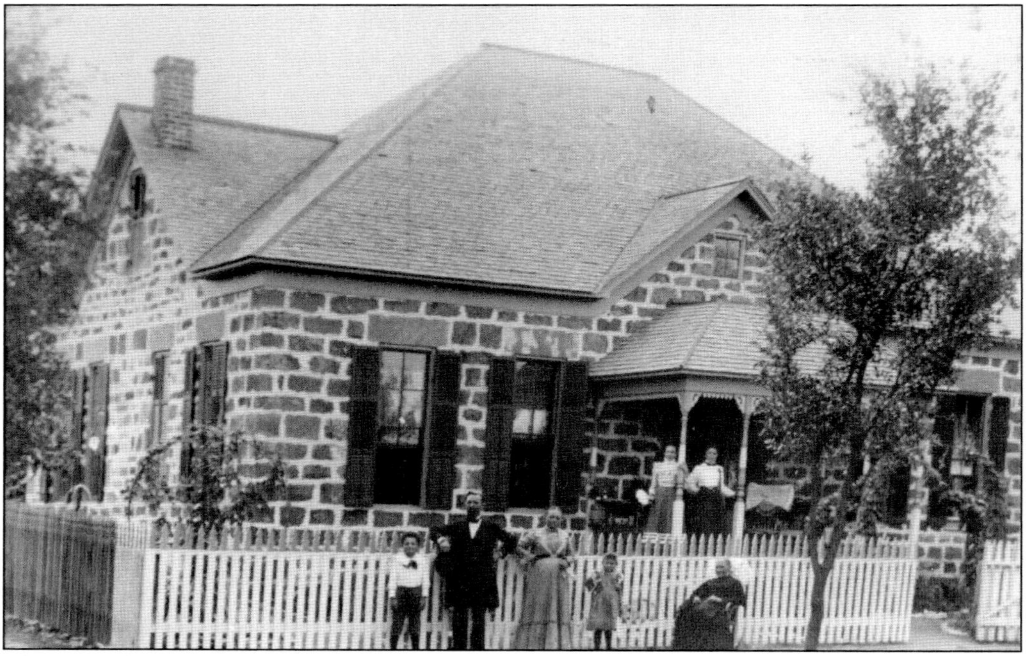

The second Hilda United Methodist Church parsonage was constructed in 1900. Standing in front is Rev. William Buehrer, who served the church from 1899–1905, his wife, Lydia, and their family. In 1929, a kitchen, bathroom, and screened porch were added. The building was last used as a parsonage in 1955. (Courtesy of the Hilda Methodist Church.)

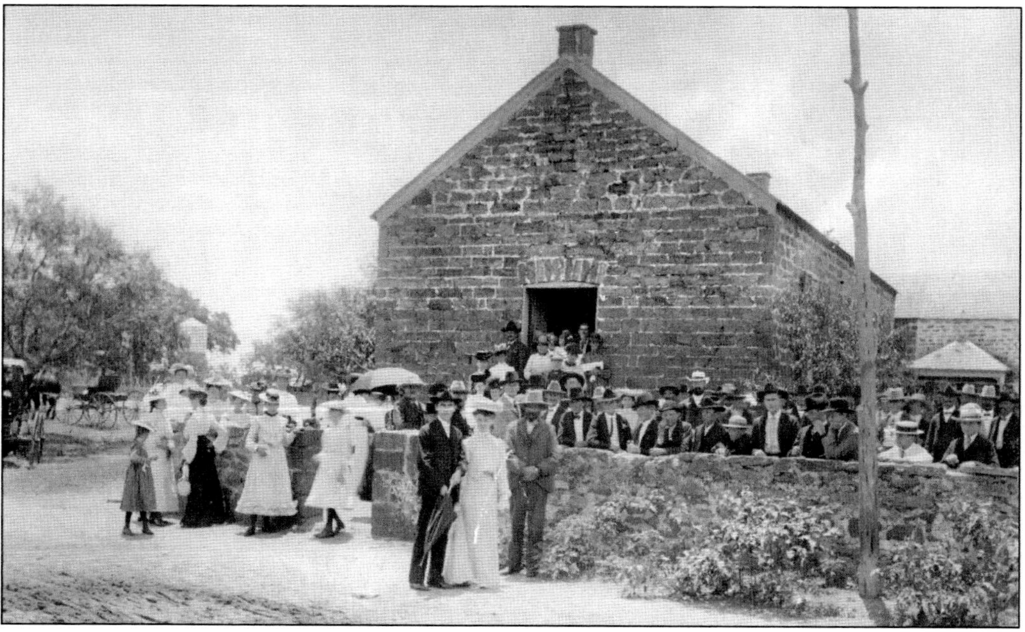

The first St. Paul Lutheran Church, built of native sandstone in 1873, is pictured on May 23, 1904, just after the members had voted to construct a new church. The parsonage in the background was constructed in 1877 and is still standing to the south of the present-day church on the Llano Highway, although its appearance was greatly altered by the addition of a second floor and exterior plastering in 1922. (Courtesy of the Arthur Geistweidt family.)

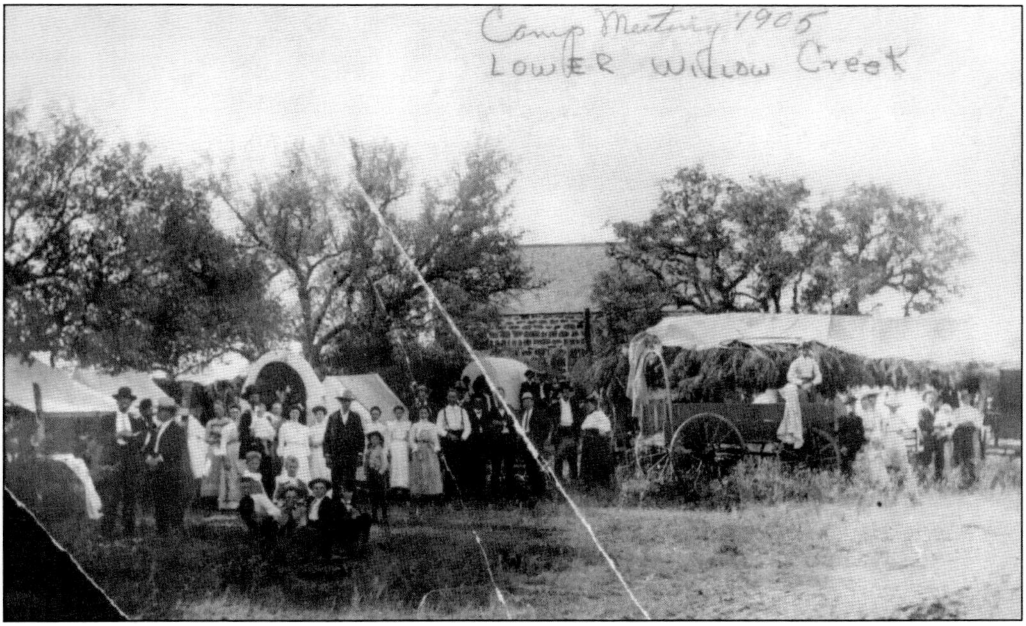

This Methodist camp meeting was held in 1905 on Lower Willow Creek. In the background is the sandstone church that was built in 1868 by the German settlers. The first camp meetings were held in the late 1860s under brush arbors and tents, and the tradition continued until 1914. The advent of the automobile made the journey to the meeting site seem shorter and easier, but it also made it more tempting to go places other than the camp meeting. (Courtesy of the Hilda Methodist Church.)

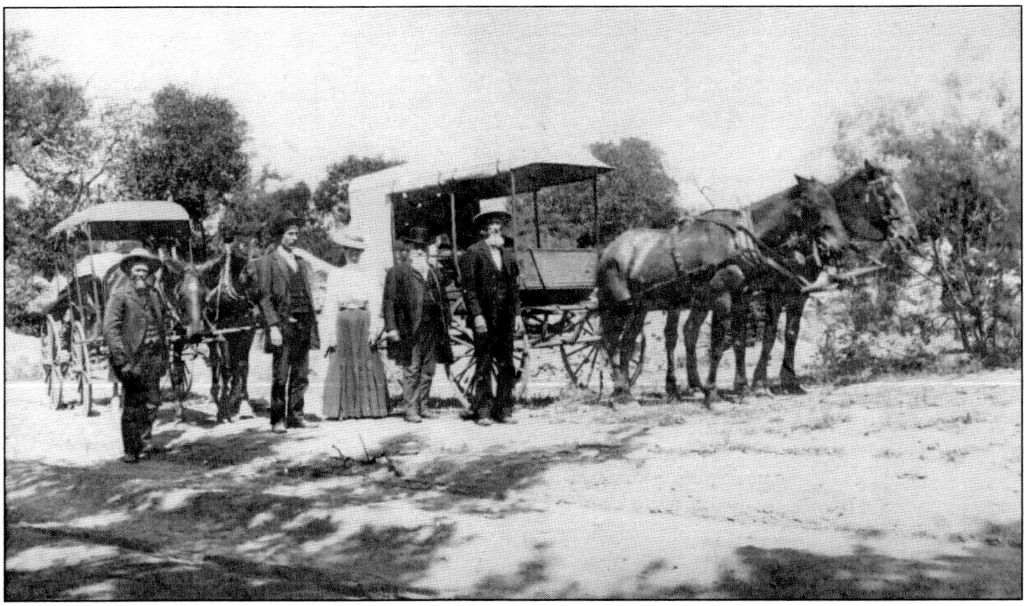

This group is heading to the 1906 District Methodist Conference, probably being held in Hilda. Standing from left to right are Christian Loeffler, Rev. Alfred D. Mohle and his wife, Emma Mohle, Rev. William Felsing, and Theodore Wiedemann. Ministers and lay leaders from surrounding areas attended these annual conferences, which were held in different churches each year. Out-of-town attendees stayed in church members' homes. (Courtesy of the Hilda Methodist Church.)

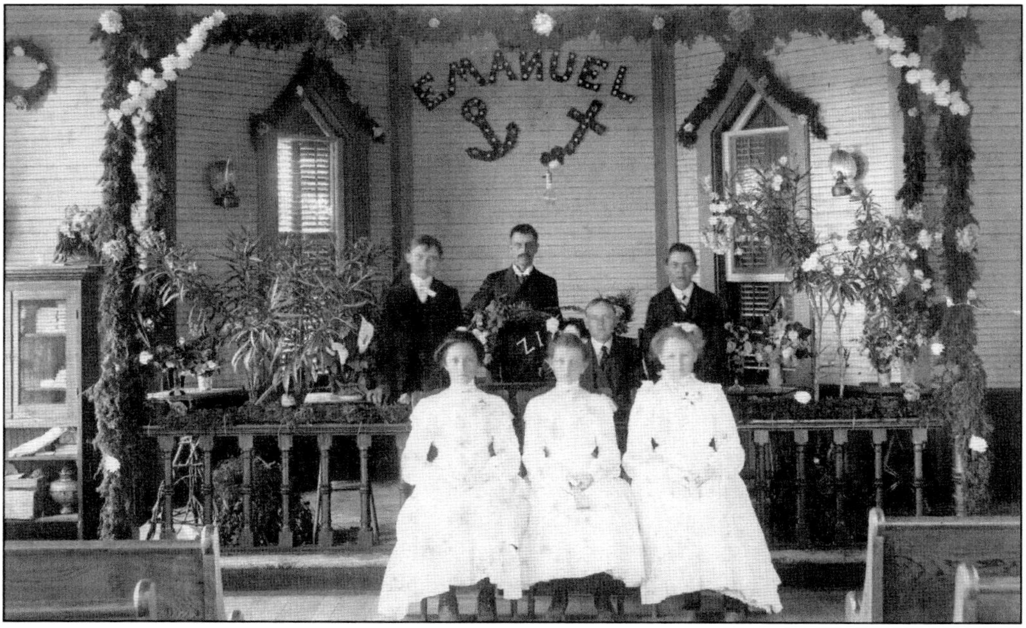

These young ladies and gentlemen are possibly members of a confirmation class at Spring Street German Methodist Episcopal Church. The interior of the church has changed little since its construction in 1892 at a cost of $1820.60. Interior details of the original structure include handmade pews, pine floors, and 3-foot wainscot. This is the only one of Mason's four oldest churches not constructed of red sandstone. Note the "N" and the spelling of Emmanuel. (Courtesy of the Mason County Museum.)

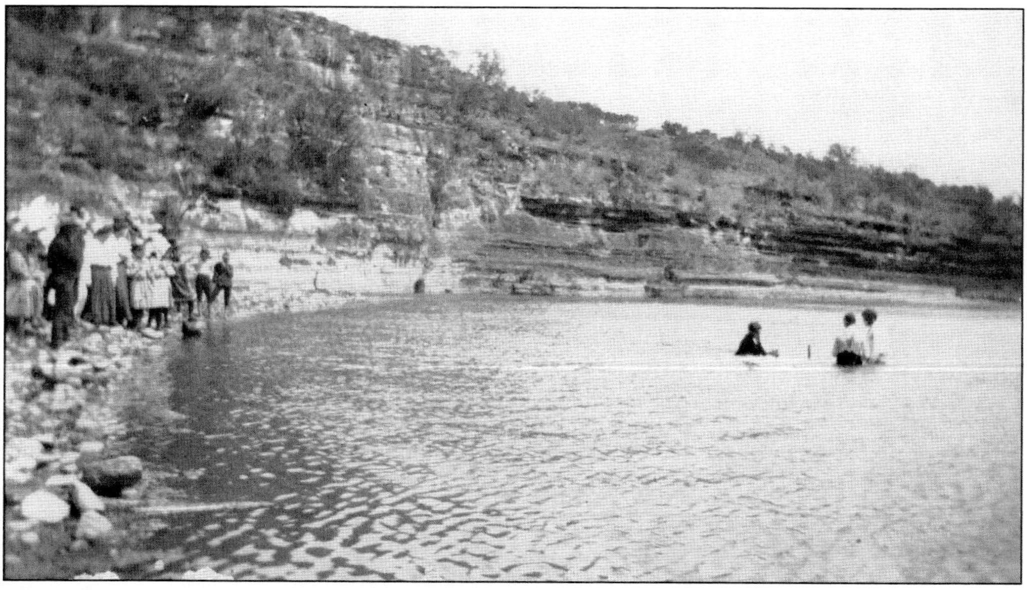

Throughout the years, the inhabitants of Mason County have used its rivers and streams for many purposes—as sources of food and water, as sites for picnicking, boating, and swimming, and as places of solitude and inspiration. This photograph, around 1920, shows some Mason County resident undergoing a spiritual renewal—a baptism in the Llano River. (Courtesy of the Mason County Museum.)

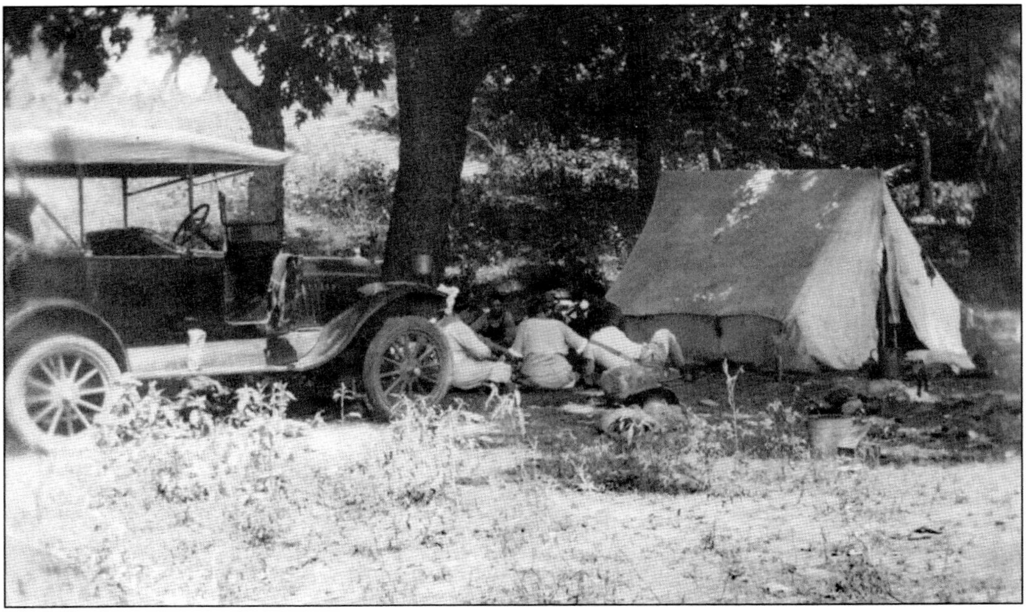

Beginning in the 1860s, German settlers, many of whom lived on isolated farms and ranches, turned to Methodist camp meetings for social interaction as well as for spiritual stimulation. Entire families loaded cots, tents, cooking utensils, chairs, bedding, clothes, and food into wagons (later automobiles) and headed to the pecan groves along the Llano River and Willow Creek for a week of singing, preaching, and praying. Worship services were originally held in German, but during World War I, English slowly began to replace German. Speaking English came easily for some, as did singing in English; however, praying to an English-speaking God proved almost impossible for many. (Courtesy of Wilburn Shearer.)

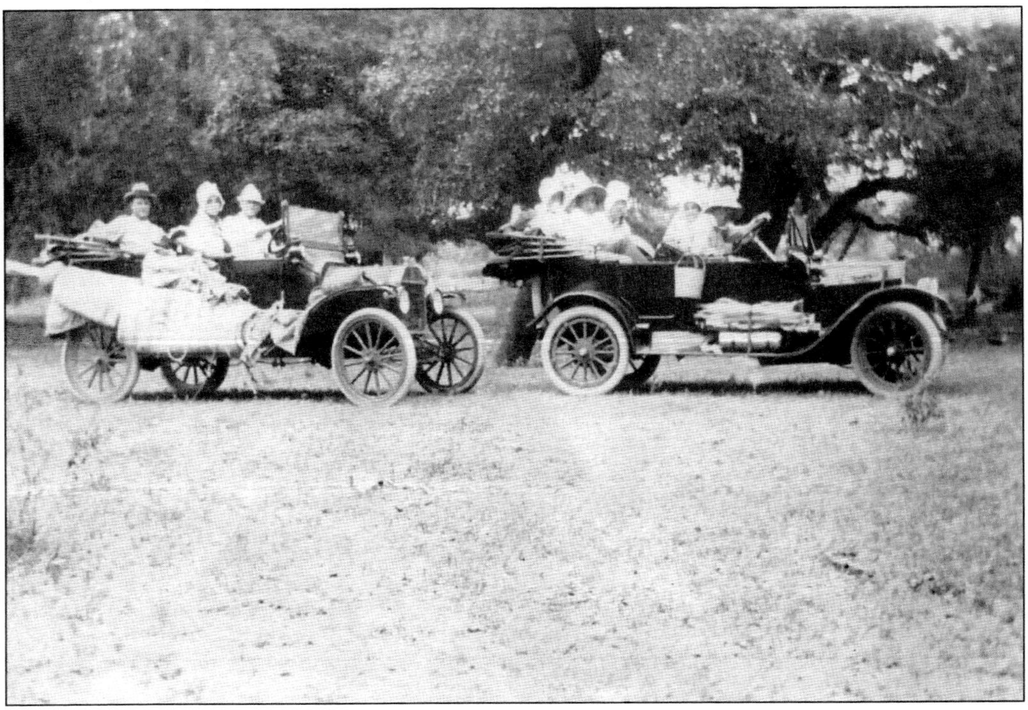

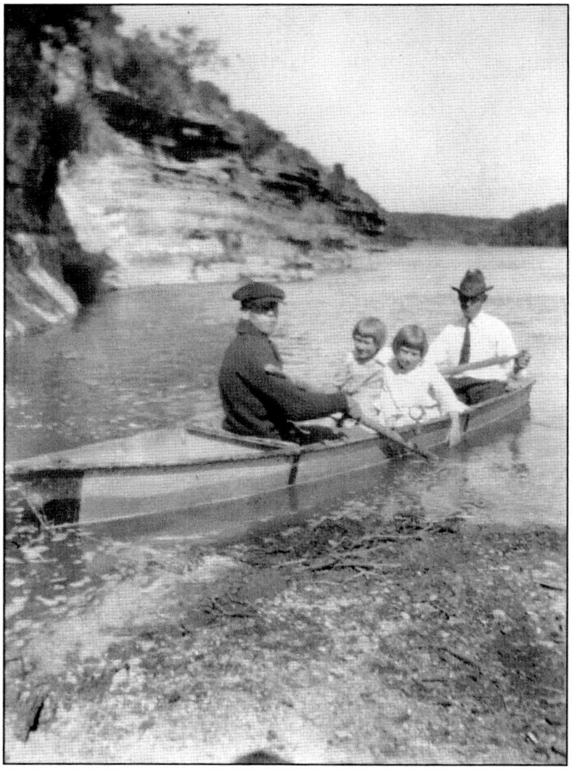

These Lutheran picnickers at the James River Crossing on the Llano River are, from left to right, Arthur Eckert, Karlita Hofmann (Lange), Anna Marie Rode, and Robert Schmidt. At the time of this photograph, around 1924, Robert and his brother Carl were active in the Luther League for young people, established in 1923 at St. Paul Lutheran Church. (Courtesy of the Arthur Geistweidt family.)

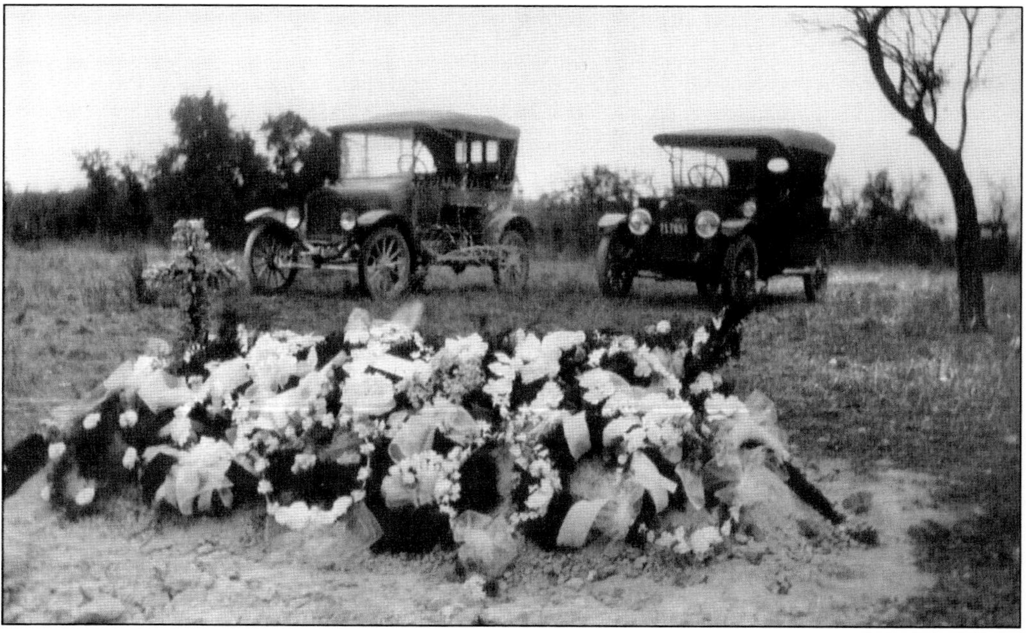

Elaborate decoration of graves was typical in the 1920s—as was taking photographs immediately after burials. This picture was taken after the funeral of Margaretha Fritze Anderegg, who died on November 30, 1924. She had arrived with John Meusebach in the first group of German immigrants to settle in Fredericksburg and later made her home at Cow Valley, 6 miles south of Hilda. (Courtesy of Charles Eckert.)

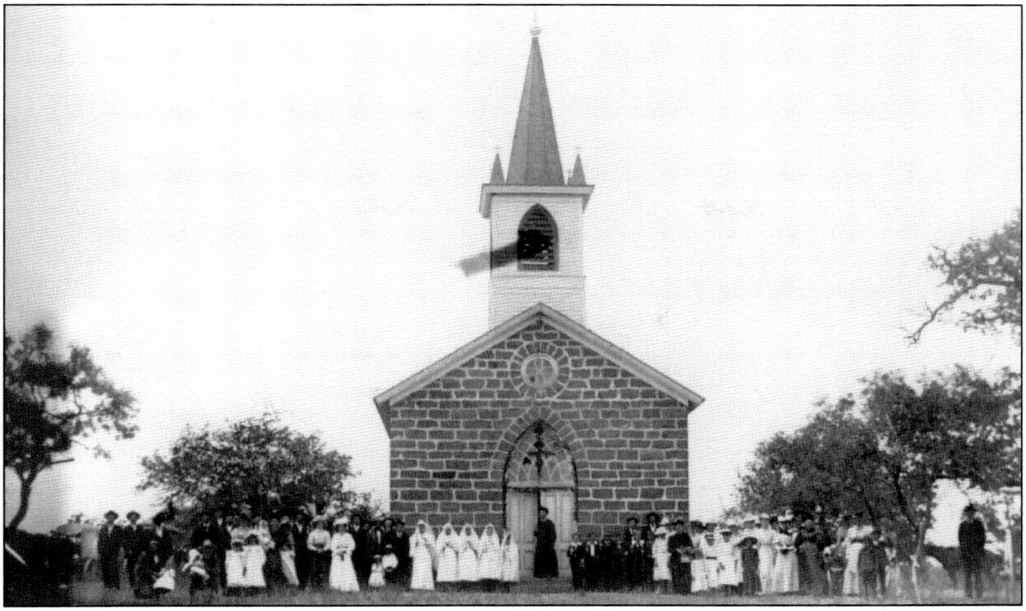

St. Joseph's Catholic Church was organized in 1873. Elizabeth Bridgett Crosby Taylor is said to have ridden horseback over Mason County collecting funds with which to build the sandstone structure, erected by local stonemasons on land donated by David and Lucy Doole. The building was dedicated in 1876, a bell was added in 1877, and a pine floor was installed in 1906. The bottom photograph shows the sanctuary. Faintly visible on the ceiling are angels, clouds, and stars painted in 1916 by Manuel Lopez, a Mason resident. Little was changed until 1963, when the church was remodeled and ceiling tiles were installed. The angels remained covered by the tiles until a rainstorm and tornado in 1989 resulted in their being uncovered, as they remain today. (Courtesy of MCHC.)

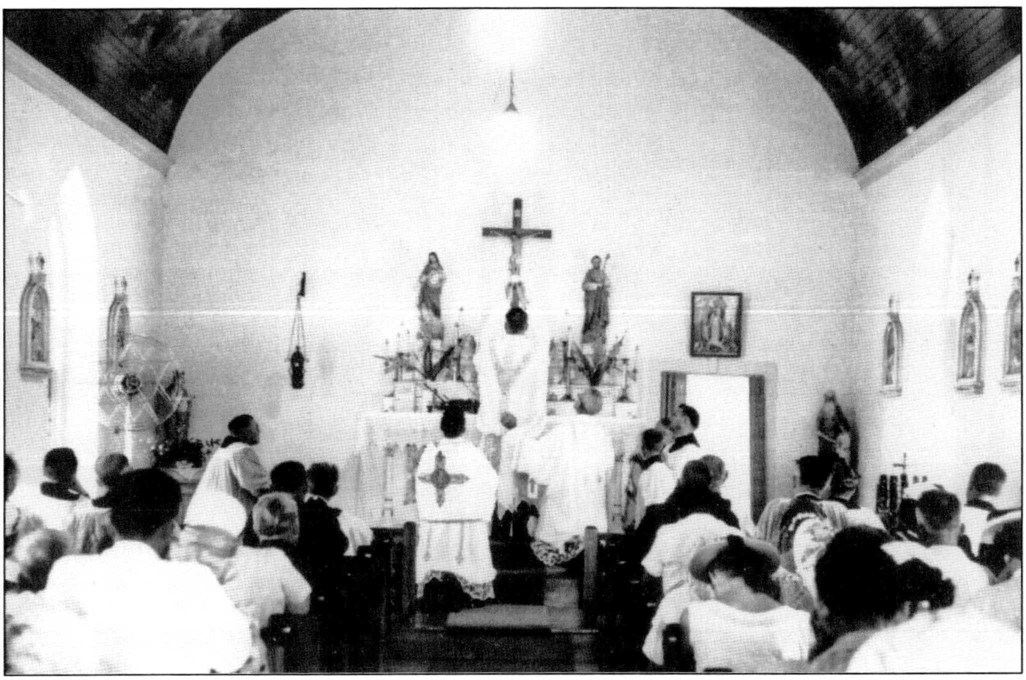

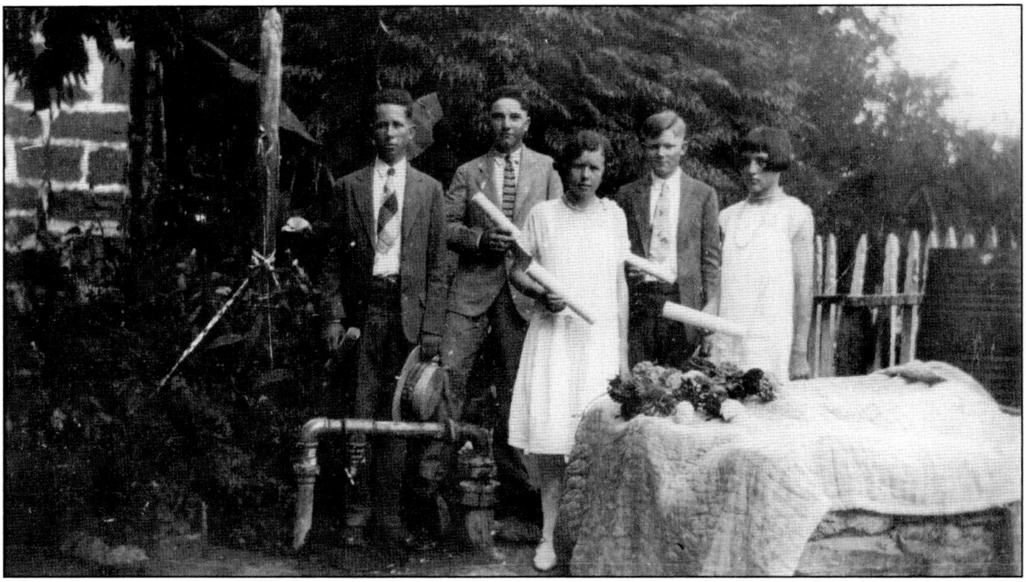

The 1926 confirmation class of the Hilda Methodist Church included, from left to right, Andrew Wiedemann, Hugo Sattler, Silas Kothmann, Evelyn Wiedemann (Stinson), and Florine Loeffler (Magee). Confirmation classes usually lasted three months, and on Confirmation Sunday the students had to answer questions in front of the congregation. This was one of the most important milestones in a Methodist teenager's life. (Courtesy of Jan Appleby.)

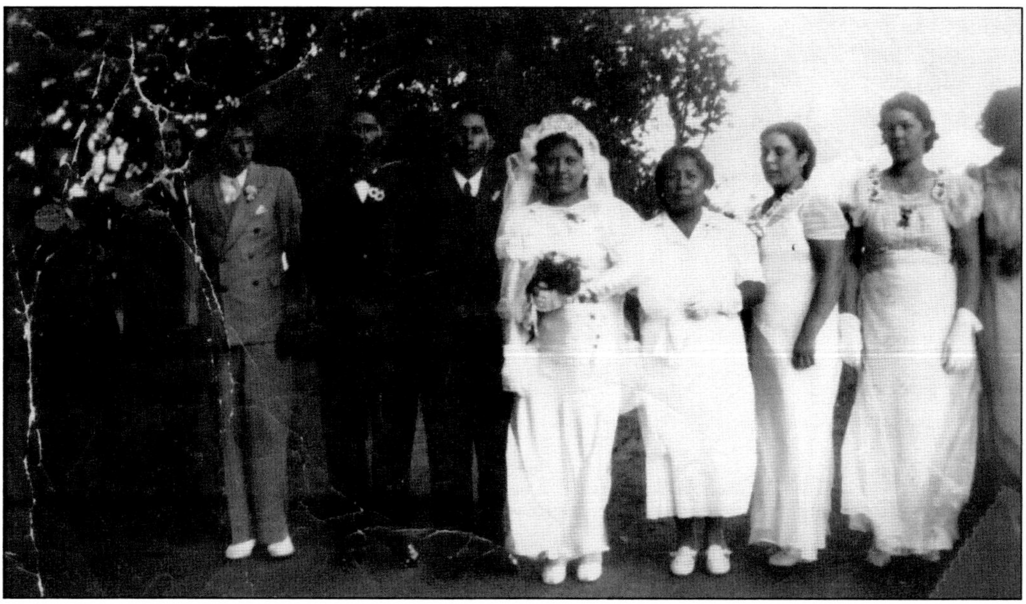

Pedro "Pete" Hernandez and Miceala "Mickey" Castorena were married on June 18, 1939, at St. Joseph's Catholic Church. This wedding photograph was taken at the reception at the Hightower Ranch, which had a dance pavilion. Carmen Florez, the matron of honor, is standing to the right of the bride. (Courtesy of Candy Luna.)

Five

At Home

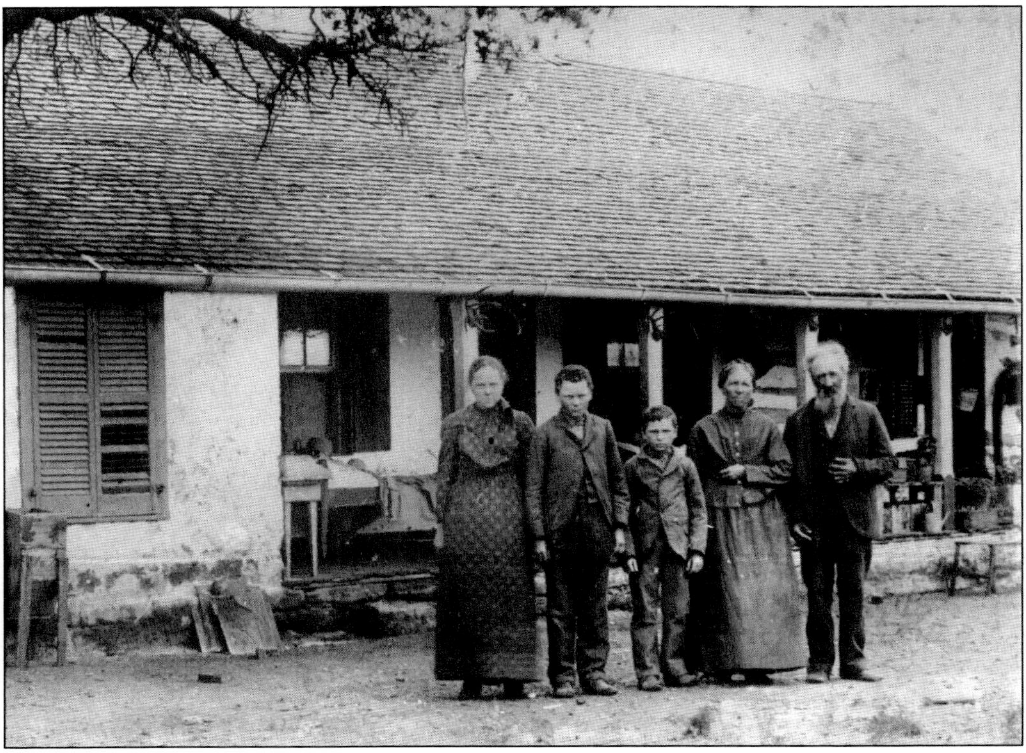

The Reichenau family poses for a photograph around 1894 at their homestead in Simonsville. From left to right are Katie, Hugo, Willie, Johanna, and Adolph A. Reichenau. Their poses and facial expressions were characteristic of the time and are often referred to as rural gothic. Adolph, a German patriarch of the old school, was a veteran of the Mexican War and an intrepid Texas Ranger. The Reichenau place was purchased in 1960 by Fred Gipson, author of *Old Yeller*. (Courtesy of Charles Reichenau.)

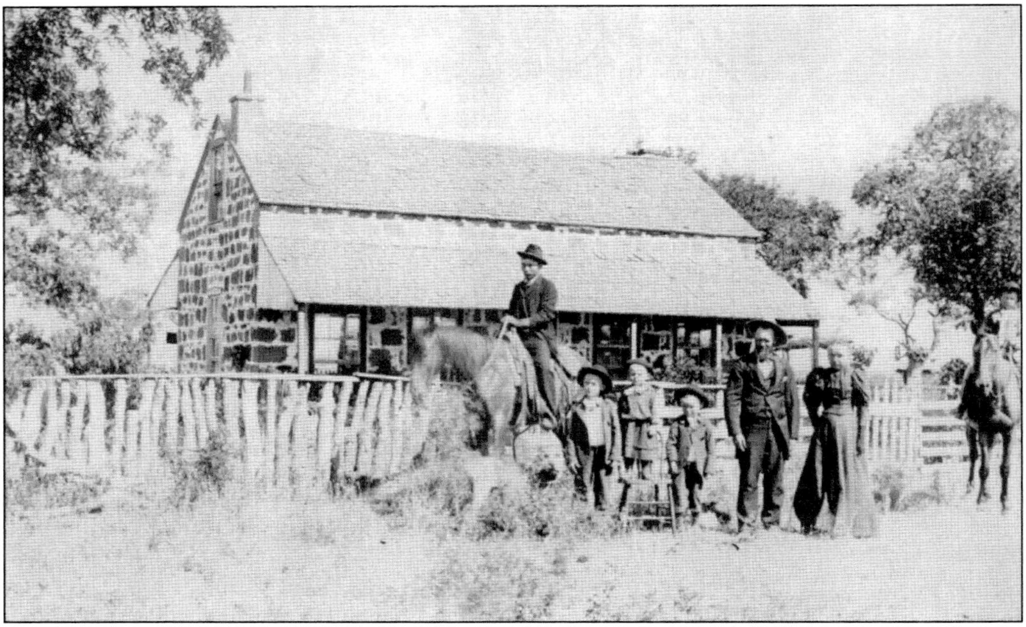

Pictured in front of their Hilda farmhouse in 1896 is the family of Christian and Maria Geistweidt Loeffler. From left to right are sons Frank Henry, Karl Daniel, Will John, Wilhelm Elias, Christian, mother Maria Geistweidt (Loeffler), and Edwin August Loeffler. Their eldest son, Frank, purchased the house from his parents when he married in 1904. (Courtesy of Jan Appleby.)

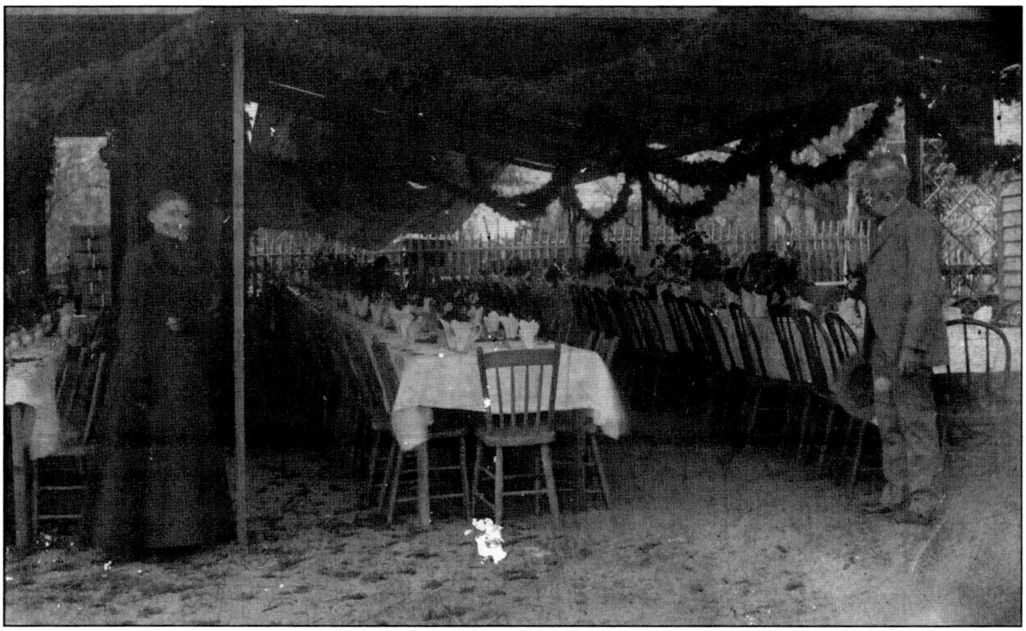

This rare photograph of a 19th-century social event at a private residence shows the wedding reception of Hugo Koock and Lena Hofmann on November 8, 1899, under an arbor decorated with cedar garlands. The reception occurred at the home of her parents, Karl and Katherine Hofmann (shown standing by the cloth-covered tables). About 300 guests were served wine, baked turkey, and stuffed pigs with glass eyes. A dance followed in Koock's Hall. (Courtesy of the Arthur Geistweidt family.)

Charlie Evers is pictured on a horse at his ranch in the Salt Branch area of southern Mason County in the early 1900s. Windmills were vital for water supply in many parts of the county. However, when the wind was light, some windmills were supplemented by engine-driven pump jacks, as seen in the background. (Courtesy of Helen Habecker.)

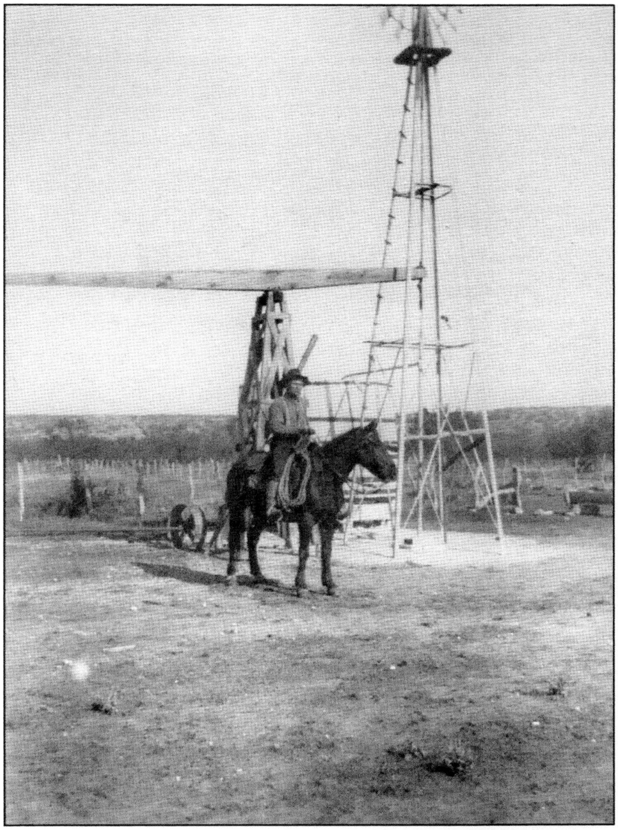

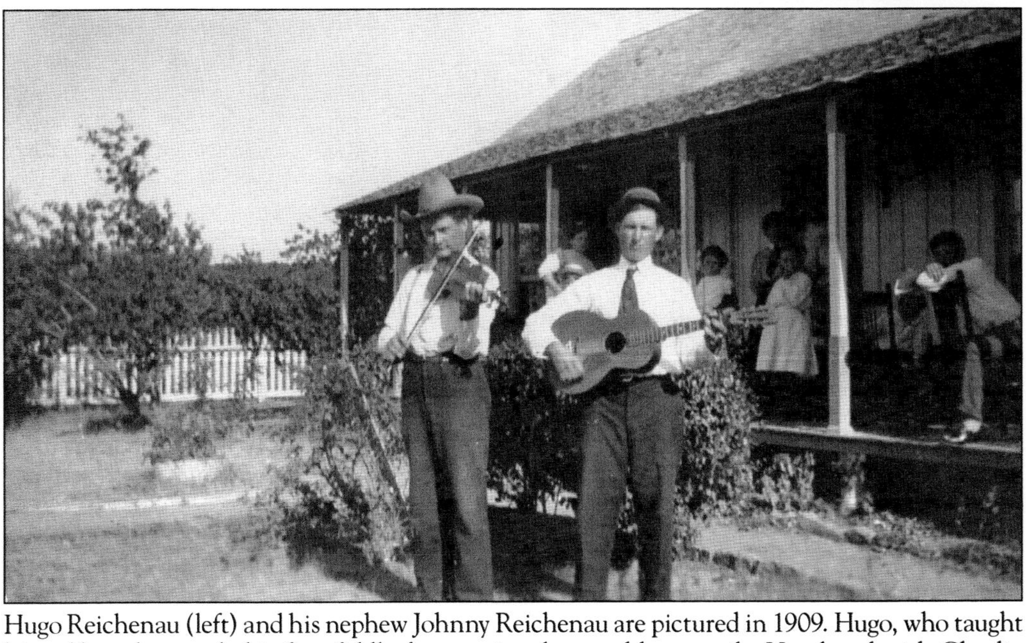

Hugo Reichenau (left) and his nephew Johnny Reichenau are pictured in 1909. Hugo, who taught himself to play, made his first fiddle from a cigar box and horse tails. He played with Charlie Hofmann's band in Mason and sometimes rode horseback more than 18 miles to play his fiddle at Cherry Spring dances. (Courtesy of Charles Reichenau.)

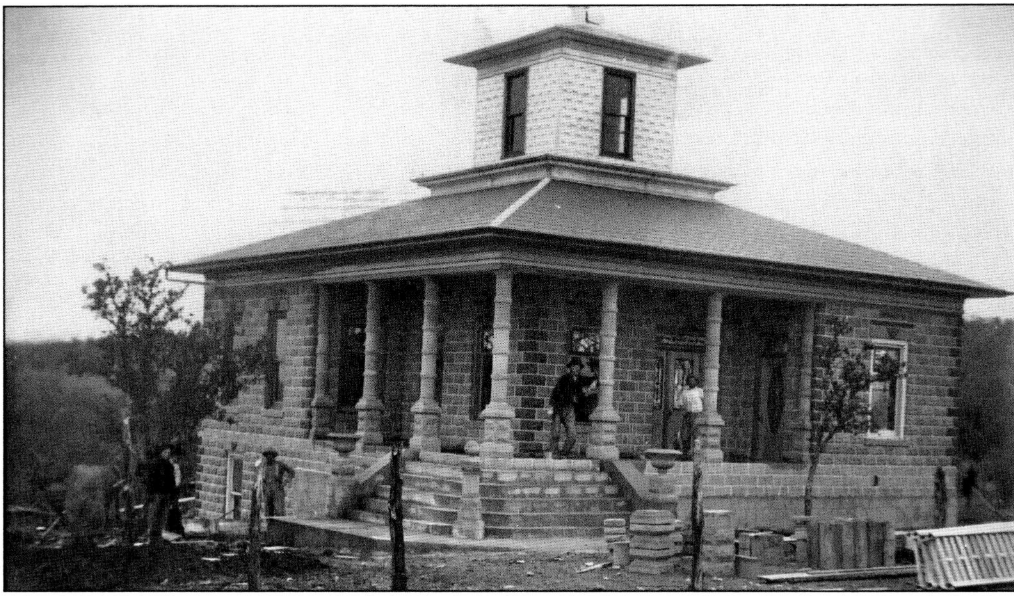

The Winkle residence on Lincoln Avenue was constructed as a "spec" house in 1911 using Basse Block, a popular building material of that era. It was purchased by Fritz Winkle in 1912 and remained in the family until 1964. When finished, the cupola on top would be decorated with the white railing seen in the front yard on the right. Used as a children's playroom, it was later removed because it was not watertight. The stone blocks in the yard became railings for the front porch. (Courtesy of Bobbye and Marshall Frazier.)

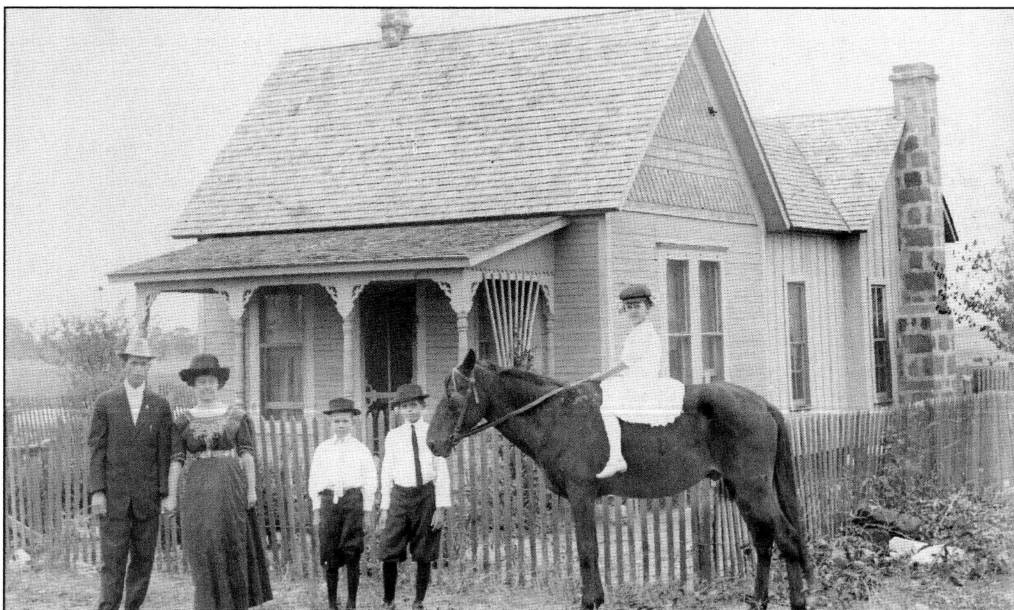

Maud Mason McWilliams Ross, second from the left, holds hands with her second husband, Charles Ross, outside their house near Double Knobs around 1912, the year they were married. The children are, from left to right, her son Guy McWilliams, Charles's son Dorset Ross, and her daughter Irlene McWilliams (Underwood) on the horse. The house was located along Streeter Lane and is no longer standing. (Courtesy of Patsy Zesch.)

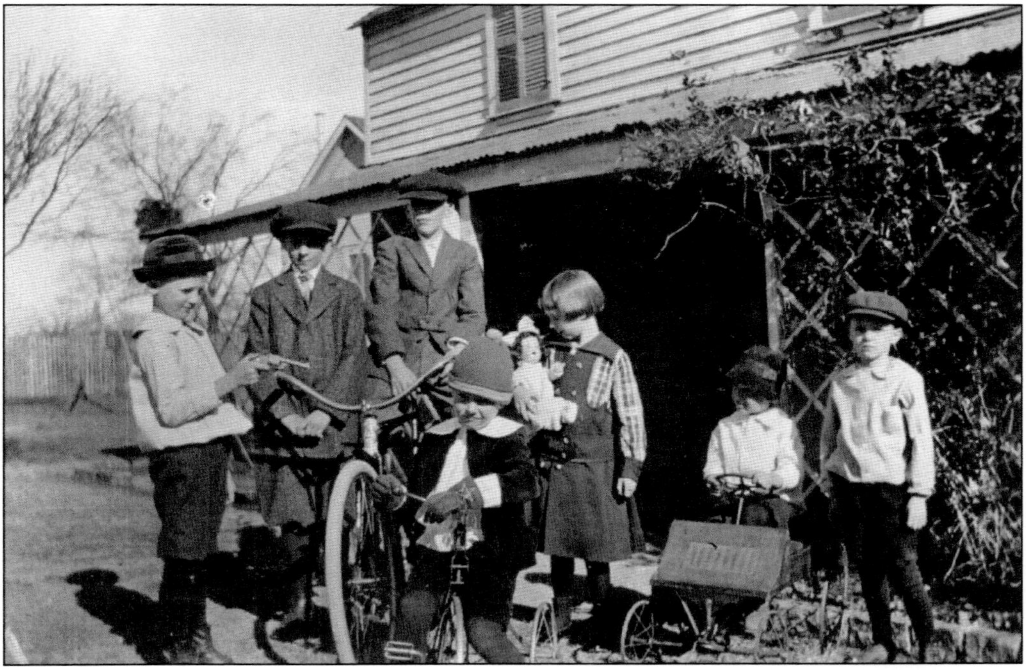

These children, all dressed up in 1916, are standing in front of the Karl and Katherine Hofmann house on Smith Street. The Hofmanns were the grandparents of Anna Marie Koock (Geistweidt), in the center holding her doll, and her brother William "Koockie" Koock, the tall boy to the left of Anna Marie. They and their mother, Lena Hofmann Koock, moved into this home after their father, Hugo, died of pneumonia in 1911. (Courtesy of the Arthur Geistweidt family.)

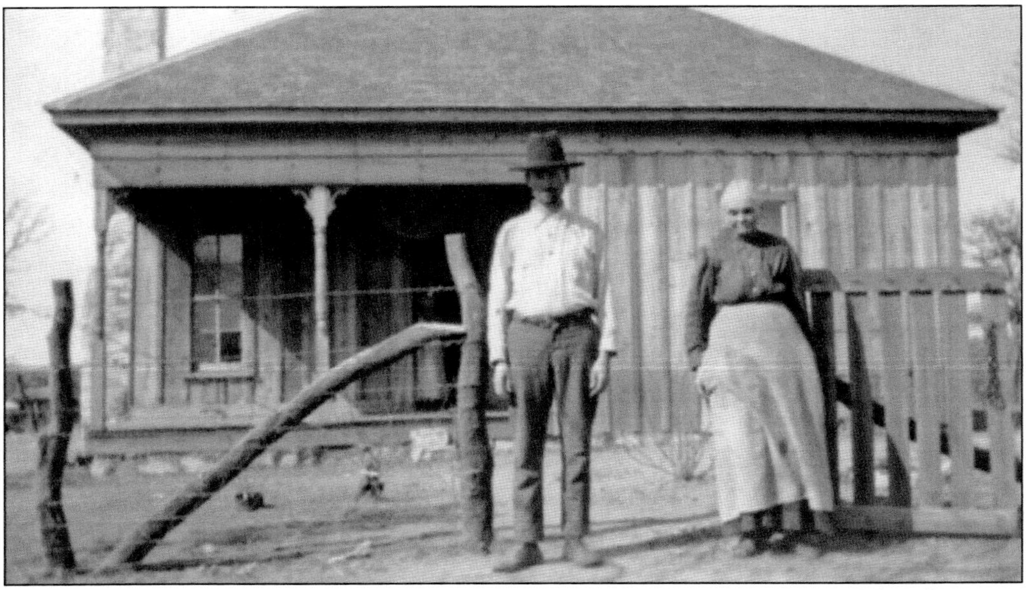

Edward "Ed" Cavness stands beside his mother, Martha Doyal Cavness, in front of their five-room house built in 1905. It replaced the log cabin where Martha and her husband, Jasper, raised 15 children. Martha lived in the new house with her unmarried sons Ed, Alfred, and Henry until her death in 1925. She was a daughter of Matthew Doyal, a friend of James and Rezin Bowie who helped the Bowies search for the Los Almagres silver mine in 1834. (Courtesy of Emma Gene Jackson.)

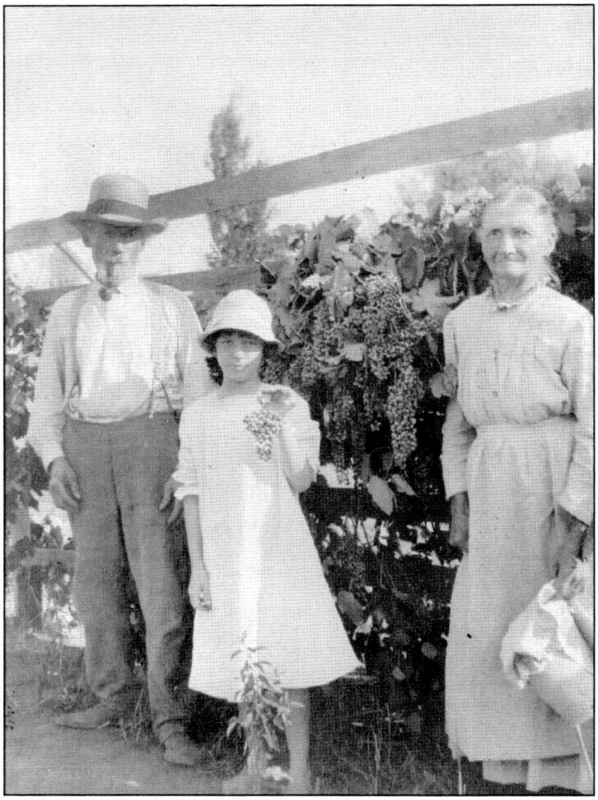

Karl Hofmann, pictured at his home on Smith Street with his wife, Katherine, and their granddaughter Anna Marie Koock (Geistweidt), made wine to give to his customers and to use at home and in church communion. He used three types of grapes. For men's wine, he used wild Mustang grapes that grew nearby on Centennial Spring Creek. In his garden, he grew Black Spanish grapes, which were used for ladies' wine. He used one other type of grape for a lesser grade of wine. (Courtesy of the Arthur Geistweidt family.)

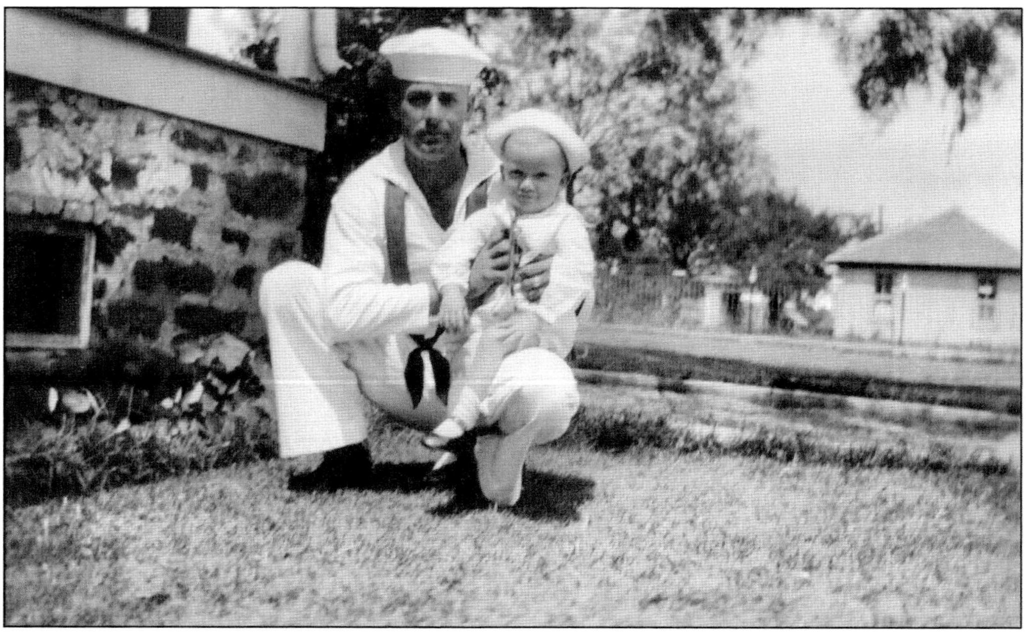

Emeth Keller is holding his nephew Hilton Moneyhon around 1919. Keller enlisted in the U.S. Navy in 1918 and was assigned to the USS *Shirlin*, which conducted submarine patrols in the Gulf of Mexico. During World War II, Moneyhon served in the U.S. Army with the combat unit that invaded Mindanao, Philippines, in 1945. (Courtesy of Rebecca Moneyhon.)

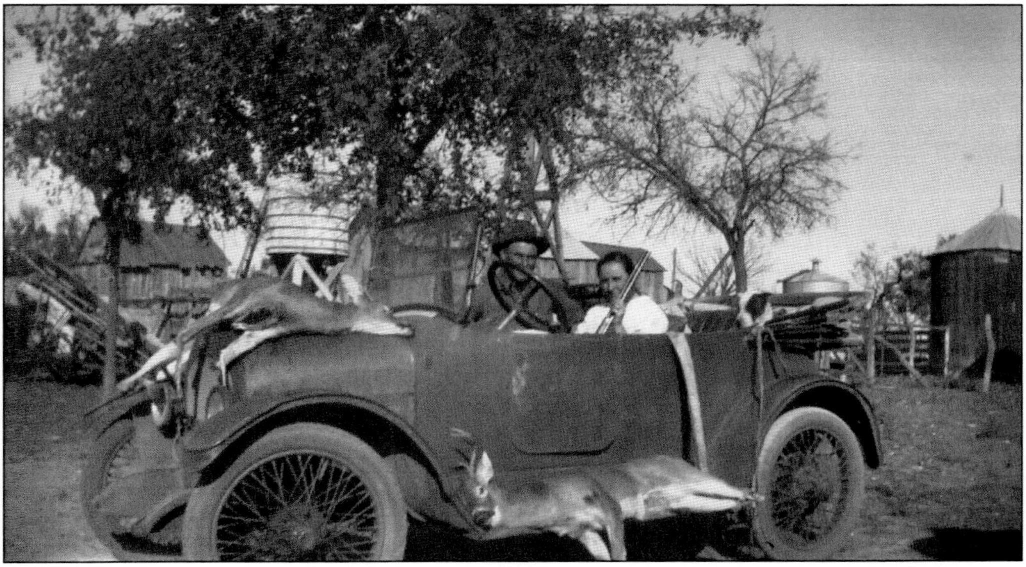

Hugh Shearer and his wife, Hulda Willmann Shearer, pose in the style of Bonnie and Clyde, displaying trophies from a Mason County hunt, around 1920. "Bonnie" holds a .30-30 Winchester. The photograph was taken at the Willmann home place. (Courtesy of Wilburn Shearer.)

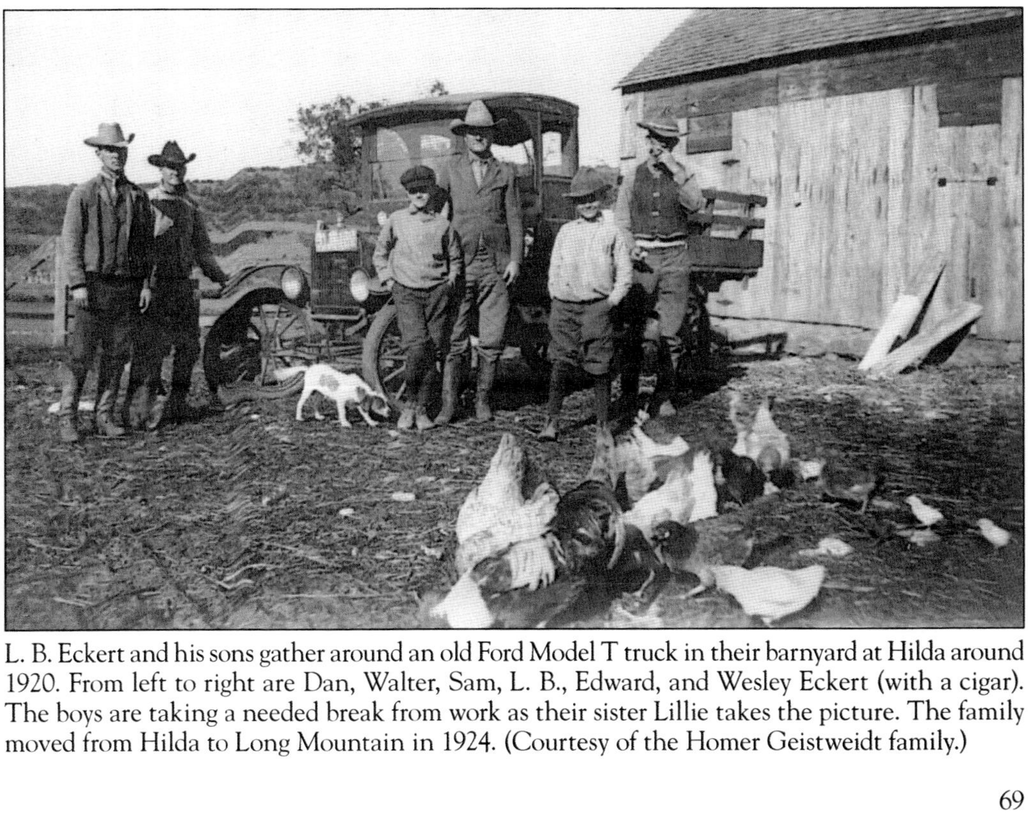

L. B. Eckert and his sons gather around an old Ford Model T truck in their barnyard at Hilda around 1920. From left to right are Dan, Walter, Sam, L. B., Edward, and Wesley Eckert (with a cigar). The boys are taking a needed break from work as their sister Lillie takes the picture. The family moved from Hilda to Long Mountain in 1924. (Courtesy of the Homer Geistweidt family.)

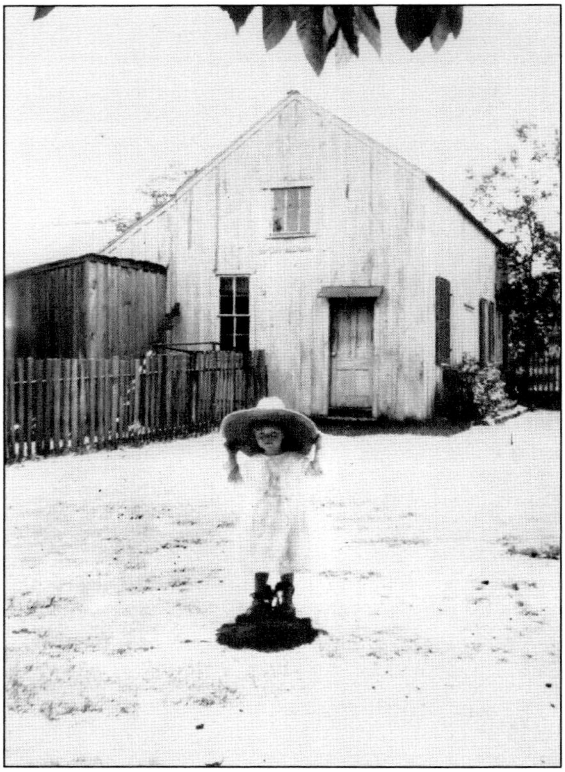

Marie Louise Bielfeldt (Loeffler) is pictured in 1922, standing in front of her grandfather Karl Hofmann's workshop. Karl, a carpenter and cabinetmaker, came to Mason around 1870. He started building coffins in his workshop located behind the family home on Smith Street and thus became Mason's first undertaker. His whole family helped with the funeral business, and his sons Henry and Ernest continued it after Karl's death in 1920. (Courtesy of the Arthur Geistweidt family.)

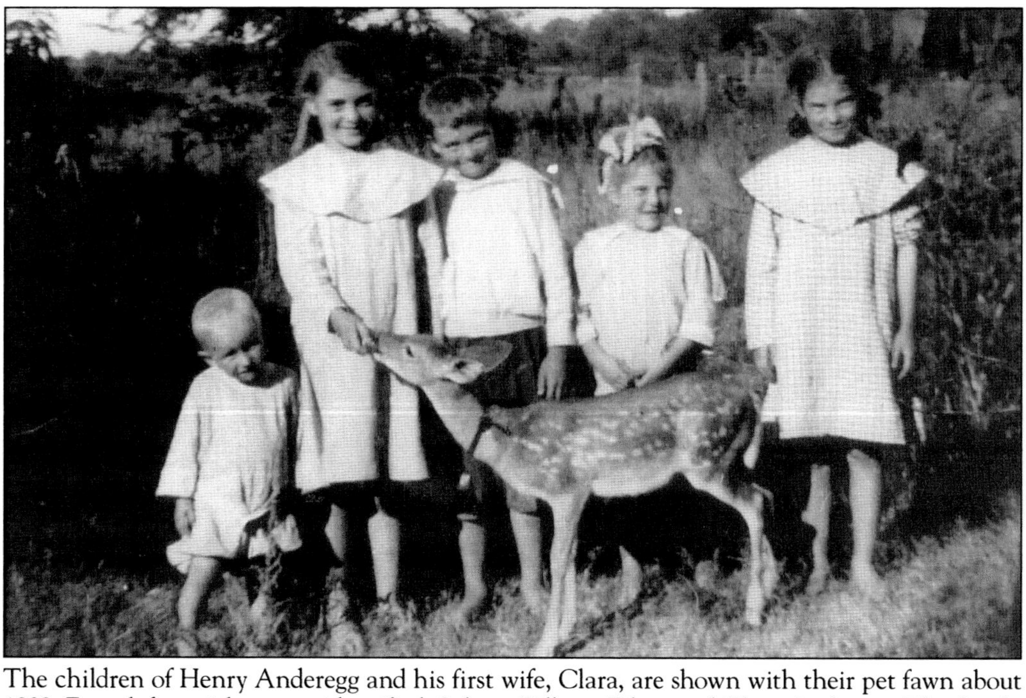

The children of Henry Anderegg and his first wife, Clara, are shown with their pet fawn about 1922. From left to right are unidentified, Selma, Gilbert, Edna, and Clara Anderegg. The family lived on the Mason-Gillespie County line in the Salt Branch area. The fawn was probably an orphan raised by the family until it was grown. (Courtesy of Charles Eckert.)

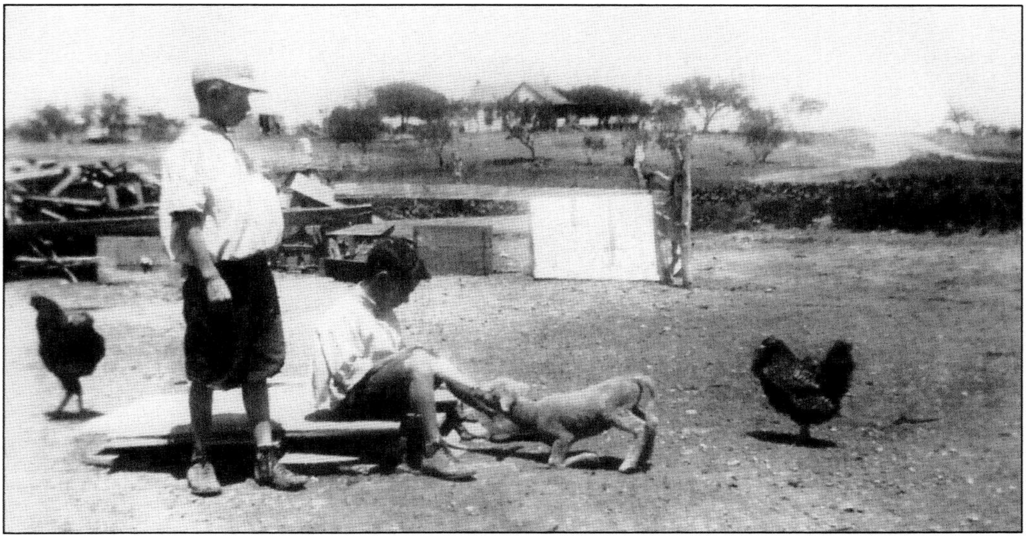

Lawrence Reardon (left) watches his brother Franz bottle-feed their lamb on the family farm near Art in the early 1920s. In 1924, T. O. Reardon, the boys' father, moved his family into the town of Mason, where he established the Reardon Grain Company. Lawrence began working at the Mason post office in 1927, became the postmaster in 1943, and retired from the postal service in 1972. Franz, in addition to ranching, worked with his father in the grain business. (Courtesy of Pat Reardon.)

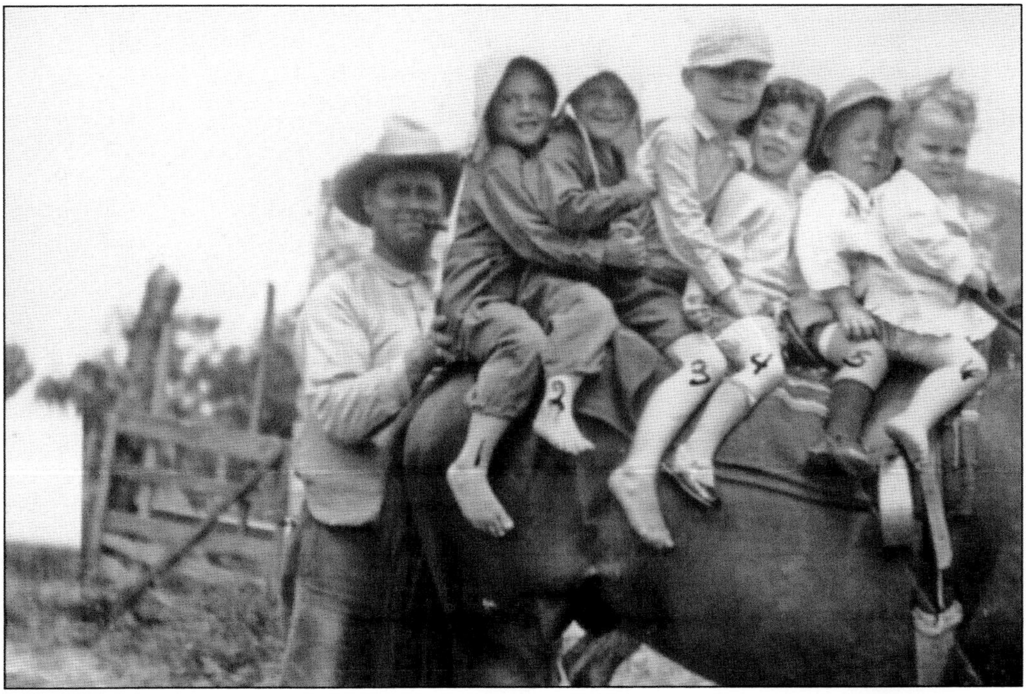

Jane Hofmann (Hoerster) (right) celebrates her first birthday on the family ranch at Grit on June 9, 1923. Her young companions are, from left to right, sisters Della Louise (Moneyhon) and Mary Maud (McMillan), cousin Bill Hofmann, friend Lena Sibyl Hey (Snyder), and cousin L. H. "Hoppy" McMillan. Jane's father, Otto Hofmann, keeps the rambunctious sextet from falling off the horse. (Courtesy of Jane Hoerster.)

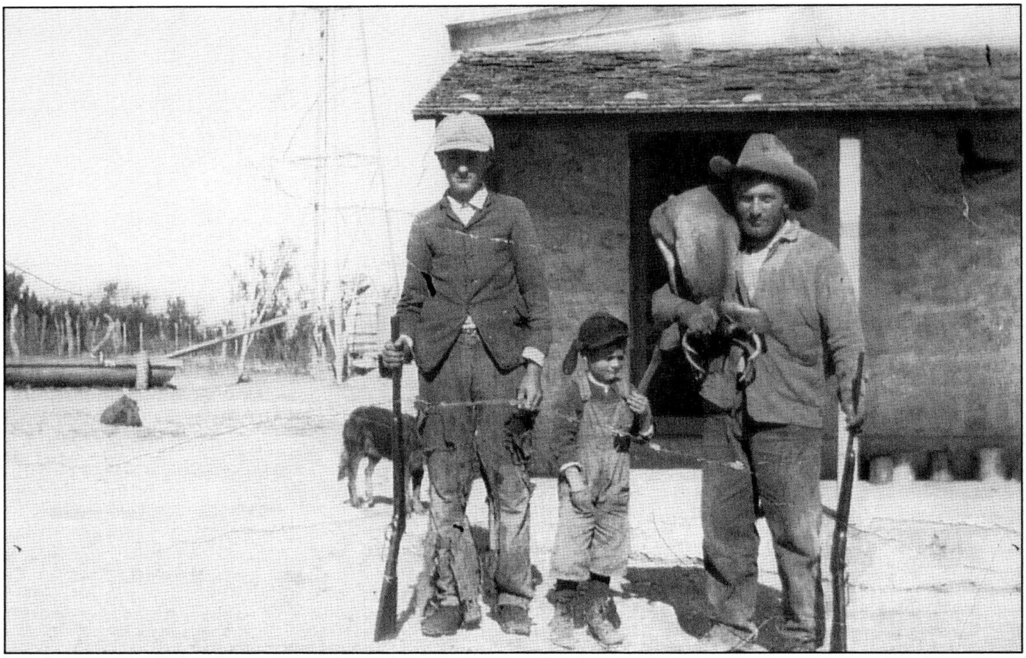

Henry Anderegg, on the right with the deer over his shoulder, loved hunting and the outdoors. His nephew Charles Siefert (left) is wearing several pairs of ragged britches and holding his .30-30 Winchester rifle. In the middle is Henry's son Gilbert. This photograph was taken at Salt Branch about 1927 at the home of Henry's oldest sister, Louise Siefert. (Courtesy of Charles Eckert.)

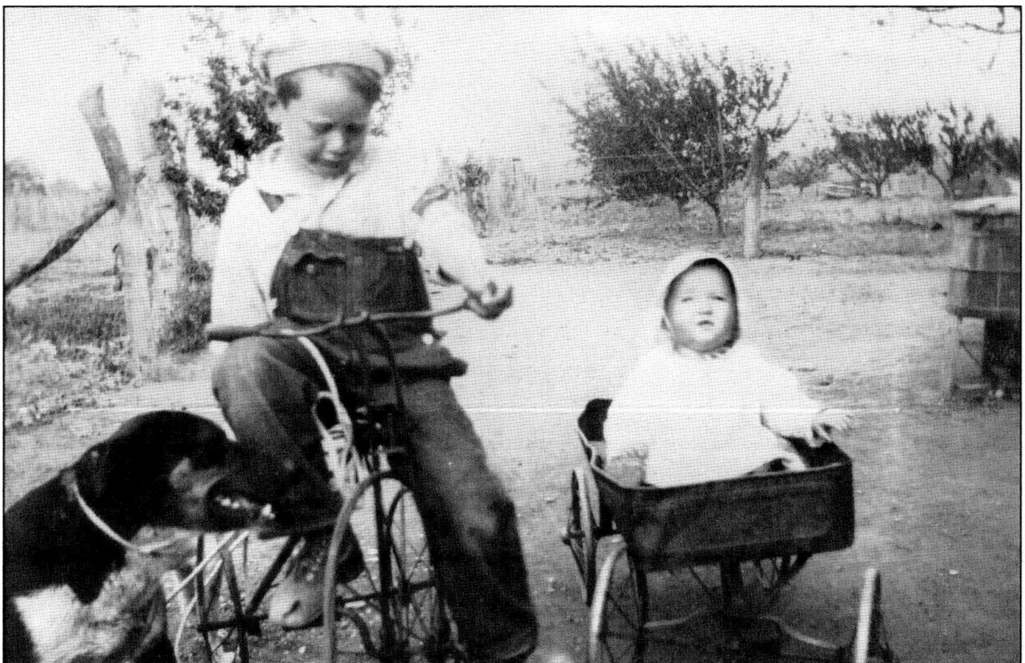

Richard "Dick" Pluenneke, on the tricycle, is enjoying an afternoon outing with his little brother Howard on their parents' farm near Hilda. Dick farmed and ranched in Hilda all his life. Howard died in 1928 when he was only nine months old. (Courtesy of Jan Appleby.)

Socorro Martinez (Avalos) (left) and her mother, Maria Martinez, are shown at the Keyser Ranch near Castell around 1930. Maria was the second child of Raphael Menchaca and his wife, Annie King. Annie was raised by Amy Perryman ("Amy the Seminole"), a cousin to Chief Osceola who worked as a laundress at Fort Mason. (Courtesy of Yolanda Garza.)

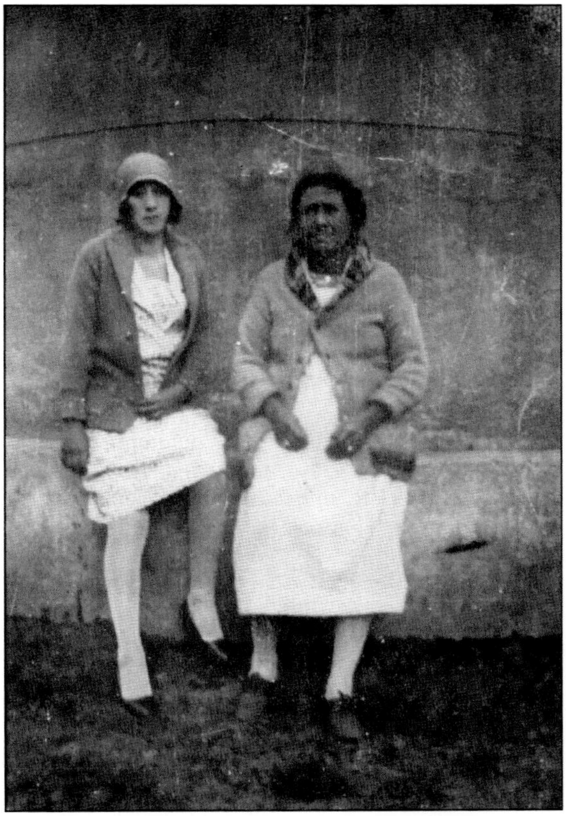

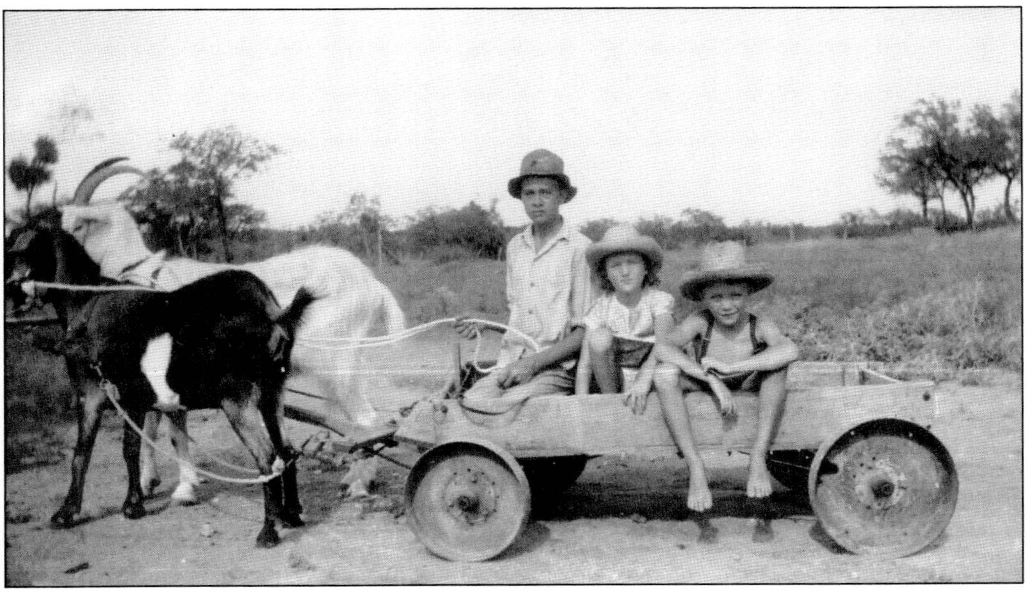

Gordon Geistweidt, the "wagon master," is entertaining his cousins Joan and Charles Pluenneke, who were visiting during summer vacation in 1938. Joan and Charles were living in Luling at the time, although they later returned to Mason. The photograph was taken at the ranch of Gordon's father, Eugene Geistweidt, near Hilda. These may have been the only goats in the county that would pull a wagon! (Courtesy of Charles Pluenneke.)

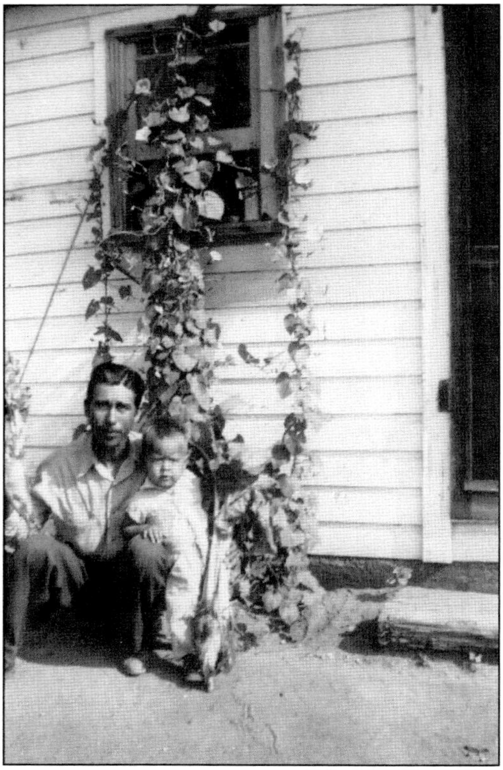

Pedro "Pete" Hernandez poses with his older son, Marcelo, at the family home on Millard Street in July 1942. Marcelo looks perturbed because he had eaten some sugar beets that did not agree with him. The Hernandez family first came to Mason in 1914 and settled in the county permanently in 1922. (Courtesy of Candy Luna.)

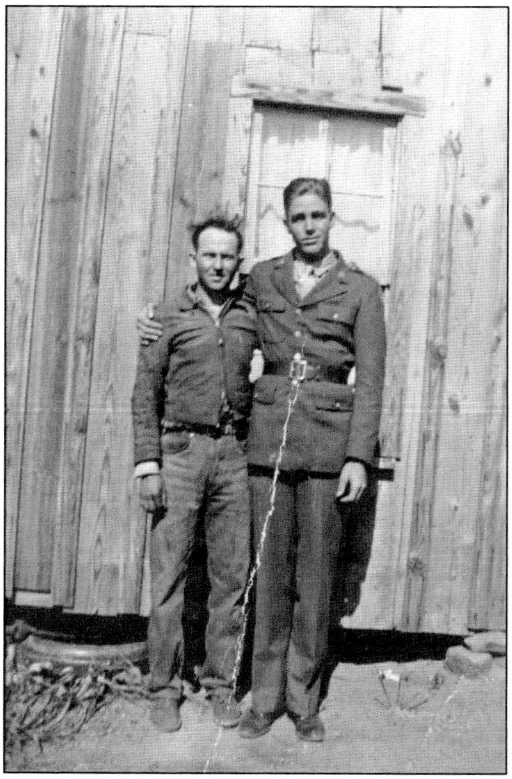

Walter Chester "Check" Airheart (left) and Carlton Crouch are pictured shortly after Carlton was discharged from the U.S. Army in 1945. Carlton served with Battalion B, 1st Anti-Aircraft Guided Missile Battalion in northern France and the Rhineland during World War II. Check ran a concrete and construction business and never knew a stranger, picking up stranded people and giving them a place to stay. (Courtesy of Carolyn Copeland.)

Clarence Airheart is strumming a guitar in the mid-1940s. His grandfather Peter Airheart arrived in Mason sometime before 1881 and spent much time trapping in a draw near White's Crossing that became known as "Peter's Gulch." Clarence worked with his brother "Check" in the construction business and loved to spend days at a time fishing on the Llano River. (Courtesy of Carolyn Copeland.)

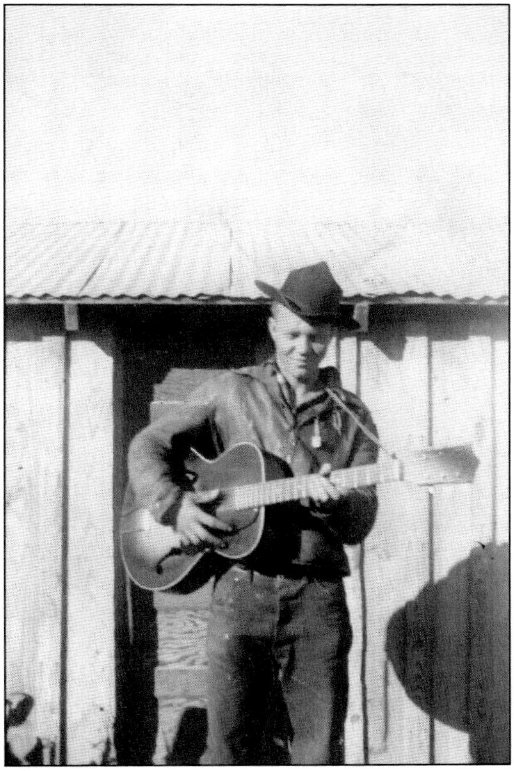

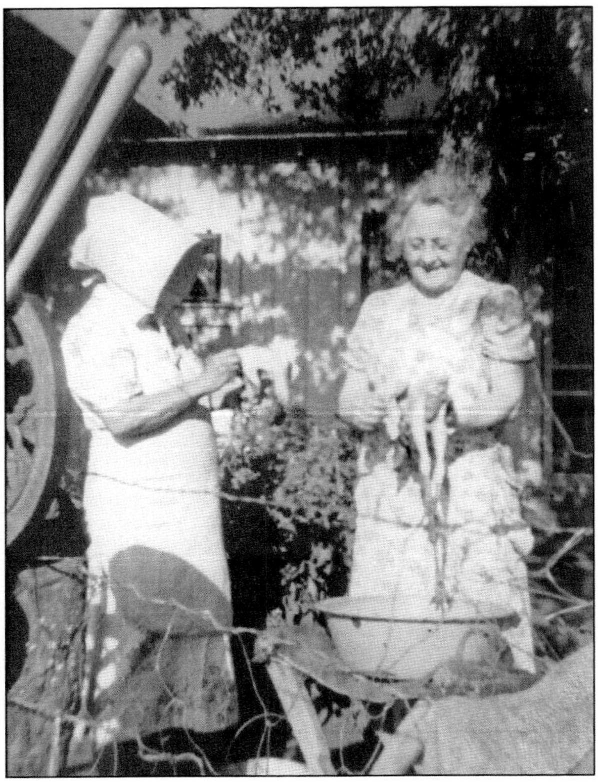

This 1940s photograph captures a common sight at many homes: chickens being cleaned in the backyard. These ladies, Oppie Barret Birk (left) and Ilda Krewitz, are preparing chickens for canning at the Birk farm between Pontotoc and Fredonia. The chickens lost their heads in one of two ways: either by having their necks wrung or by hatchet. The larger feathers were plucked by hand; then the chickens were dipped into hot water to help in removing the pin feathers. (Courtesy of Ron Birk.)

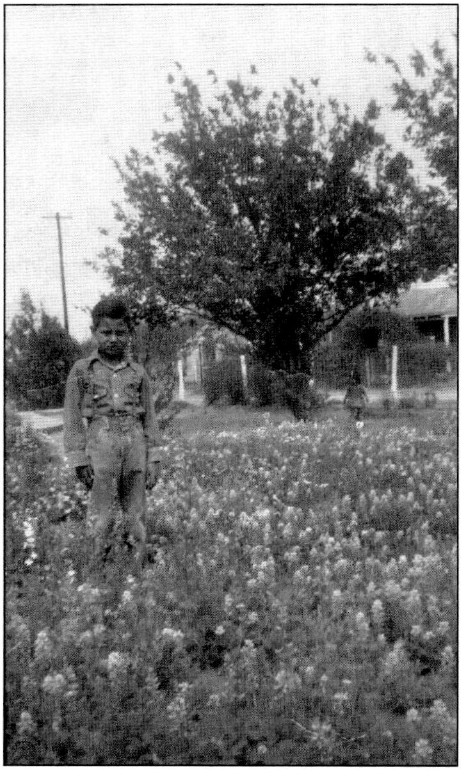

An annual springtime ritual in Mason County is taking photographs of the children in the wildflowers. In this one, Heraclio Avalos is shown standing in a field of bluebonnets near the home of his parents, Raymundo and Socorro Avalos, in the mid-1940s. The girl in the background is probably his younger sister Maria (Dominguez). The children's great-grandfather was Raphael Menchaca, a freighter who settled in Mason in 1876. (Courtesy of Yolanda Garza.)

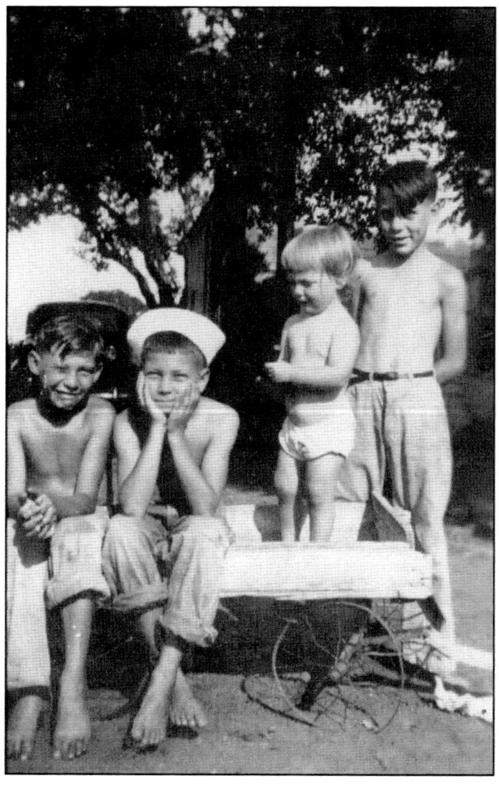

From left to right, Leighton Brown, Donald Loeffler, Janell Magee (Appleby), and Franklin Brown are enjoying a summer day in 1945 at the Hilda farm of their grandparents, Frank and Nellie Pluenneke Loeffler. This land was part of the original Fisher-Miller Grant. (Courtesy of Leighton Brown.)

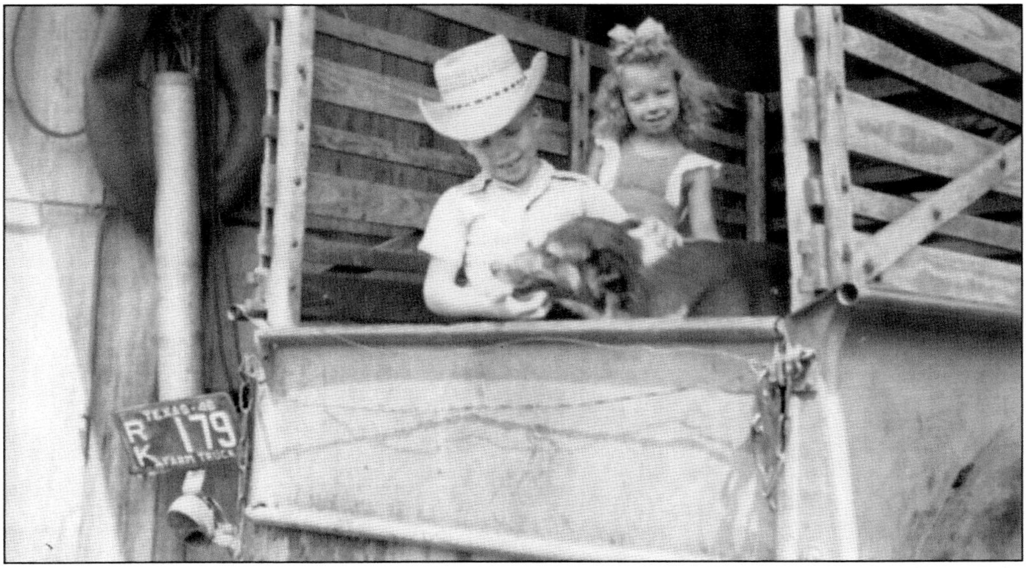

Kenneth Durst, his sister Doris, and their dog are playing in the back of their dad's pickup truck. Note the 1946 Texas license plate. For kids in Mason County, riding around in the back of a pickup was a favorite activity (before it became illegal). Even the dogs loved it, and, of course, they still get to ride back there. (Courtesy of Doris Dannheim.)

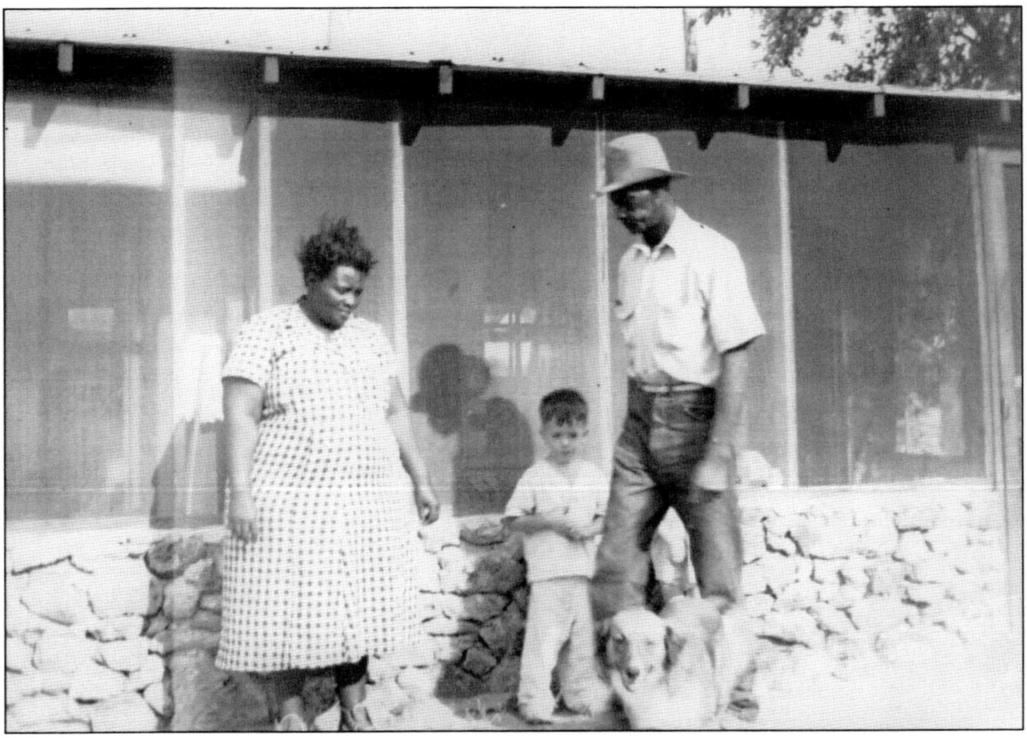

Nellie and Dave Peters are standing in front of the house where they lived at the Kurt Zesch Ranch in 1948. Dave, who worked as a cowboy, was a son of Sam Peters, possibly the first African American to settle in Mason County. The youngster is Ben Hissem, a nephew of Benellen Zesch who was visiting from New Jersey. (Courtesy of Peggy Laverty.)

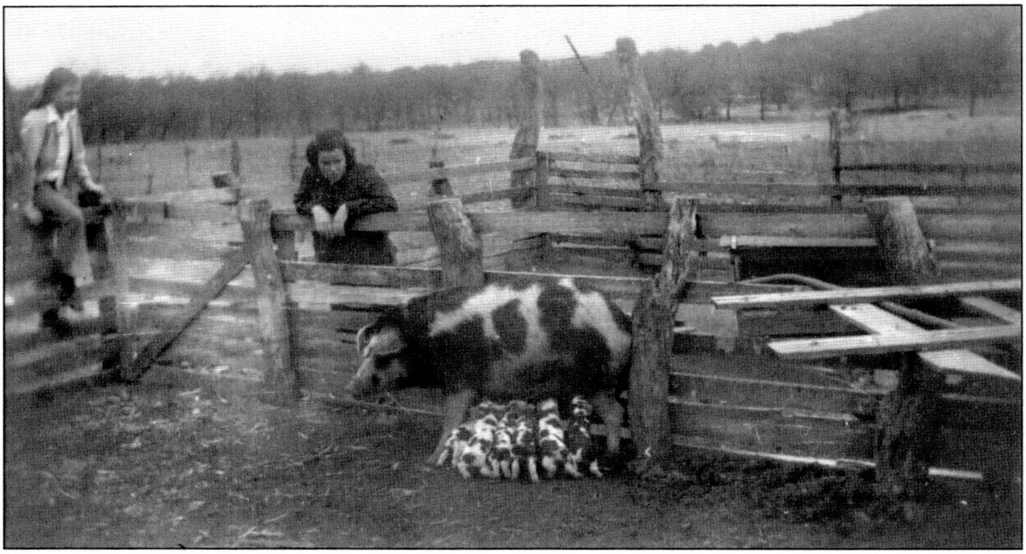

This photograph, taken in 1949, captures Ruth Jordan (sitting on the fence) and Bonnie Kruse (Hanna) (leaning on the fence) as they watch feeding time for the six piglets. The girls were attending a slumber party at Ruth Jordan's house, given for those who were graduating that year from Mason High School. (Courtesy of Sara Banta.)

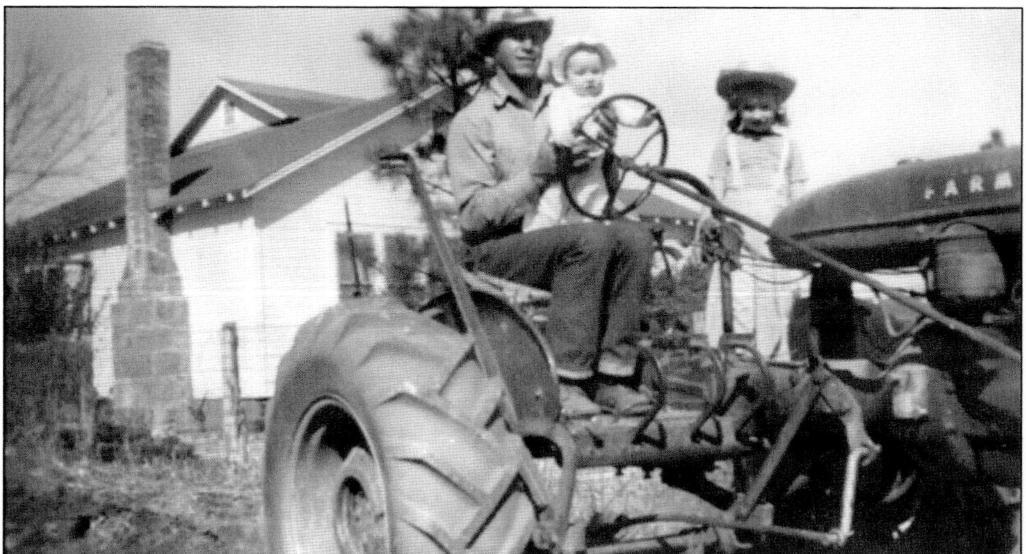

Wilbur Durst is sitting on his Farmall "B" tractor with his two daughters, Brenda (Comer) (at the wheel) and Doris (Dannheim). The photograph was taken in 1949 in front of the Durst house about 15 miles east of Mason. (Courtesy of Doris Dannheim.)

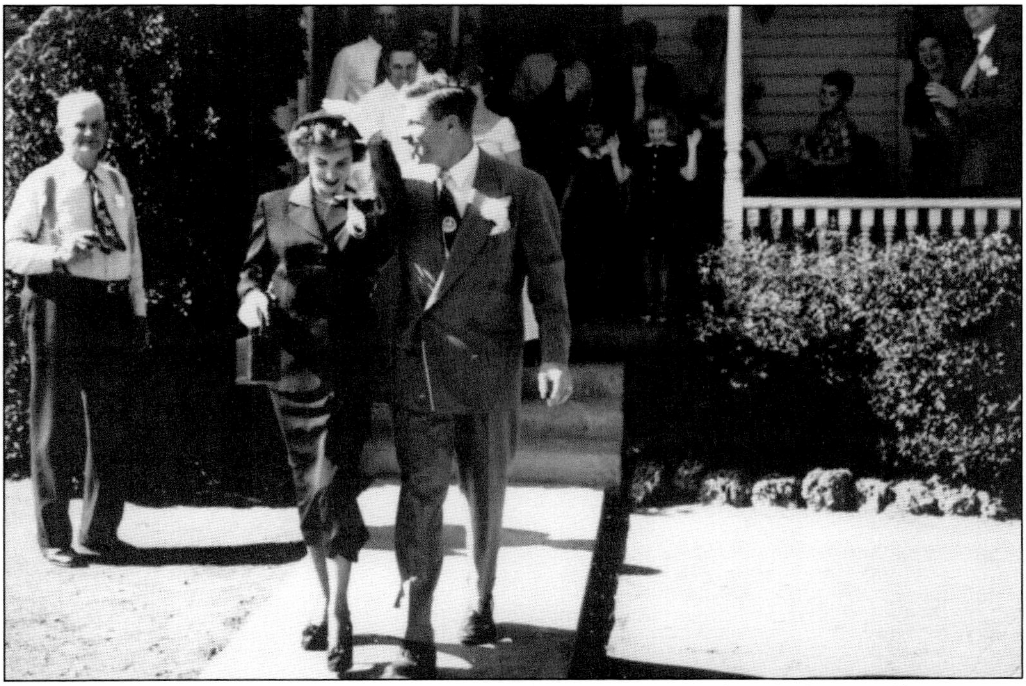

On January 25, 1950, Roy Lehmberg and Jean Roberts were married at the home of his parents, Walter and Lydia Lehmberg, on the south side of the Llano River between Hedwig's Hill and Castell. Walter is standing to the left of the happy couple. The girl on the porch with her arms raised is Linda Lehmberg (Terrell). To the right of her are Larry Lehmberg, Martha Jean Myers, and her husband, Wayne Myers, Roy's college roommate. (Courtesy of Judy Lehmberg.)

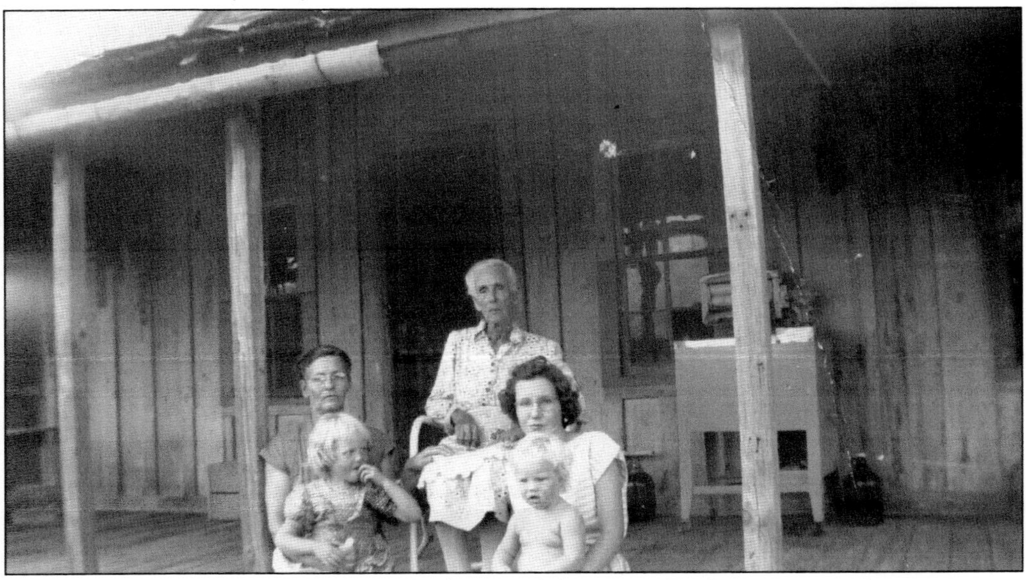

This photograph, taken in 1950 at the Charles Creech home near Fredonia, captures four generations of one family. Seated in the chair is the great-grandmother, Martha Maxwell Creech. Seated on the left is the grandmother, Mary Elizabeth Creech Ake; she is holding her granddaughter Sandra Cottle (Banks). The mother, Nina Bell Ake Cottle, is holding Shirley Cottle (Reed), her daughter. Note the hand-wringer washing machine on the porch. (Courtesy of Shirley Cottle Reed.)

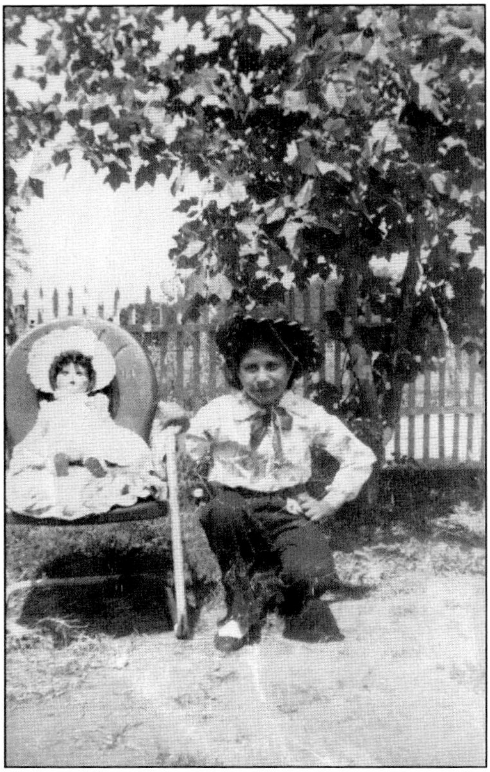

Amada "Amanda" Medrano (Orozpe), age 11, is dressed as a boy for a performance of the *garabe tapatio* (Mexican hat dance) at Mason High School in 1951, the year she came to Mason from Temamalta Edo de Mexico. She is pictured at the home of her aunt, Carmen Florez. (Courtesy of Amanda Orozpe.)

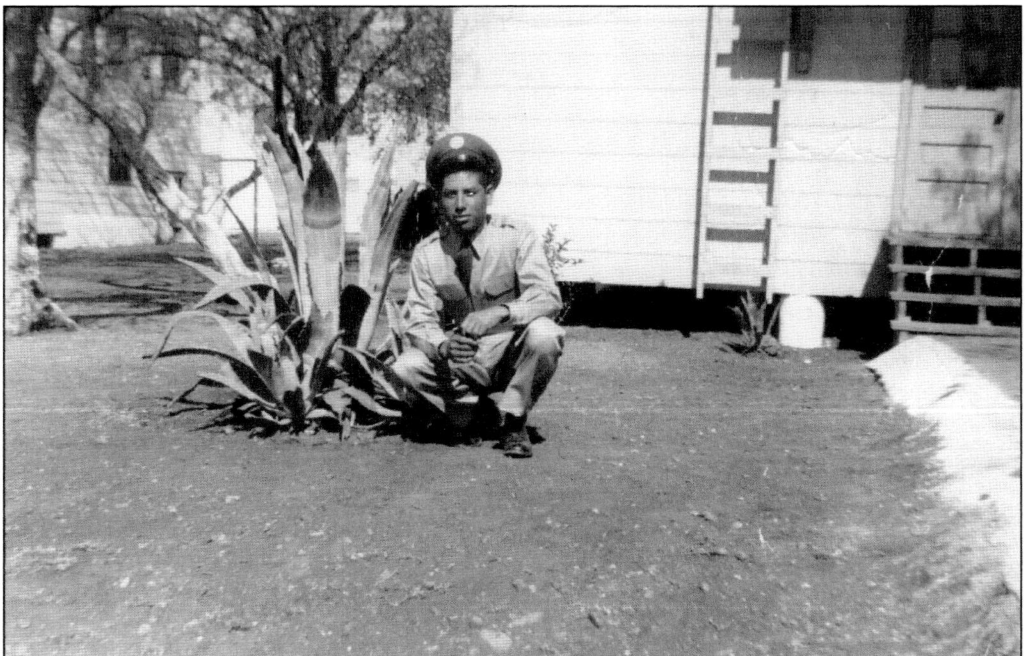

Frank "Pancho" Sanchez, who served in the U.S. Air Force during the Korean War, is pictured in 1954. He was also stationed at several places stateside, including Lackland Air Force Base and Walker Air Force Base. (Courtesy of Yolanda Garza.)

Carolyn Airheart (Copeland) (left) and Christine Airheart (Cortez) are holding their Easter baskets and wearing new dresses that their aunt brought from Austin, around 1954. Their parents, Walter Chester "Check" and Ethel Airheart, purchased this place on Bluebonnet Road in Mason with money they earned doing seasonal farmwork in California. They used the truck in the background to travel back and forth, camping out while they were away from home. (Courtesy of Carolyn Copeland.)

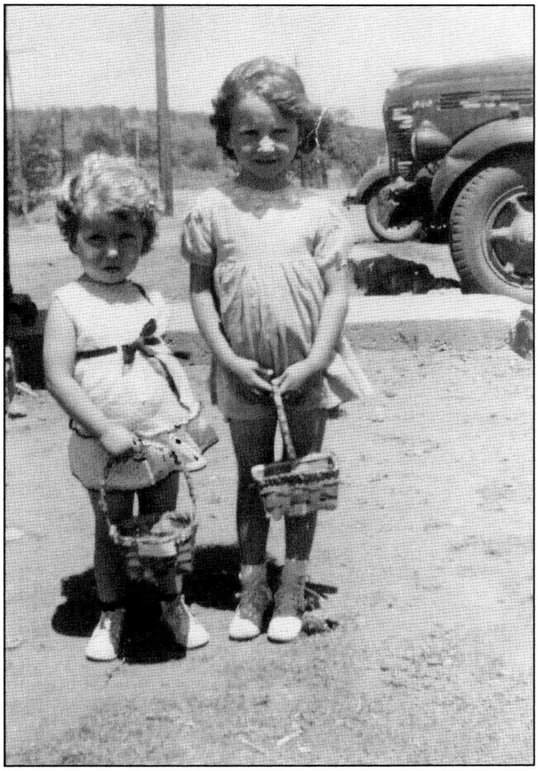

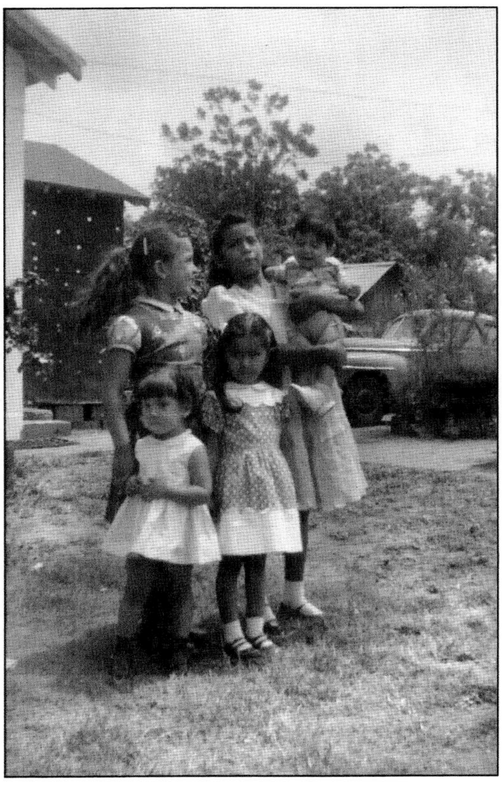

From left to right are (first row) Alejandra Garza and her sister Aida Garza; (second row) Candy Hernandez and her sister Vivian Hernandez, who is holding Johnny Garza. This photograph was taken around 1956 at the property that the Hernandez sisters' grandparents, Tranquilino "Frank" and Candelaria "Cande" Hernandez, purchased in 1931. They used the building in back as a *tiendita* (grocery store), and Tranquilino also operated a barbershop on the premises. (Courtesy of Candy Luna.)

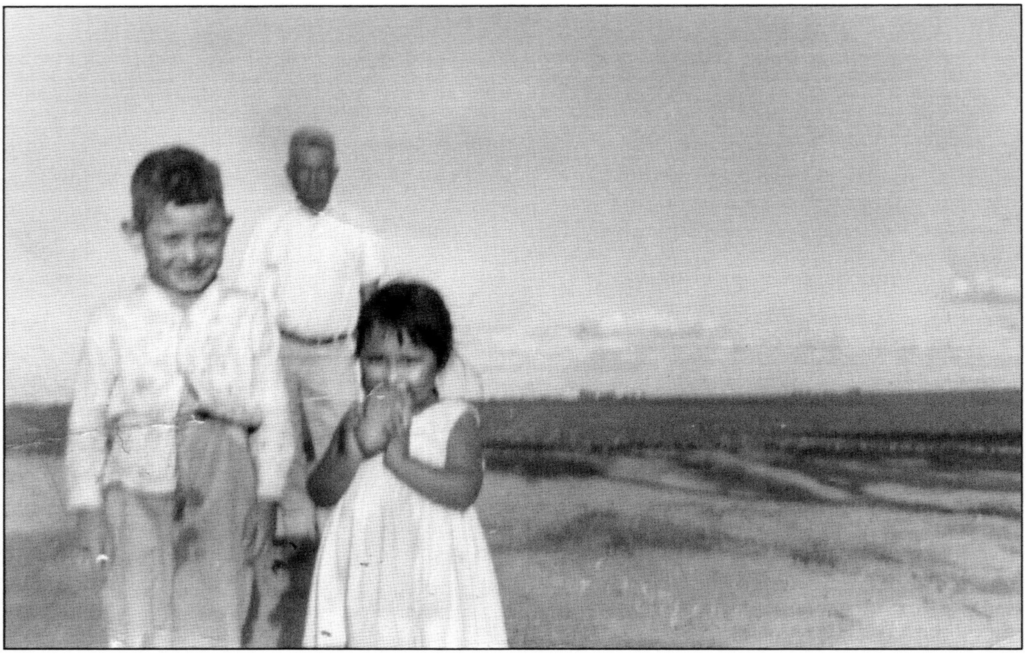

From left to right, Jerry Cantu, Eleno Castillo, and Eleno's daughter Vicki Castillo (Montez) are pictured in 1958. Eleno, born in 1900 in Jimenez, Coahuila, Mexico, arrived in Mason from Langtry in 1936. He and his wife, Rita, spent much of their lives in Fredonia, where Eleno did a variety of farm and ranch work. He also loved to hunt and fish. (Courtesy of Jane Zavala.)

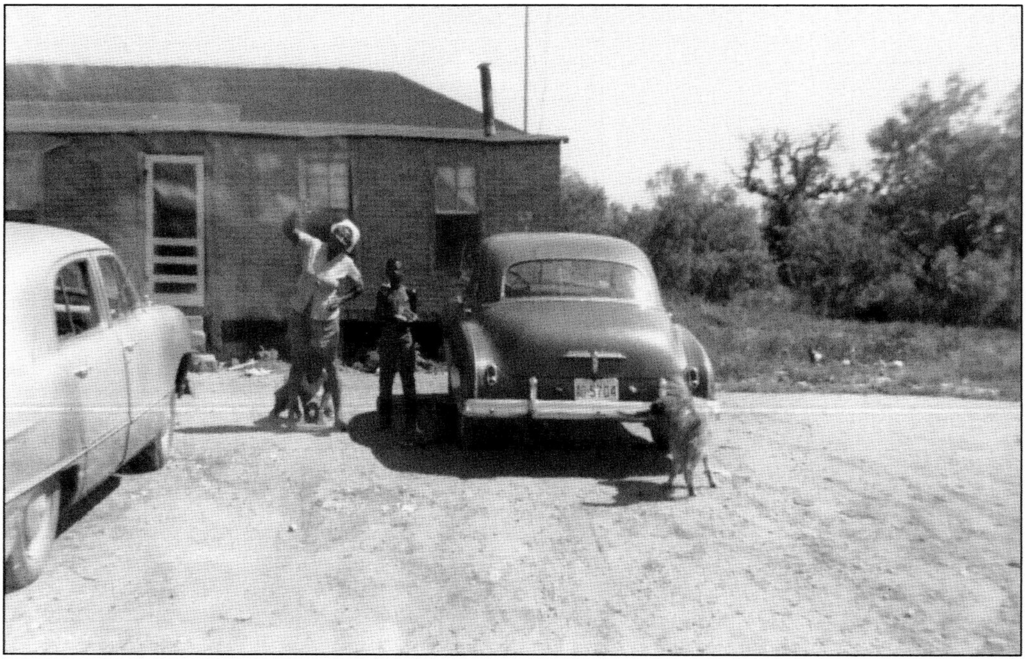

Beulah "Mae" Mason waves at the camera in front of her house, north of the square near Comanche Creek, in the late 1950s. Her grandsons James Miller and Terry Miller are with her. Mae's family purchased this land from Al Lindsay in 1914 for $150, and the area became known as the Mason-Jackson community. (Courtesy of Sandy Miller.)

Six

ON THE ROAD

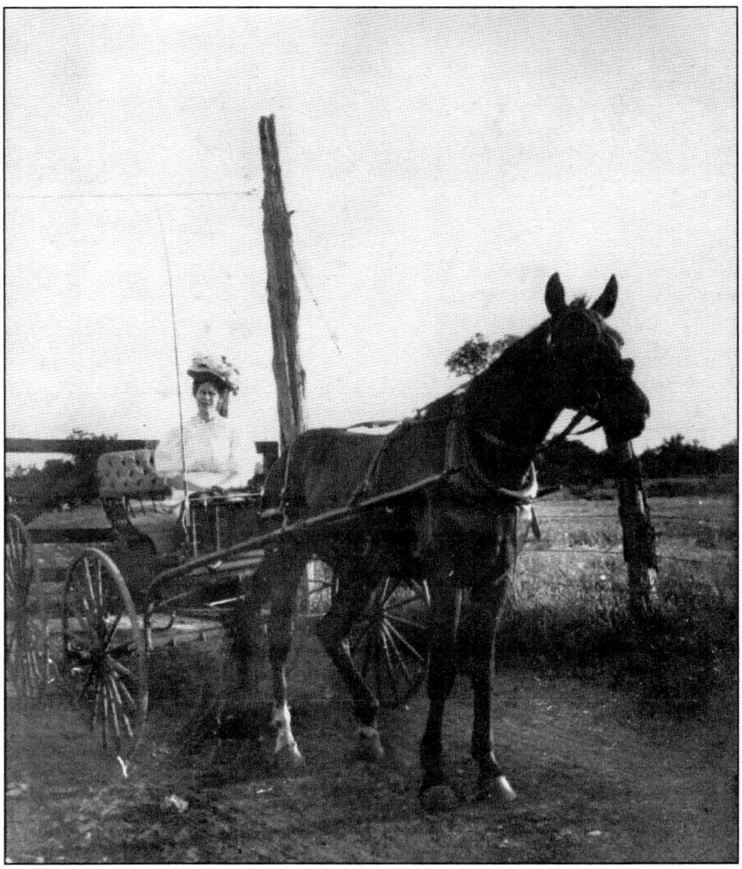

Bertha Eckert (Ochs), born to Louis and Karoline Eckert near Hedwig's Hill in 1869, is shown driving a hack, probably in the 1890s. The horse and hack were a common mode of transportation during the settlement of the Hill Country. With a tame horse, it was a safe way to travel. (Courtesy of the Mason County Museum.)

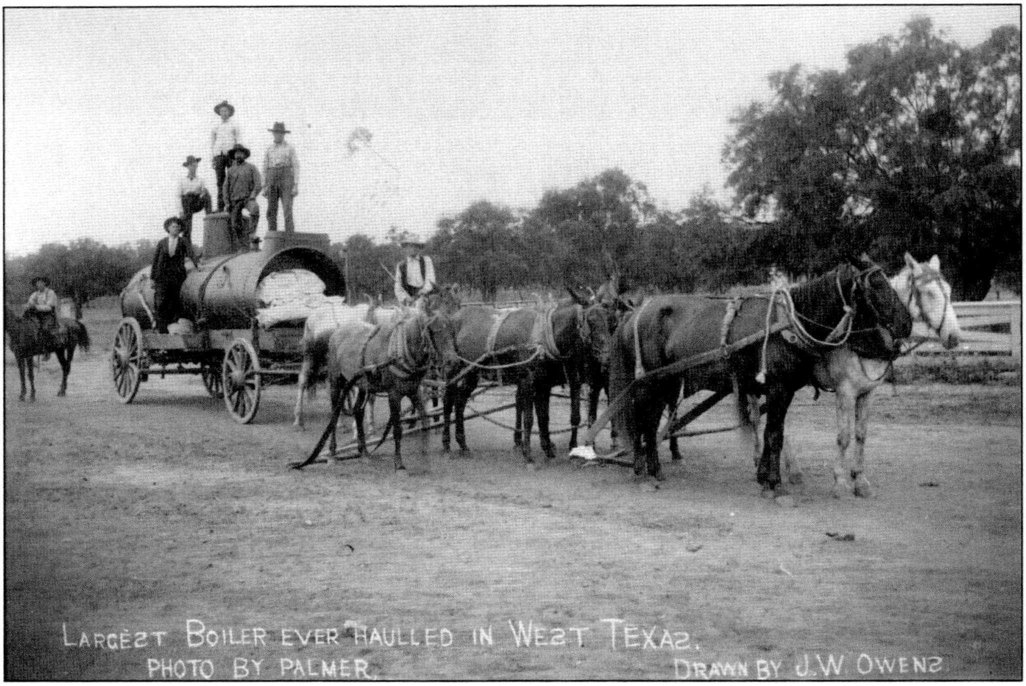

This photograph from 1900 shows the "largest boiler ever hauled in West Texas," bound for Mason. The driver of the wagon is John W. Owens. The mounted horseman is Will Schuessler. Will Ellebracht, in the dark suit, stands by the boiler. (Photograph by Palmer; courtesy of MCHC.)

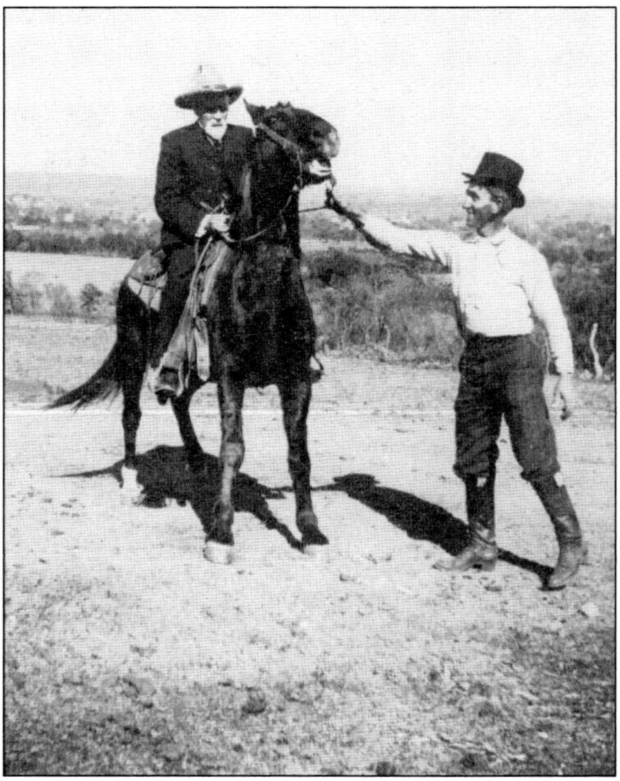
John Hey of Keighley, England, does not look very comfortable on a horse. His nephew, Jim Hey, stands to the right. The two men literally switched hats for this posed photograph on Post Hill, which they titled "The Highwayman." John arrived in Mason on November 2, 1908, the night before his brother Wilson died. They had not seen each other in 54 years. (Courtesy of Peggy Laverty.)

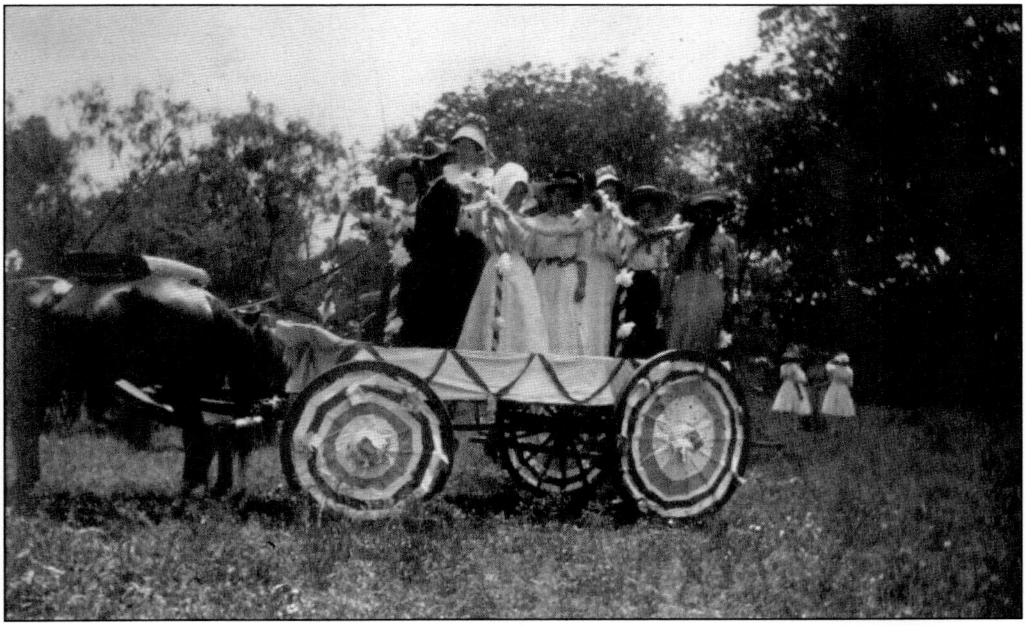

This photograph, taken in 1910, records a popular activity associated with the end of the school year in the Art community. The students decorated their wagons, buggies, saddles, and bridles with brightly colored crepe paper and rode from school to the pecan groves along Willow Creek. There, parents had built a wooden platform on which the students presented a program of songs and poems they had learned during the school year. (Courtesy of Wilburn Shearer.)

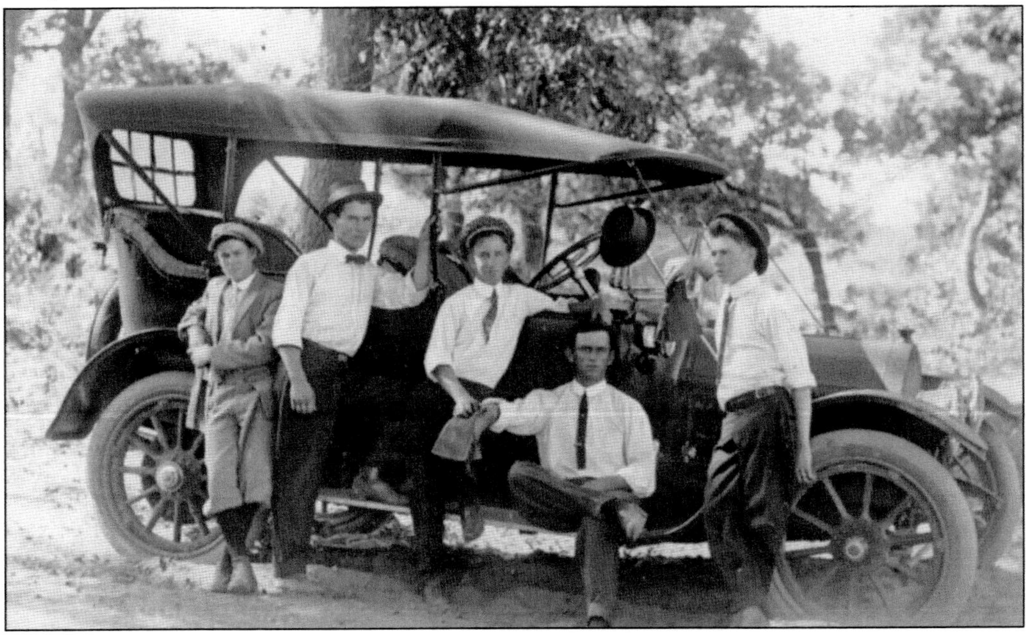

From left to right in this 1914 photograph are Lloyd Huckaby, Hugh Shearer, Seth Baze, Kimsey Shearer, and Pete Schmidt. The automobile is a Cadillac owned by Anna Martin, a successful business owner and rancher. In 1901, she established the Commercial Bank in Mason and thus became the first woman to found a bank in the United States. She did not like to drive and frequently had a chauffeur. (Courtesy of Marilyn Mahon.)

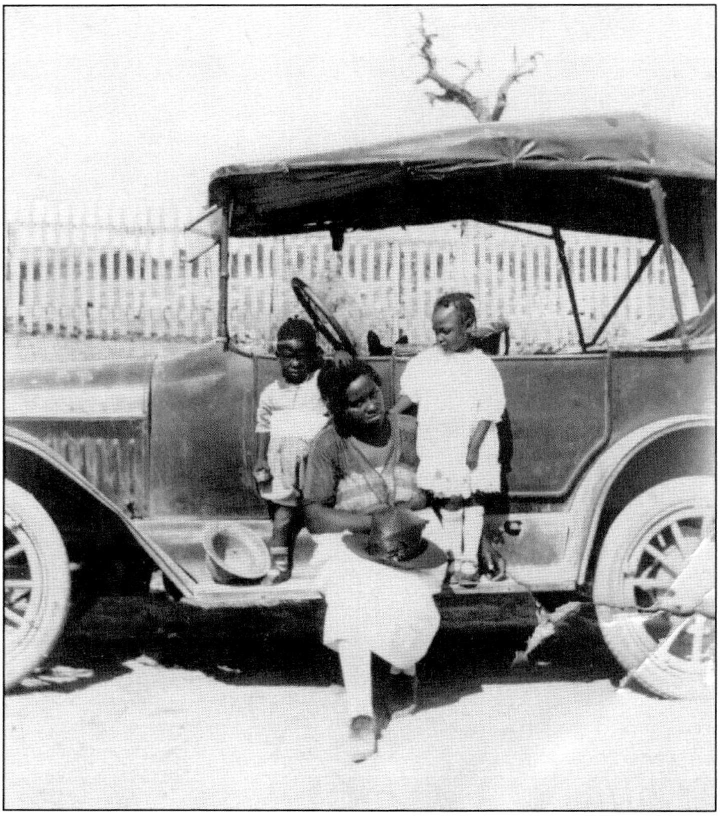

Rufus Brazil Jr. and Elizabeth "Little Nance" Brazil pose with their mother, Evelyn Brazil, on the running board of a Ford Model T touring car around 1915. Evelyn was one of 12 children born to Charles Mason Sr. and his second wife, Matt Mason. (Courtesy of Sandy Miller.)

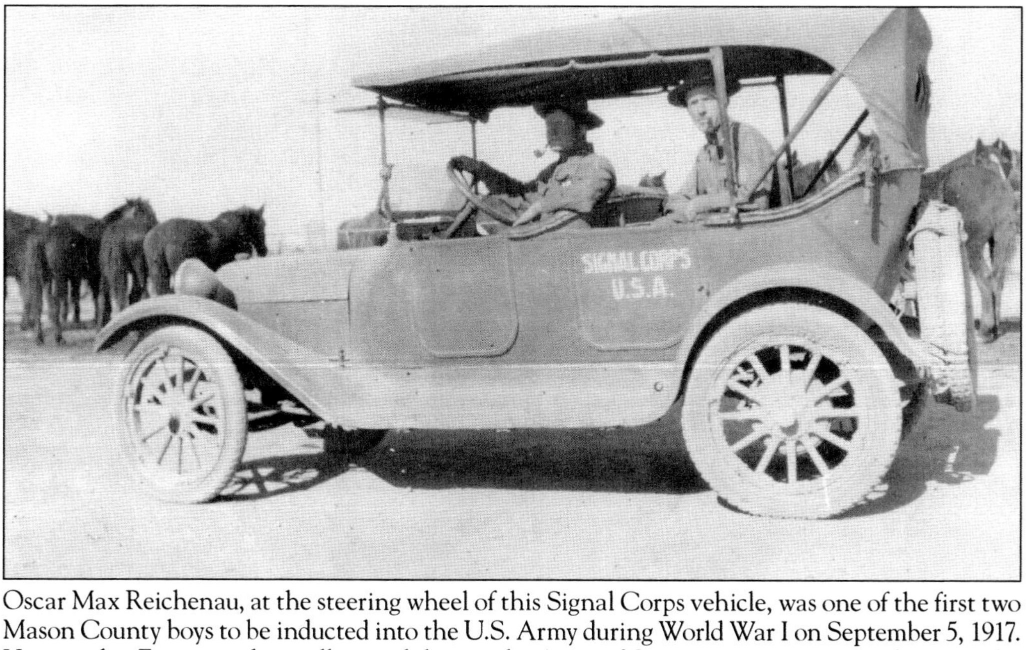

Oscar Max Reichenau, at the steering wheel of this Signal Corps vehicle, was one of the first two Mason County boys to be inducted into the U.S. Army during World War I on September 5, 1917. He served in France in the artillery and then in the Army of Occupation in Germany, living in the homes of German families until he was discharged in June 1919. Oscar was trained at Camp Mabry in Austin, where this photograph may have been taken. (Courtesy of Charles Reichenau.)

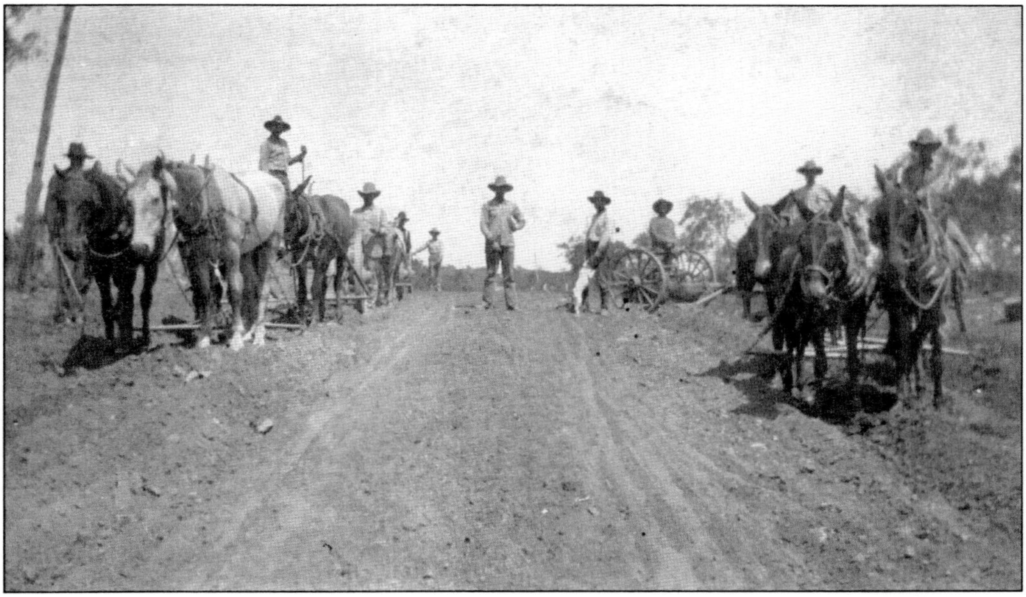

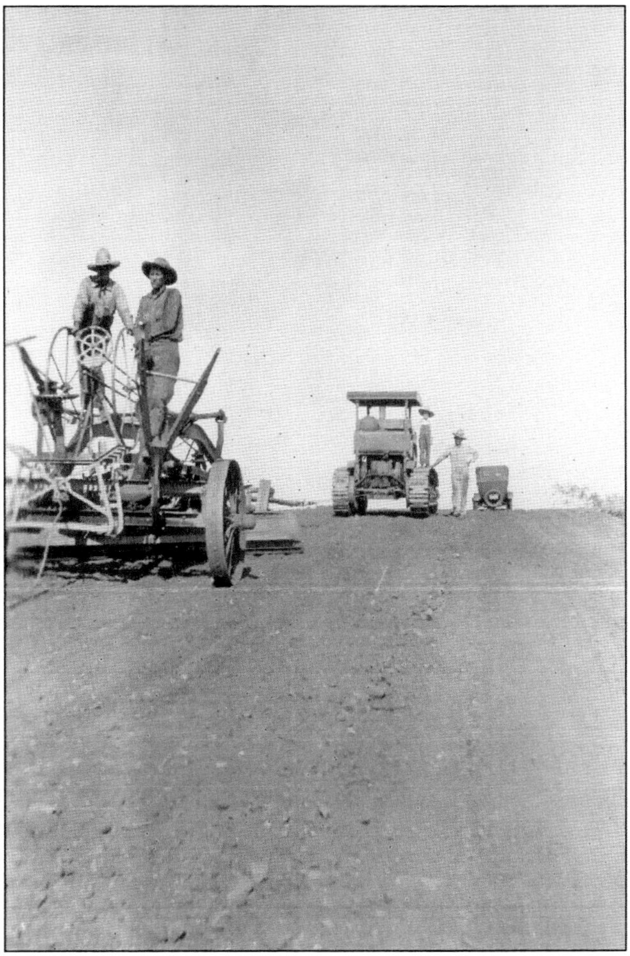

In the late 1800s and early 1900s, every able-bodied male in Mason County who owned property was assigned roadwork duty. Assignments were made by precinct each year in February, and the assignees were responsible for keeping the roads usable for the next year. "Usable roads" was a subjective term; they were often rough and sandy and only partially graded. Some Anglos in the area complained about the "damn Dutchman's dumps," i.e., diverter dams built across the roads to turn the rainwater. The above photograph, around 1900, shows road crews using only horse-drawn equipment and hand tools. The photograph at right, around 1920, shows two operators on the wheel scraper; one controlled the scraper's angle and the other its depth. It is being pulled by a cable attached to the crawler tractor. Gene "Sie" Banta, the operator on the left, recalled working on "most of the roads in Mason County." (Above photograph courtesy of the Koock family; right photograph courtesy of Charles Banta.)

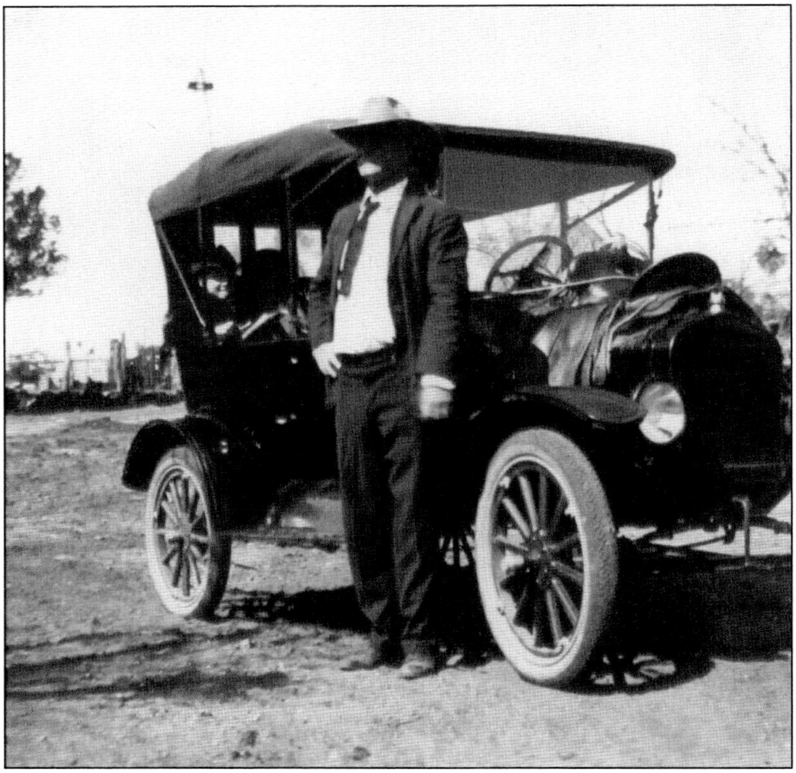

L. B. Eckert of Hilda poses with his prized 1920 Ford Model T, outfitted with a saddle placed backwards on the hood. L. B. was known as a great roper who could throw a loop on hogs, goats, steers, and strays at roundup, and he seems to have turned his automobile into a roping machine. The children in the back seat may have been his youngest sons, Dan and Walter. (Courtesy of Kathryn Martin.)

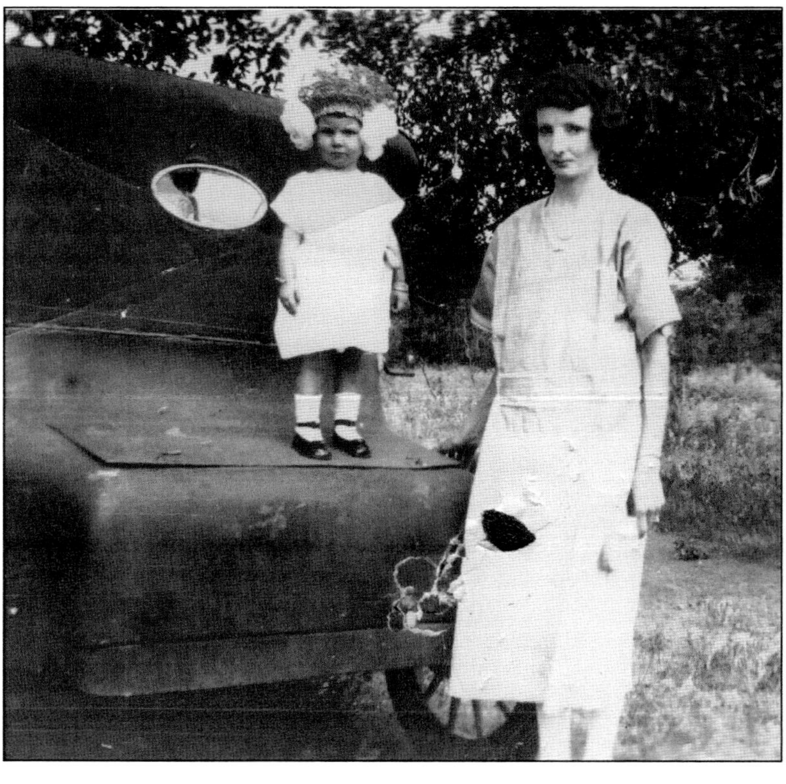

Alma Eckert is pictured with her oldest daughter, Lucille (Leach), in 1922. Lucille is wearing her fancy Easter hat and is standing on the back of a 1920 Ford. (Courtesy of Sara Banta.)

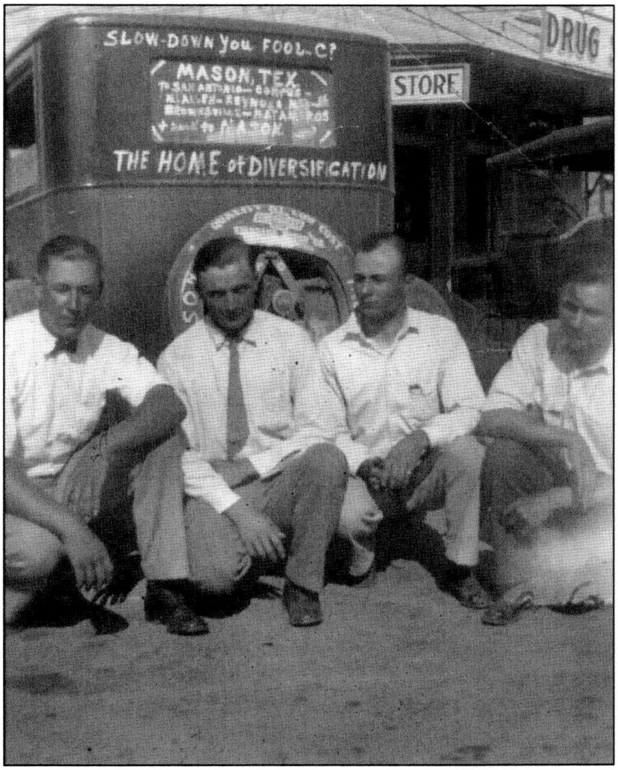

Returning from a road trip to Mexico in the latter 1920s are, from left to right, Henry Keller, Arthur Geistweidt, Milton Loeffler, and unidentified. The sign on the back of their car reads: "Slow-down you fool—C? Mason, Tex. to San Antonio—Corpus—McAllen—Reynosa, Mex.—Brownsville—Matamoros & back to Mason. The home of diversification." (Courtesy of Carolyn Loeffler.)

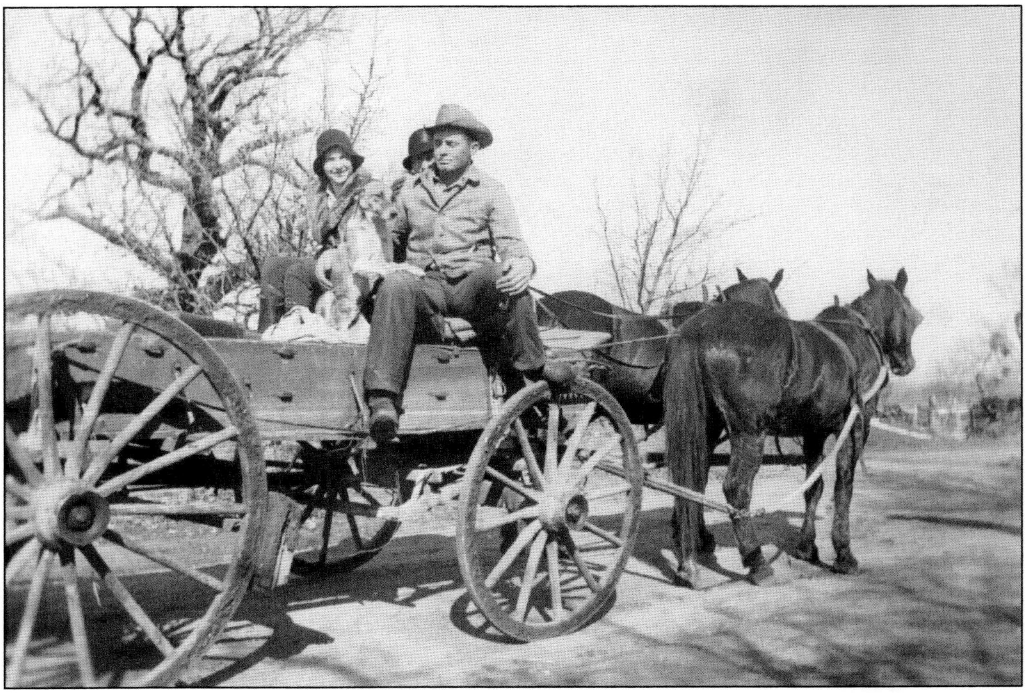

From left to right, Estella Zesch (Hoerster), unidentified, and Estella's brother Arno Zesch of Simonsville are pictured around 1930. The Zesch family settled in that part of the county in 1856. (Courtesy of Linda Owen.)

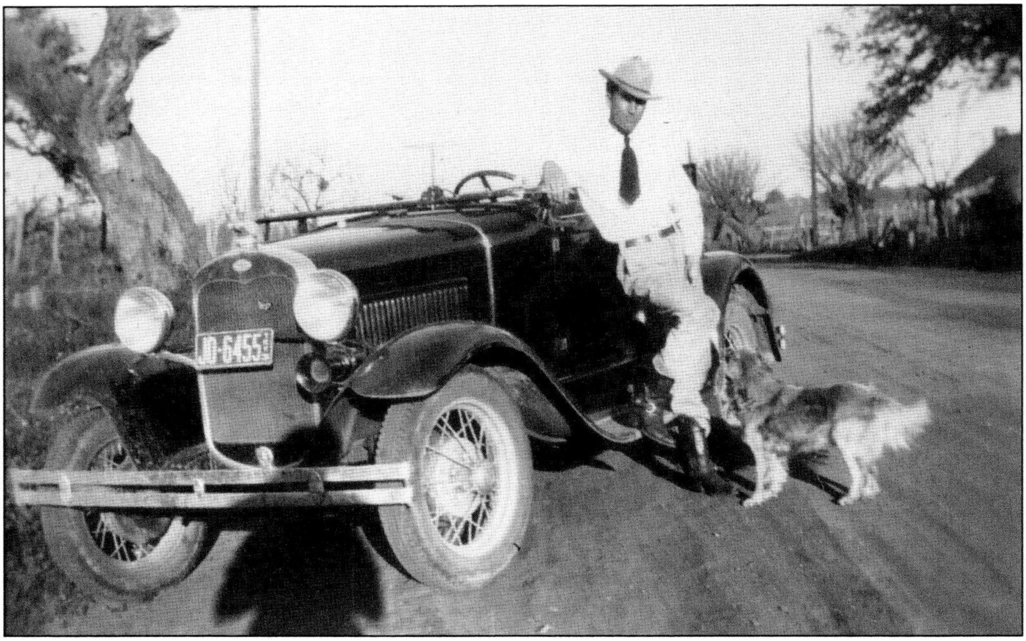

This 1931 photograph of Glenn Capps shows his sports car of the day—a 1931 Ford Model A Roadster with a rumble seat. Capps, age 26 at the time, is standing directly across the street from his parents' home in Mason, located on what is now East Pontotoc Street. (Courtesy of Sally Capps.)

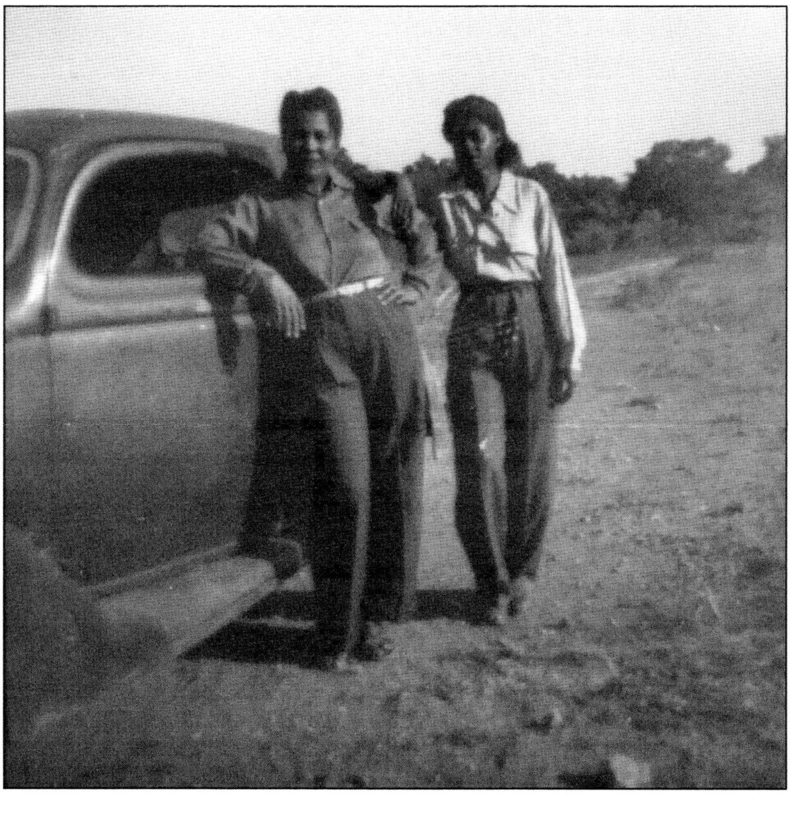

Beulah "Mae" Mason (left) and her daughter Sandy are standing beside Mae's first car. It was a Ford purchased in the 1930s from the Lee F. Eckert Motor Company, located at that time in the Louis Schmidt building on the square. Mae's father was Charles Mason Sr., who came to Mason from the Marble Falls area in the 1850s or 1860s and had 24 children by his two wives, Harriet and Matt. (Courtesy of Sandy Miller.)

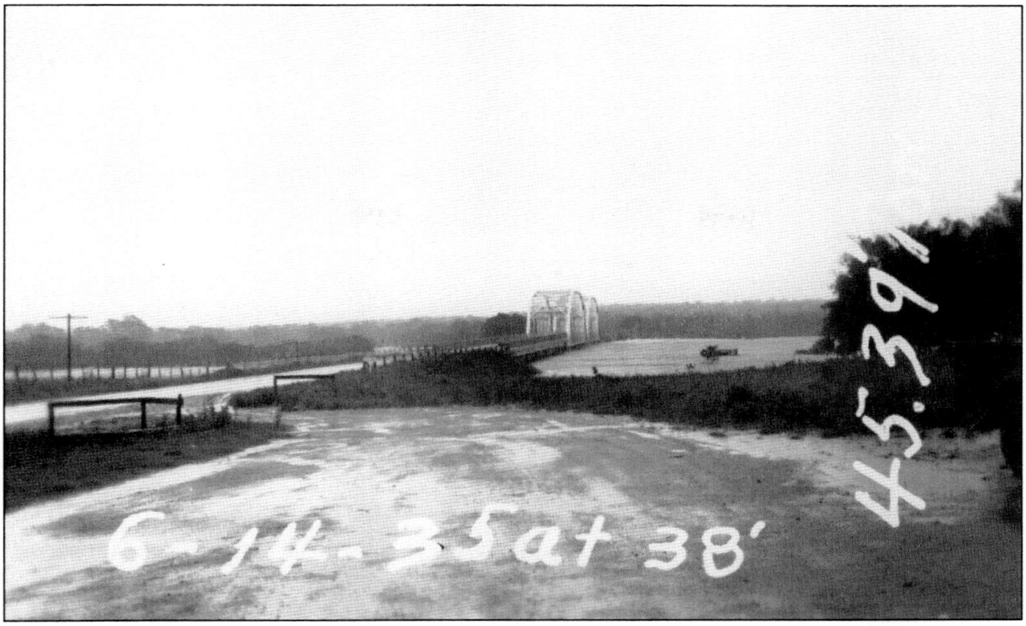

The above photograph shows the Llano River Bridge still in place on June 14, 1935, with the river level at 38 feet above average. The bottom photograph shows driftwood and other debris along Highway 9 (now Highway 87), with the bridge no longer standing. The water level rose to 45.39 feet; the bridge washed away on either June 14 or 15. Pecan groves, which grew thickly upstream along the river's banks, simply added to the force of the swollen river as the trees washed downriver toward the bridge. One of many events affected by the loss of the bridge was the marriage of Myrtle Hoerster and Vernon Fritze. Their planned wedding at the Art Methodist Church, located on the north side of the Llano River, had to be postponed until Tuesday, June 18, when Vernon could cross by boat from the south side of the river. (Courtesy of Doug and Sherry Willmann and Reuben Geistweidt.)

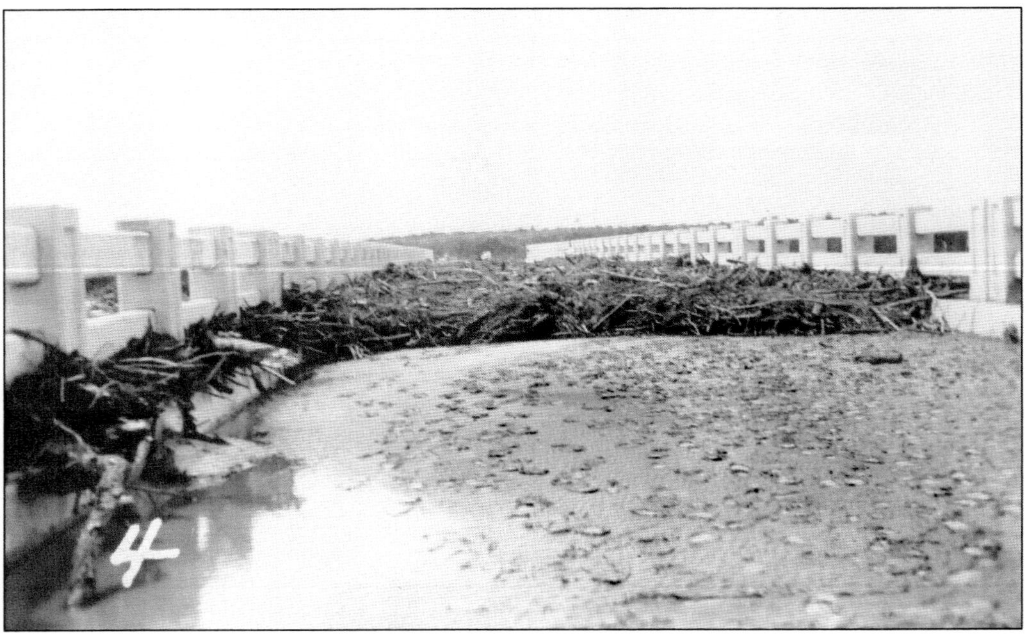

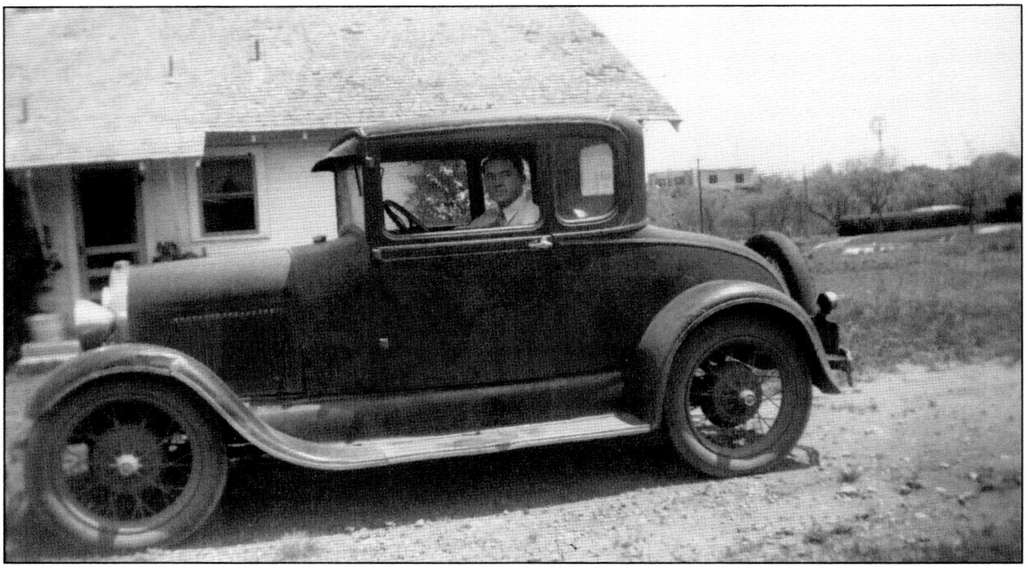

Lee "Buck" Shearer, one of the owners of the Piggly Wiggly grocery store, poses in "Little Willy," the store's delivery car. This picture was taken in 1940, shortly before Buck and his partners sold the store to Ray Hudson. Buck then enlisted in the U.S. Air Force and was stationed during World War II at San Angelo, where he performed aircraft maintenance. (Courtesy of Beverly Baker.)

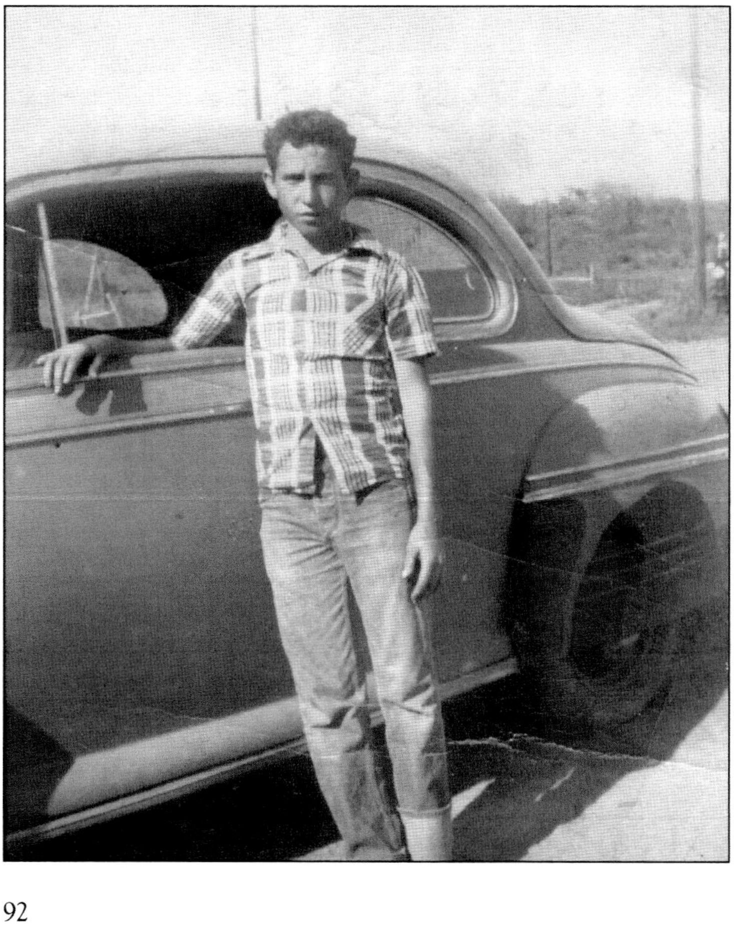

Could this be a Mason "rebel without a cause"? Gordon Airheart, age 16 in this 1955 photograph, is standing beside his family's 1946 Ford Coupe. Like any cool teenager of that period, he has rolled up his jeans on one leg. (Courtesy of Carolyn Copeland.)

Seven

At Work

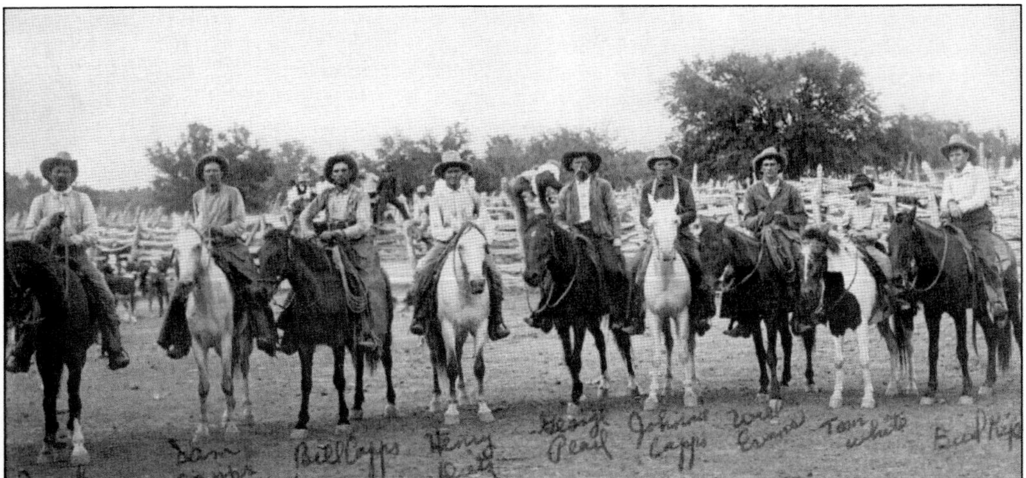

These cowboys are rounding up calves in 1903 on the Littlefield-White Saline Ranch, which extended into three counties. The pens were located near London. From left to right are Jack Ivy, Sam Capps, Bill Capps, Henry Dietz, George Pearl, Johnny Capps, Will Evans, Tom White (the owner's son), and Bud Kiser. J. W. White and his uncle, George W. Littlefield, grazed as many as 6,000 steers at a time. (Courtesy of Sally Capps.)

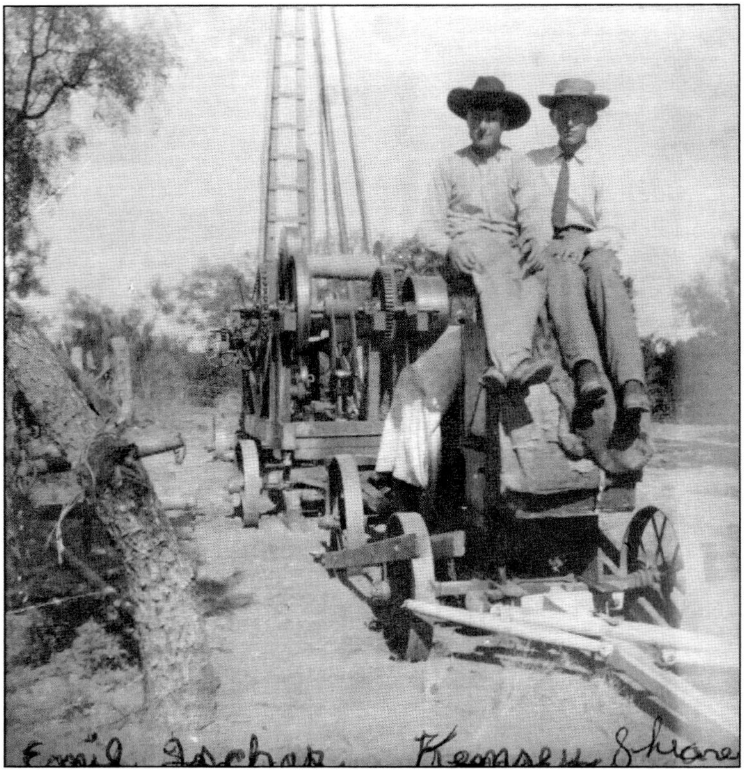

Shown on this well-drilling rig are Emil Ischar (left) and Kimsey "Kemp" Shearer Jr., around 1910. Water wells were a vital part of living in Mason County. Most of the pre-1900 wells were dug by hand, digging and blasting the rock and dirt. As mechanical drilling rigs, such as this cable-tool drilling machine, became popular in the late 1890s, they quickly replaced the wearisome hand techniques. (Courtesy of the Mason County Museum.)

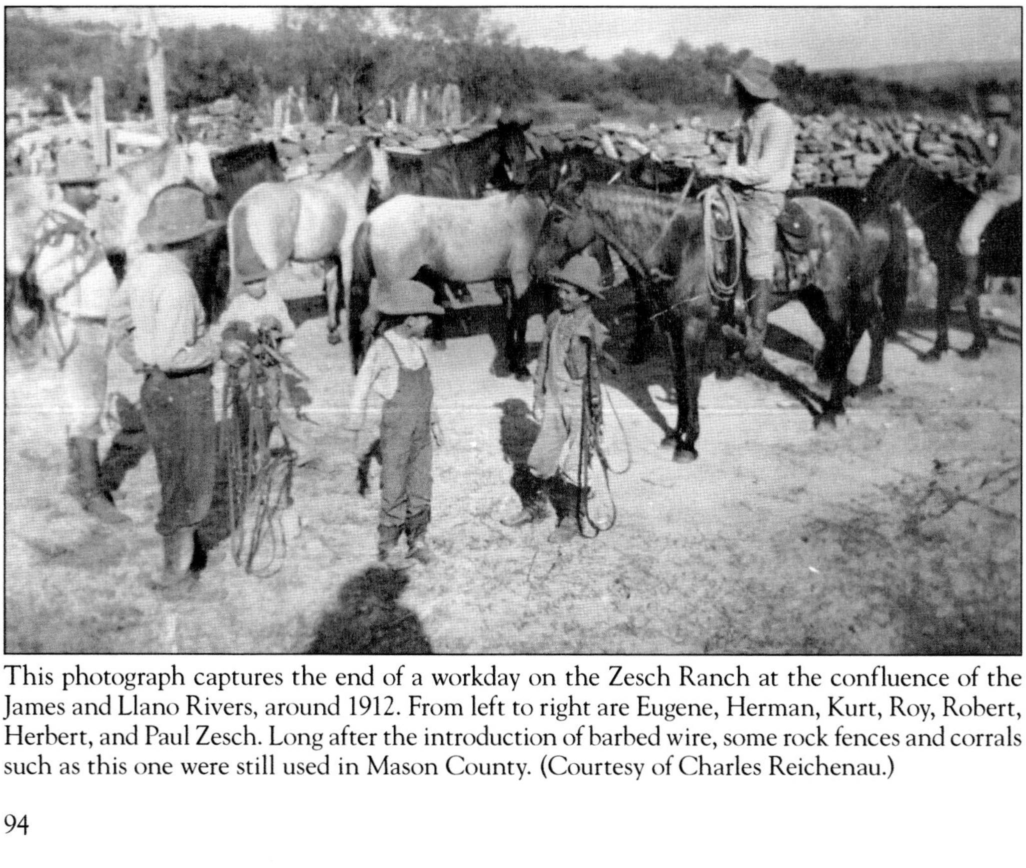

This photograph captures the end of a workday on the Zesch Ranch at the confluence of the James and Llano Rivers, around 1912. From left to right are Eugene, Herman, Kurt, Roy, Robert, Herbert, and Paul Zesch. Long after the introduction of barbed wire, some rock fences and corrals such as this one were still used in Mason County. (Courtesy of Charles Reichenau.)

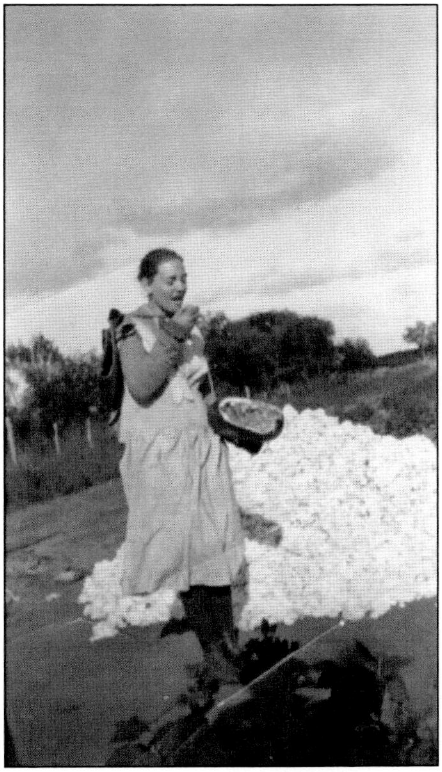

These photographs show two children of Jasper and Martha Doyal Cavness on the family farm. At right, Lucy Cavness (Koerner), age 15, takes a break from picking cotton to enjoy a juicy watermelon in 1918. The bottom photograph shows Alfred Cavness with his mules and his cart, which he built himself for hauling items. The Cavness family first arrived in Mason County in 1856 and settled on Honey Creek in 1867. (Courtesy of Emma Gene Jackson.)

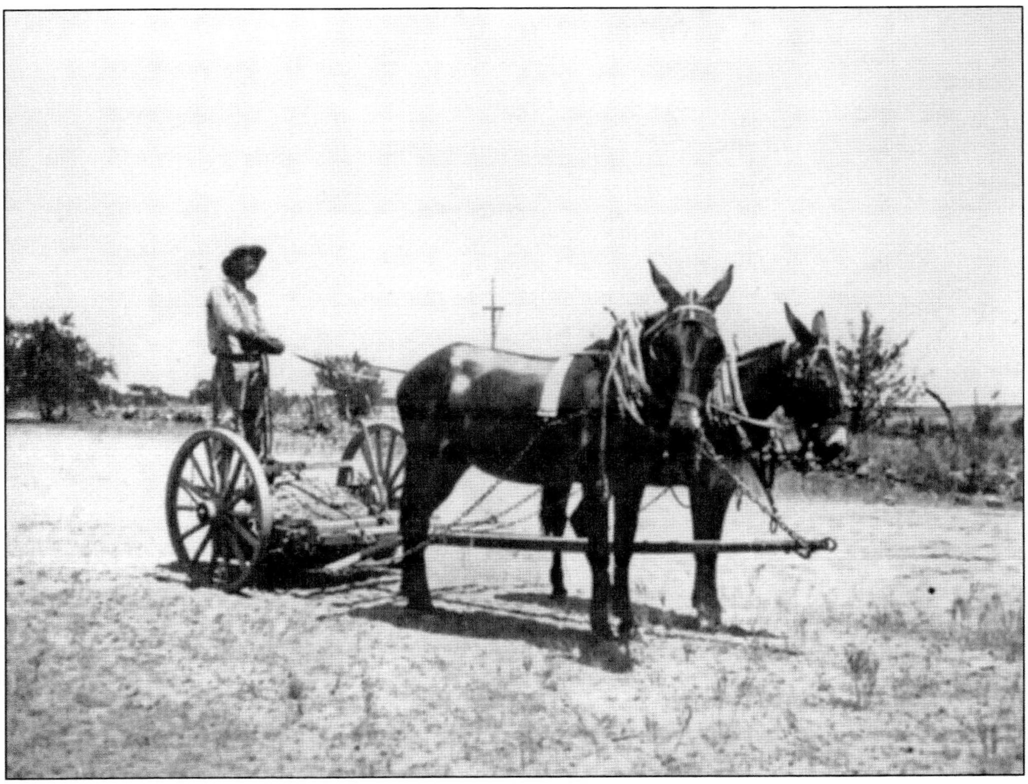

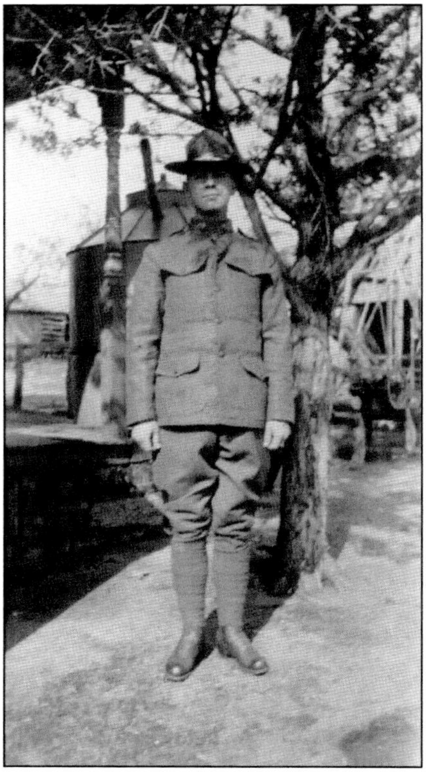

Some 225 young men from Mason County served in the "War to End All Wars." At left, George Henry Daniel "Dan" Eckert of Hilda, who served in the U.S. Army in 1918, is shown in a uniform of the World War I era. This was a difficult period for the German American citizens of Mason, who were suspected of disloyalty. In the bottom photograph, Bud F. Derby is pictured with his future in-laws in 1919, just after he returned from the Great War. From left to right are Raymond Smart, Maude Smart, Bud, and Annie Smart. Bud, who was on active duty with the U.S. Army on the Mexican border in 1916–1917, went to France with the 278th Aero Squadron (AEF) in 1918. He married the oldest sister of the Smart siblings, Gussie, in 1923. (Left photograph courtesy of the Homer Geistweidt family; bottom photograph courtesy of Steven B. Kensing.)

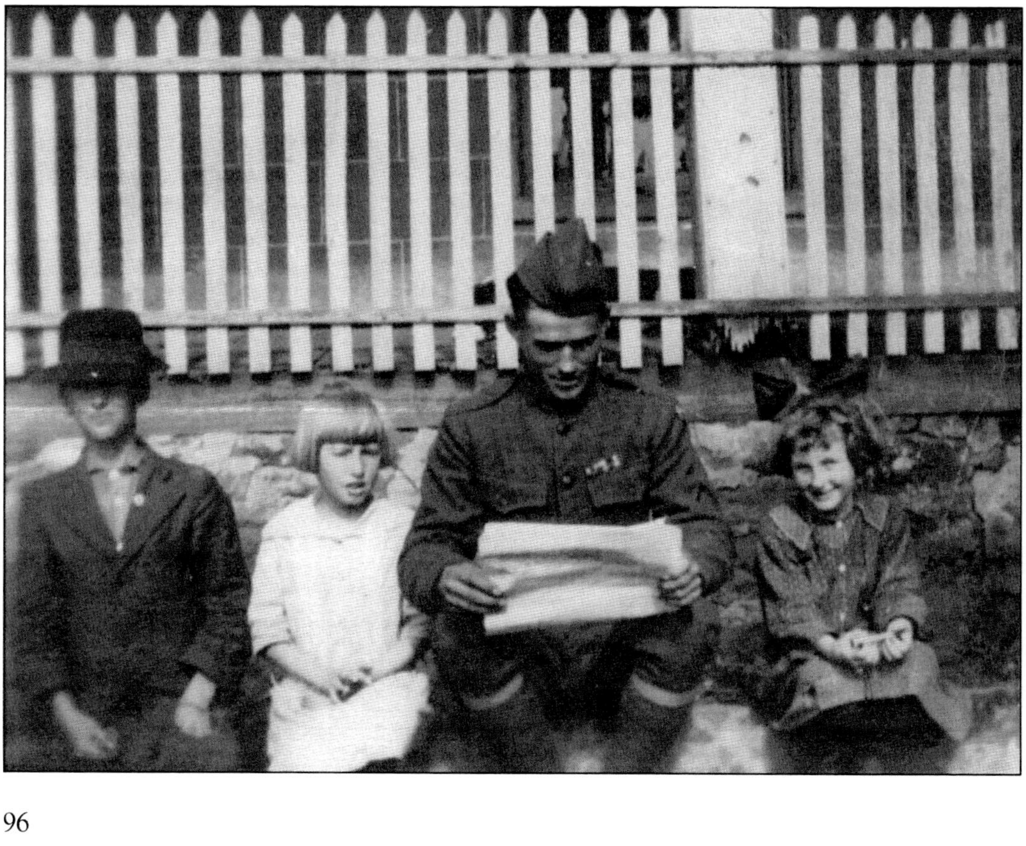

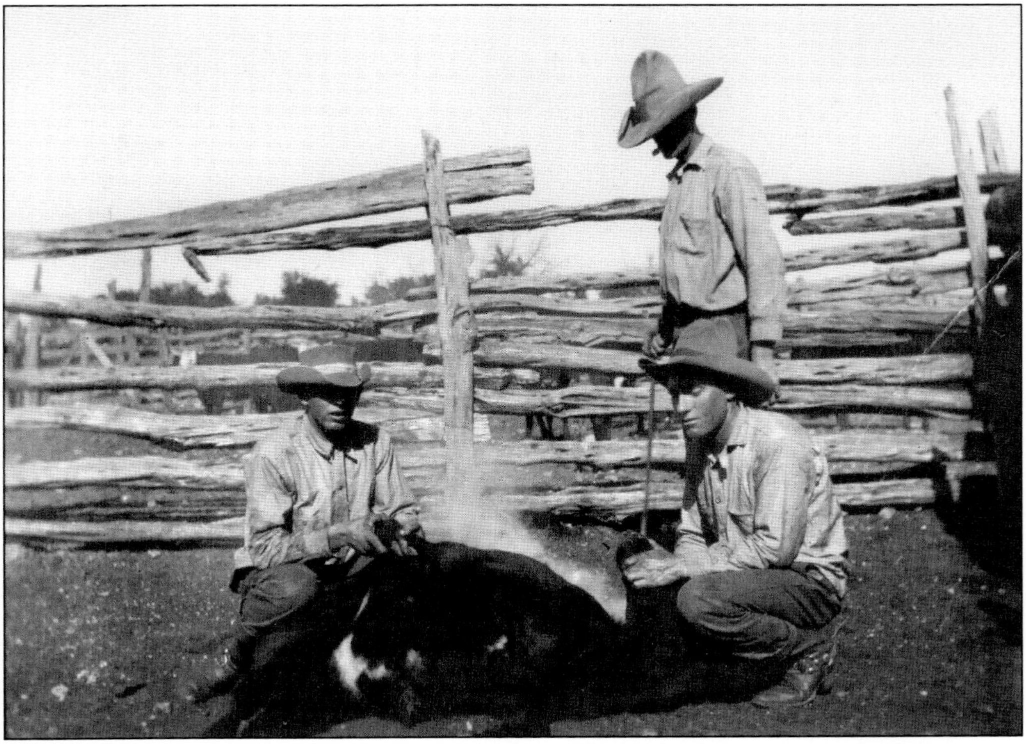

From left to right, Howard Bruce, Buck Waddell, and Gene "Sie" Banta (standing) are shown branding at J. W. White's Mill Creek Ranch in the early 1920s. Sie, a lifelong cowboy who served as foreman of this ranch, recalled in later life that he had been "bitten by one rattlesnake and one vinegar roan, shot up, cut up, chewed up, and spit out and throwed out of places and drug by horses." (Courtesy of Charles Banta.)

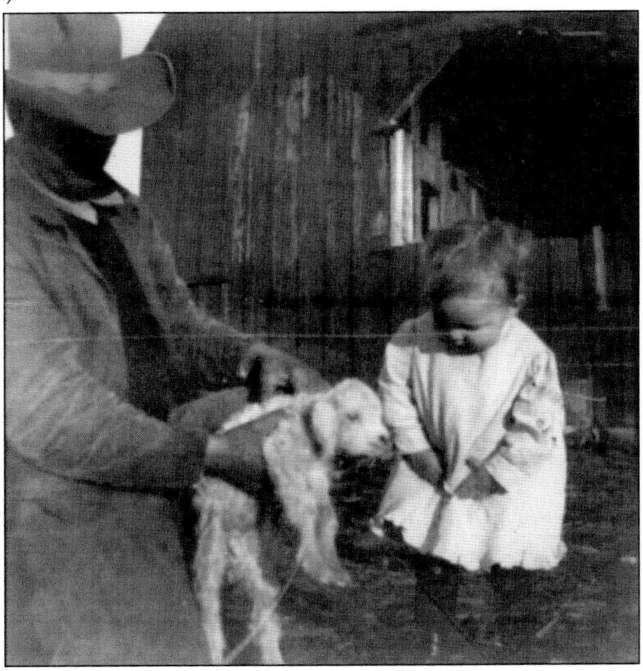

Otto Hofmann is showing his daughter Jane (Hoerster) a newborn Angora goat kid on their ranch at Grit in the spring of 1923. The goat kids had a leather strap on one hind leg tied to a peg in the ground to keep them safe from varmints while their mothers went to the pastures to eat. (Courtesy of Jane Hoerster.)

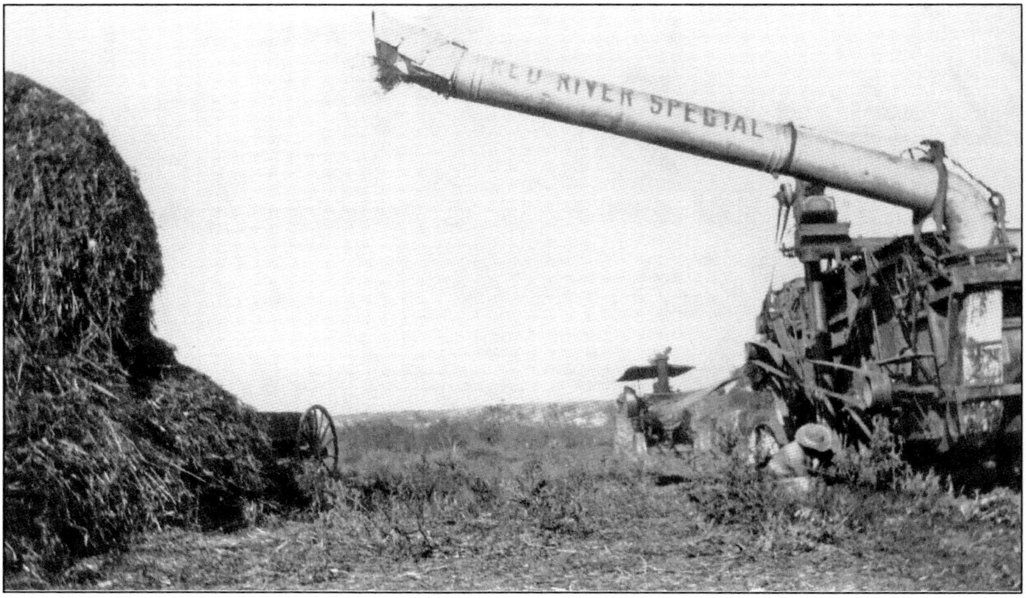

Grain harvesting was accomplished in the 1920s by these large stationary machines. The above photograph shows a Nichols and Shepard Red River Special threshing machine, owned by Oscar Geistweidt, harvesting oats on the ranch of Wanda and Charlie Evers in Salt Branch. Arnold Ellebracht is assisting. The bottom image is an excellent photograph of Oscar's Nichols and Shepard single-cylinder steam engine tractor, which was made before 1927. The tractor, using the long belt, is the powering the threshing machine in the above photograph. (Courtesy of Helen Habecker.)

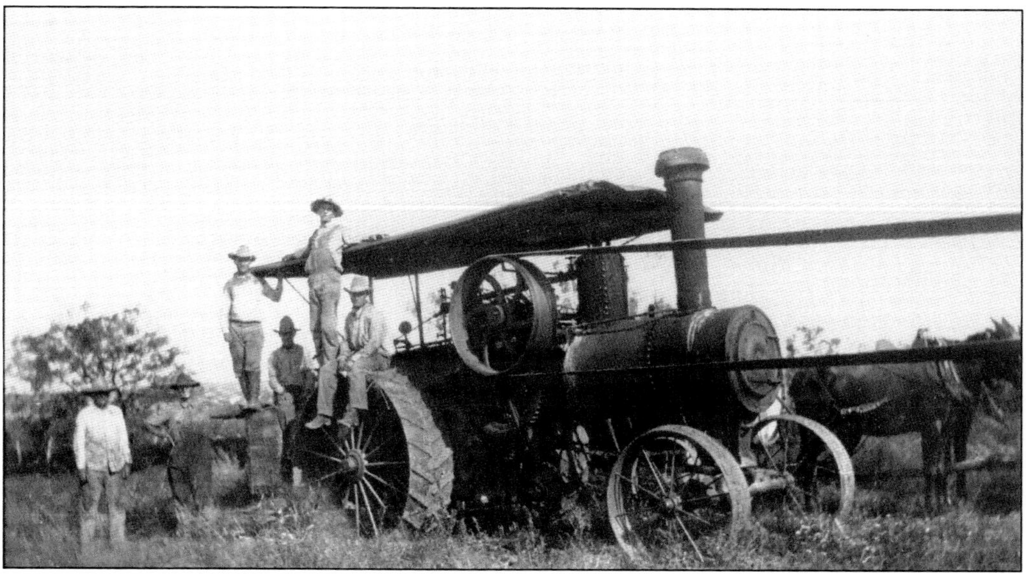

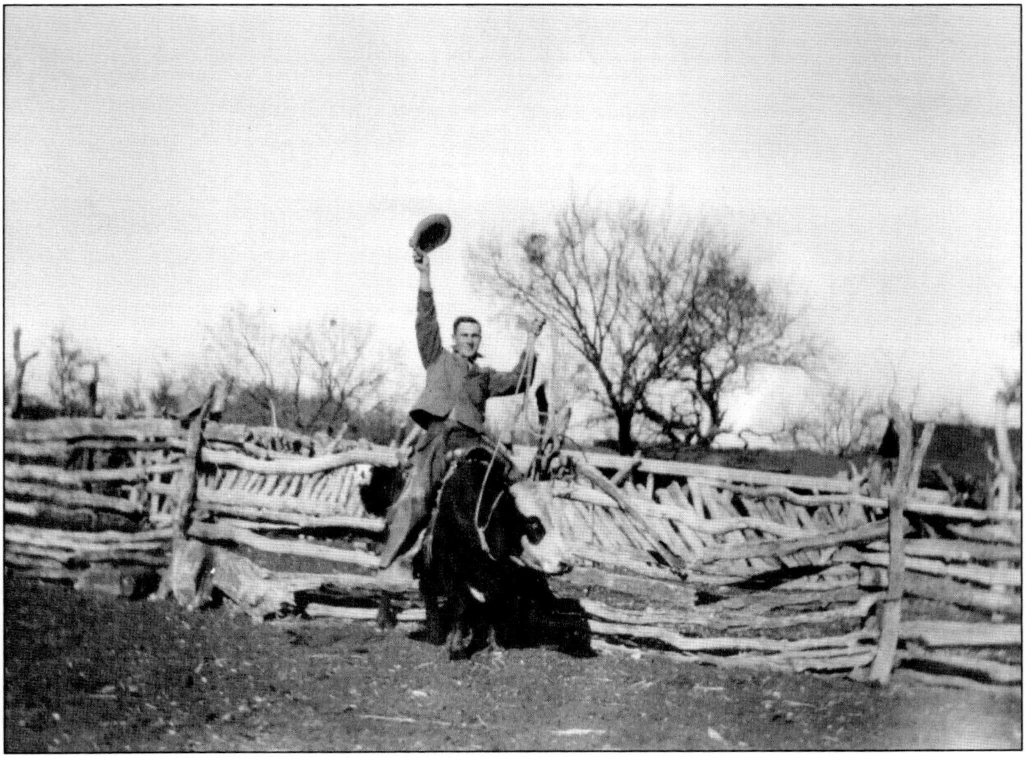

Although Johnie Eckert lived to be only 36, these images attest that he enjoyed those years to the fullest. In the above photograph, he is riding a bull on the family homestead at Ranch Branch. Johnie participated in weeklong roundups on neighboring ranches, including the Blockhouse. In the bottom photograph, he is pictured at his parents' homestead about 1925 with the dogs he trained for hunting varmints. Many nights he spent hunting raccoons with Werner Schmidt, following their hounds on horseback. The hides were collected and sold to fur traders in Mason. (Courtesy of Sara Banta.)

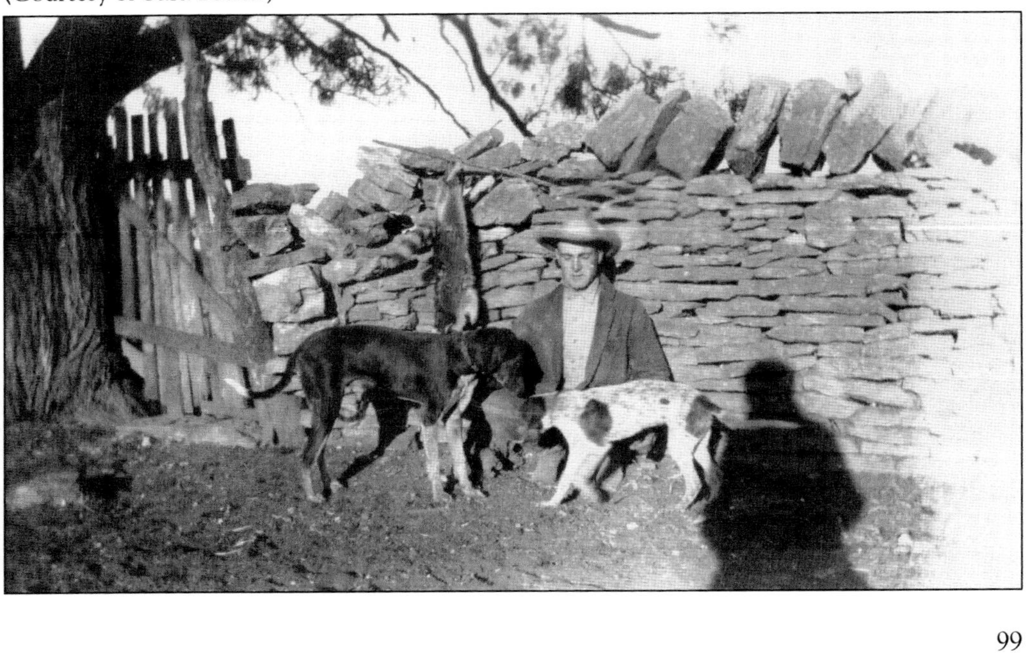

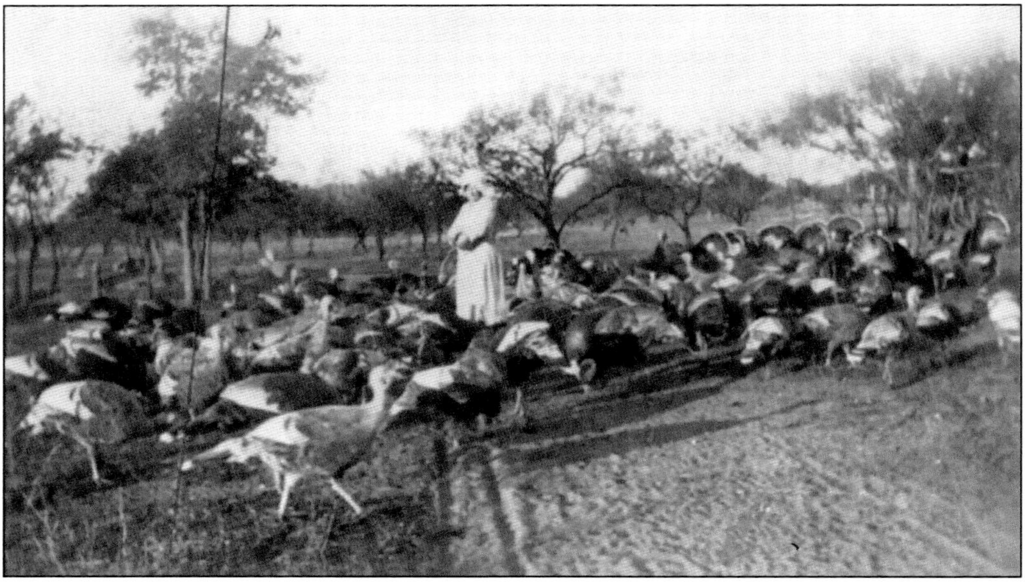

Ellie Durst feeds turkeys on the Emil Durst place at Union, around 1926. The *San Antonio Express* of November 13, 1926, reported that Mason County turkey raisers would market in excess of $100,000 worth of turkeys that season. Emil Durst sold $673.75 worth of turkeys to the Mason Produce Company during the first week after the market opened and still had 50 turkeys left on his farm. (Courtesy of Doris Dannheim.)

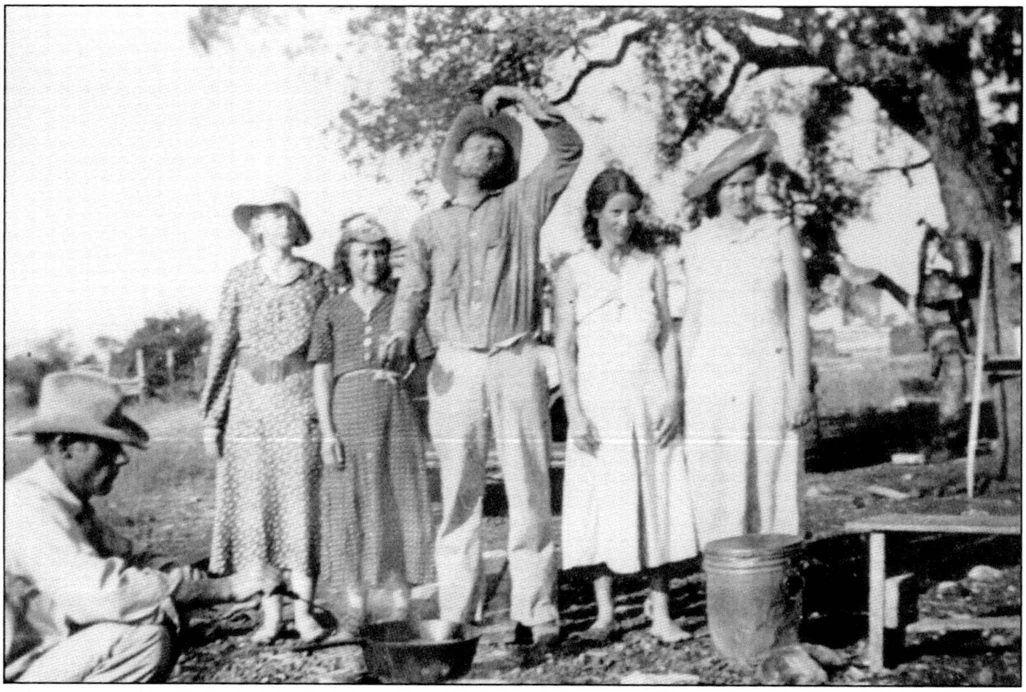

The Morris family is camped on a ranch in Mason County while building a fence, around 1928. From left to right are Earl Morris, Elsie Morris (Carter), Juanita Morris, Elzie Morris, Dovie Morris, and Nettie Ray Morris (McWilliams). Earl is frying something, probably venison or wild turkey, and Elzie appears to be sampling his brother's cooking. (Courtesy of Fae Danz.)

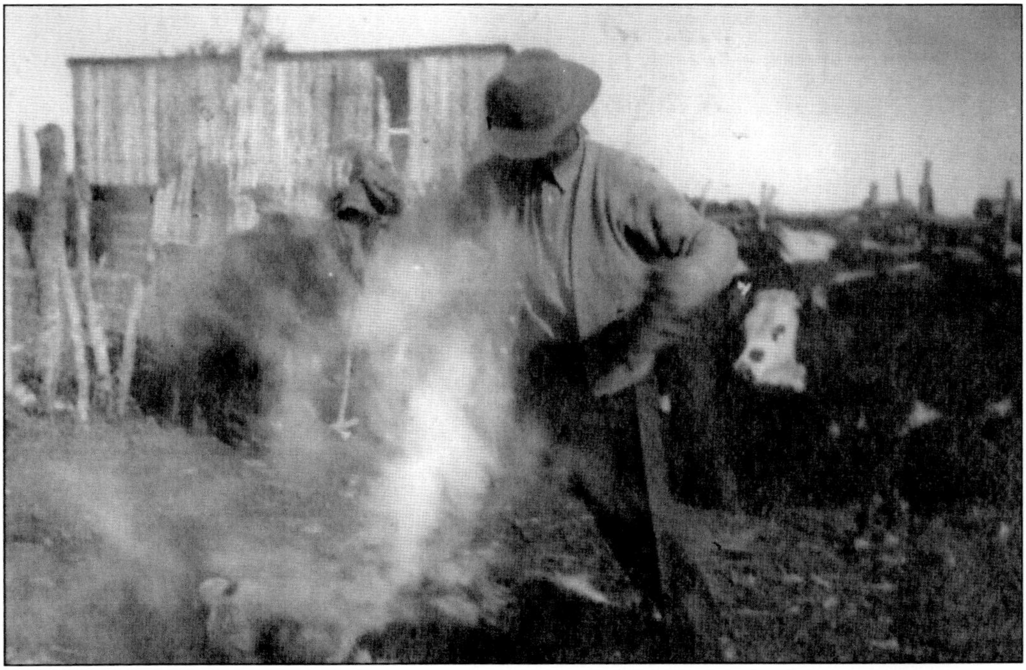

Mason County sheriff Allen T. Murray is shown branding around 1928. First elected sheriff in 1924, Murray was murdered by bootleggers in 1929 not far from the place where his grandfather Tom Milligan, Mason County's first sheriff, was killed by Indian raiders in 1860. One of the Texas Rangers who searched for Murray's killers was Frank Hamer, best known for tracking down Bonnie Parker and Clyde Barrow in 1934. (Courtesy of Ruth Dannheim.)

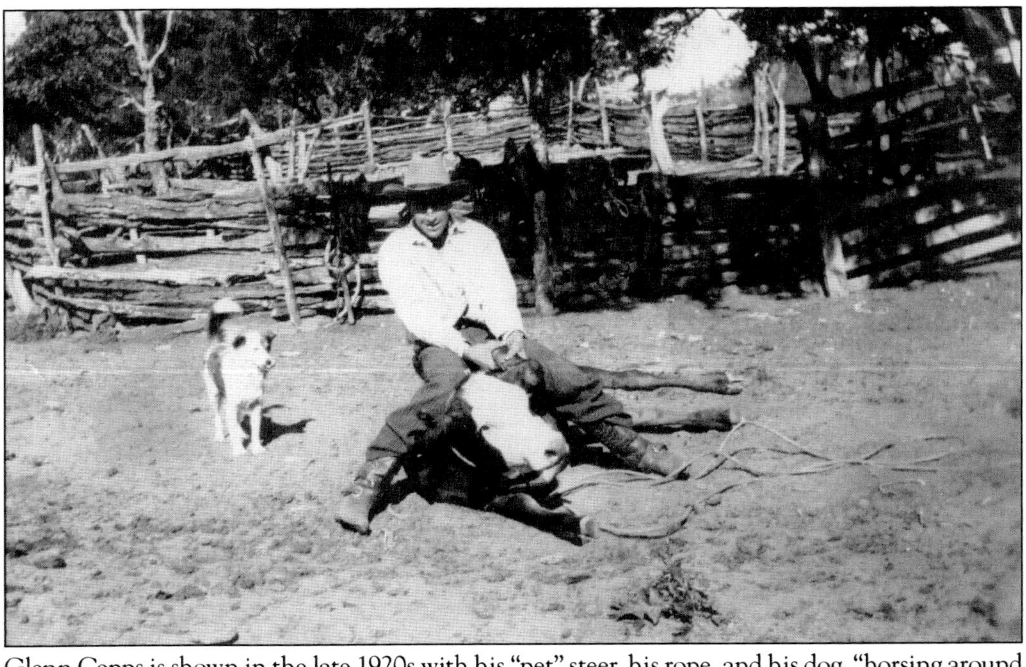

Glenn Capps is shown in the late 1920s with his "pet" steer, his rope, and his dog, "horsing around without his horse in sight," as his daughter Sally says. The wooden pens were typical of the era. (Courtesy of Sally Capps.)

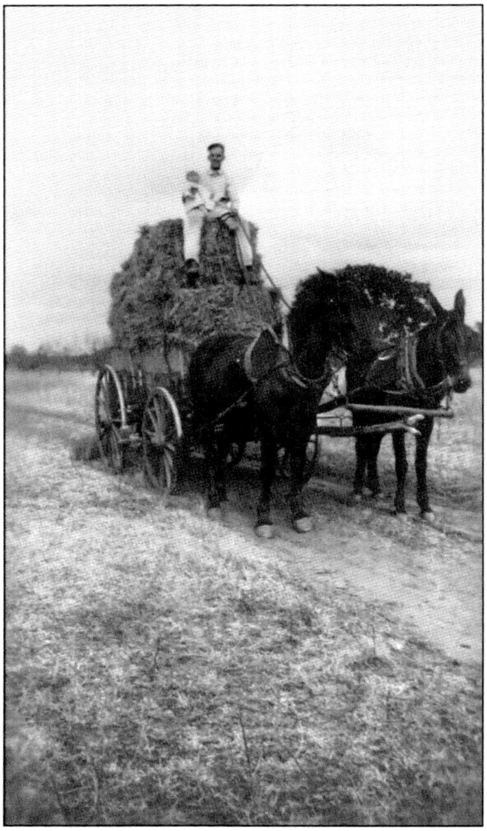

Wilbert Meyer holds his infant daughter, Carolyn (Loeffler), as he hauls a load of hay in 1935. Mason County farmers and ranchers produced 7,500 tons of hay for local consumption in 1930. (Courtesy of Carolyn Loeffler.)

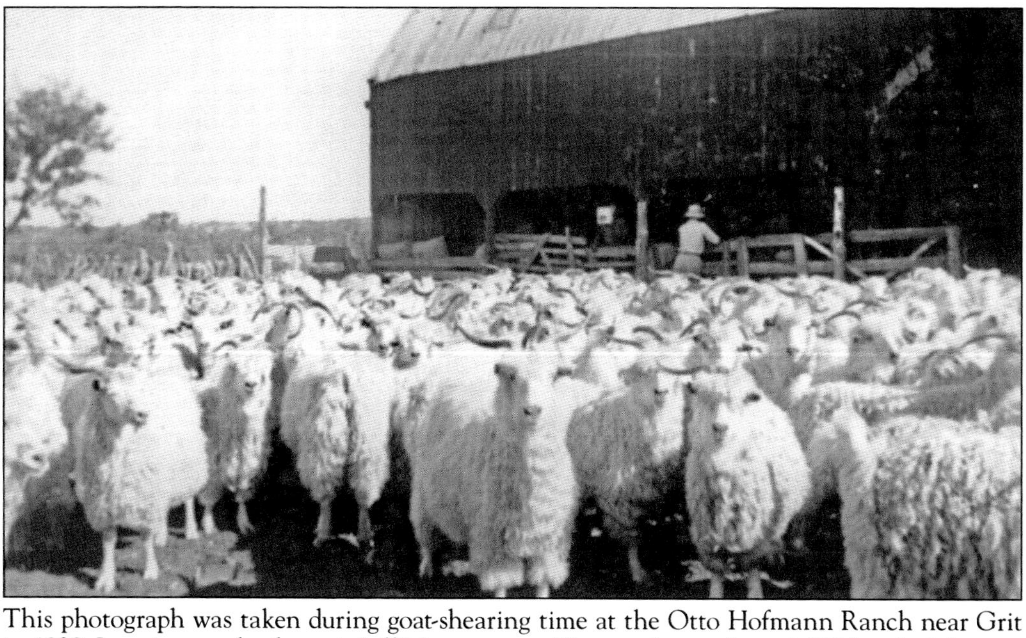

This photograph was taken during goat-shearing time at the Otto Hofmann Ranch near Grit in 1938. Leaning on the fence is Jeff Montgomery. The ranch ran about 2,000 head of Angora goats, which were raised for their mohair and were shorn twice a year by a Mexican American crew. (Courtesy of Jane Hoerster.)

Manuel Castillo, an experienced horseman, is seen on a ranch in Mason County, where he worked as a cowboy. He inscribed the back of this photograph to his brother Eleno Castillo in 1942. (Courtesy of Jane Zavala.)

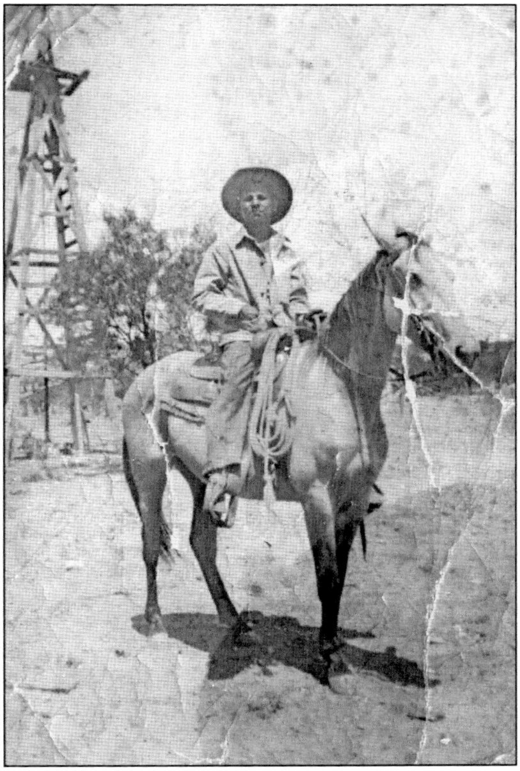

Sam A. Hoerster Sr. is pictured on his horse, Dick, in a cutting horse competition at the Mason rodeo arena in the 1940s. Local friends encouraged Sam, who was already in his 50s, to enter a major cutting horse competition in Houston. He loaded Dick in the back of his pickup truck and drove to the city, where he won third place in three of the events, competing against much younger men. (Courtesy of Sam and Maribelle Hoerster.)

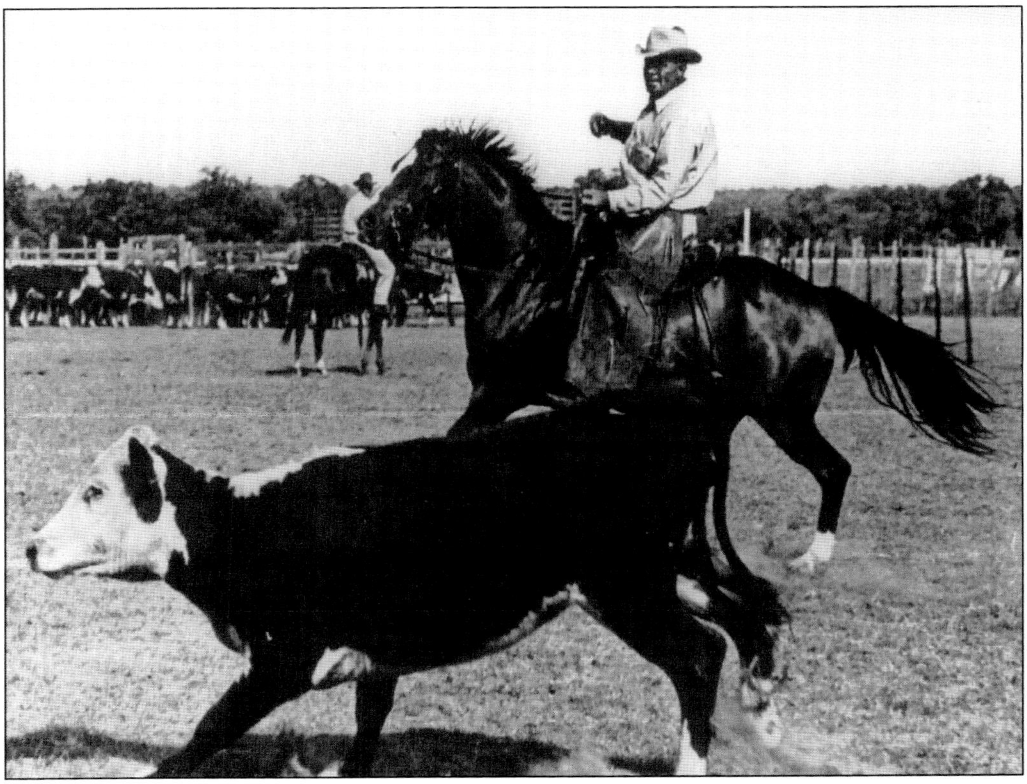

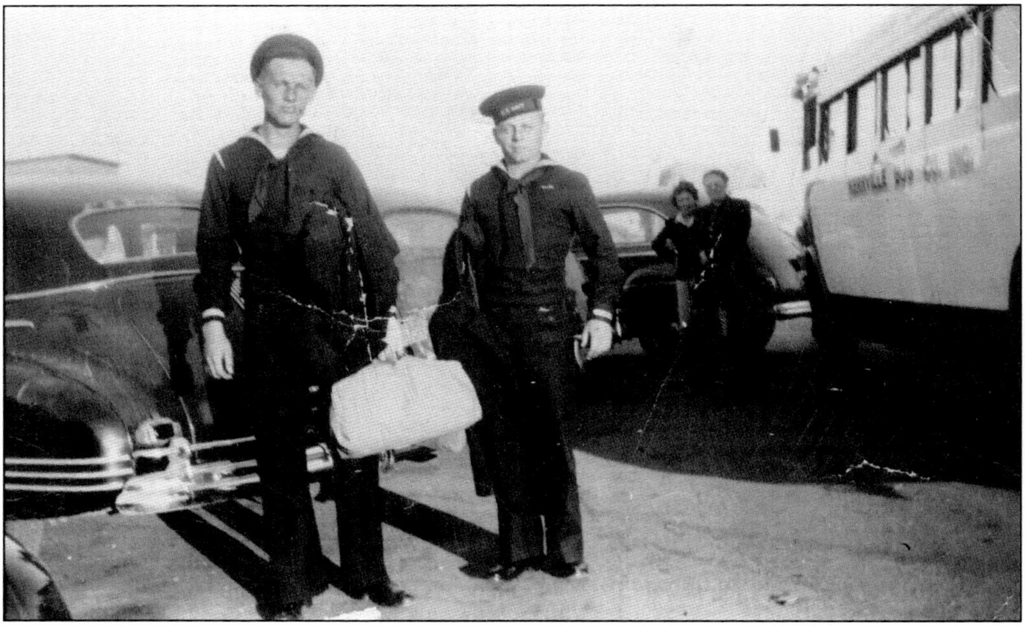

Alex Grosse (left) and Jack Hofmann are getting ready to board a Kerrville Bus Company coach. The two young men, who were next-door neighbors, served their two years and eight months in the U.S. Navy without ever being separated. They were discharged on March 23, 1946. (Courtesy of Florene Hofmann.)

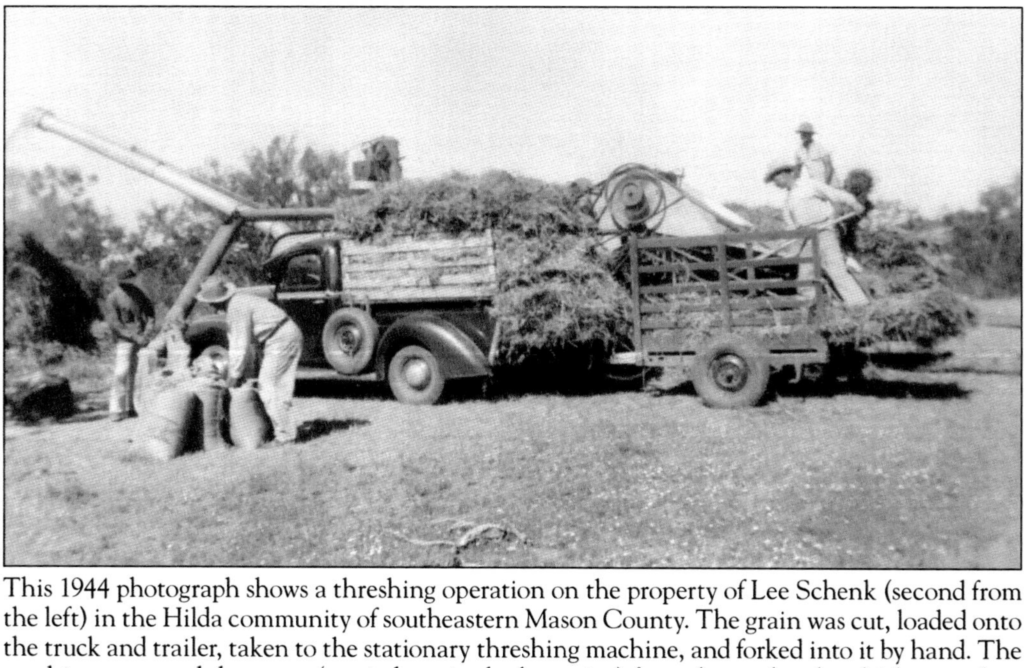

This 1944 photograph shows a threshing operation on the property of Lee Schenk (second from the left) in the Hilda community of southeastern Mason County. The grain was cut, loaded onto the truck and trailer, taken to the stationary threshing machine, and forked into it by hand. The machine separated the stems (carried out in the long pipe) from the oat heads, which were then bagged. (Courtesy of the Homer Geistweidt family.)

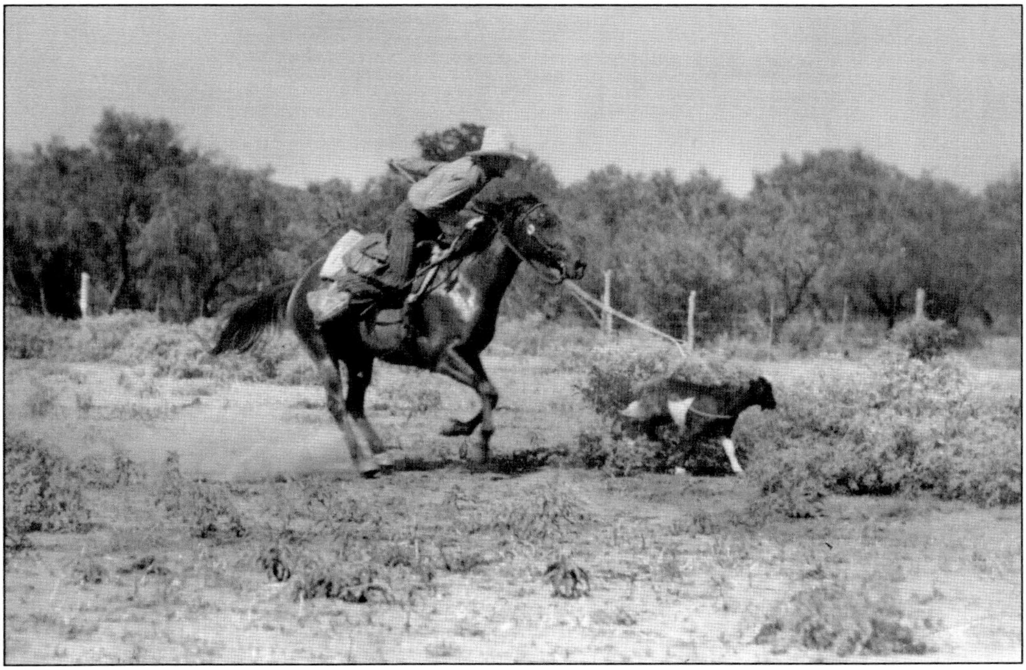

Ivan Johnson was a real cowboy. However, even cowboys will stoop to roping goats when they get bored. Ivan is shown in action here in the 1940s as he throws a perfect loop. People roped goats for fun at rural social gatherings. (Courtesy of Ron Birk.)

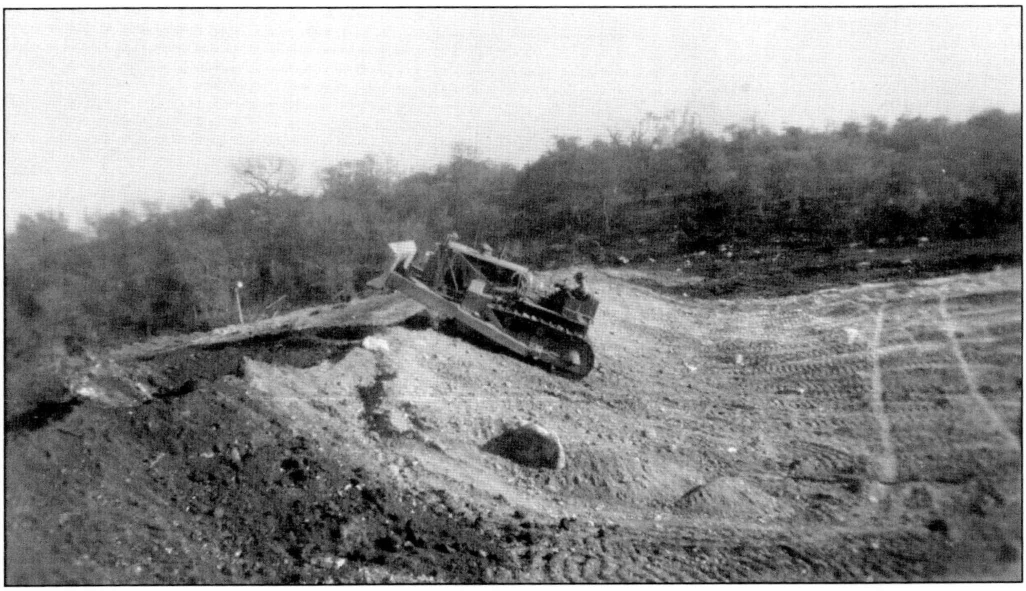

Homer Geistweidt is at the controls of his bulldozer in 1946, putting the finishing touches on a dam for a large tank on his ranch near Streeter. Except for the few streams and rivers of Mason County, much of the region has little available perennial surface water flow. Thus, it became commonplace to construct earthen catchment ponds or tanks to collect the runoff from the rains. Homer enjoyed working with Caterpillar tractors and developed the idea of linking two "Cats" together to "chain-out" the brush between them. (Courtesy of the Homer Geistweidt family.)

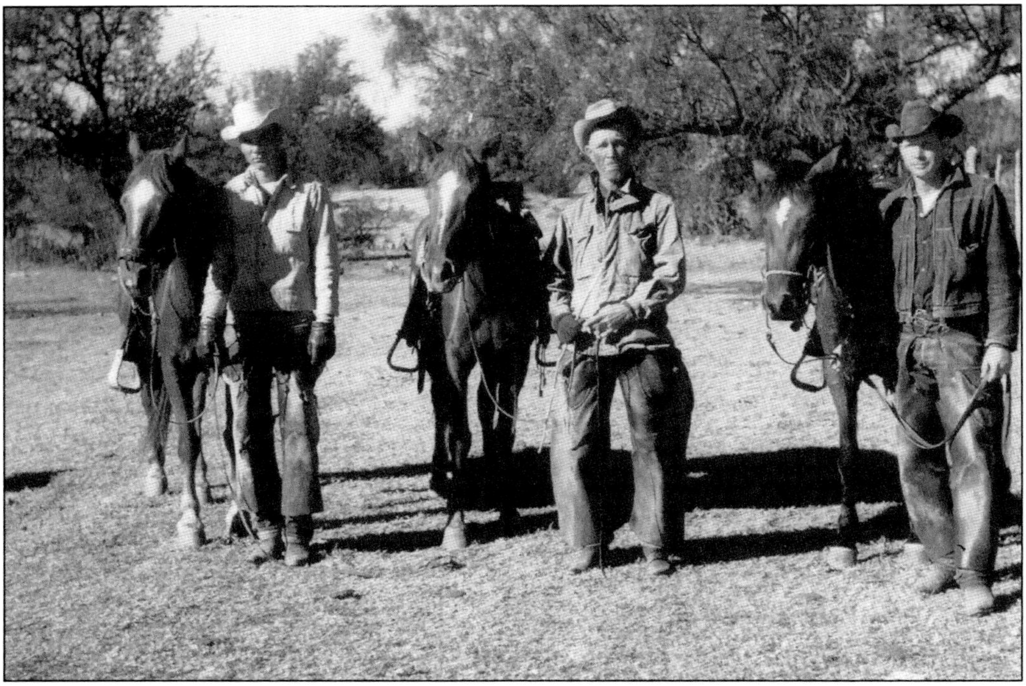

These photographs were taken in 1951 on the Blockhouse Ranch, which was one of the oldest and largest ranches in Mason County. From left to right in the above photograph, Vernon Lively, Leo Starks, and Jack Crouch are pictured after rounding up cattle. In the bottom photograph, Leo Starks is burning the thorns off prickly pear leaves for the cattle to eat. During the severe drought of 1950–1956, ranchers burned pear for livestock year-round because there was no grass. (Courtesy of Glenn Ruthven.)

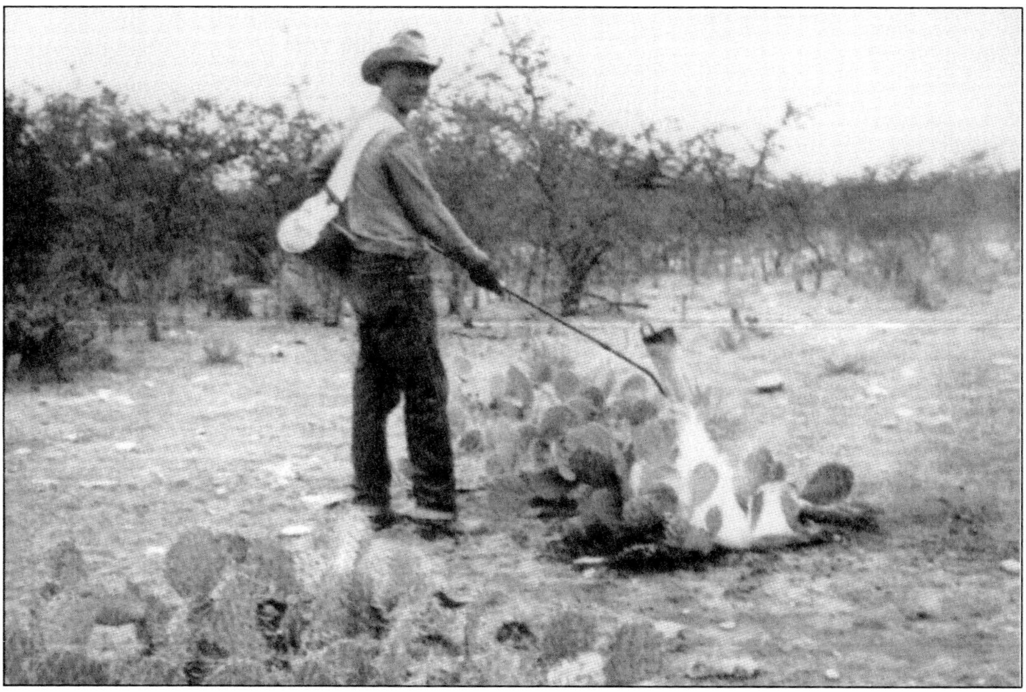

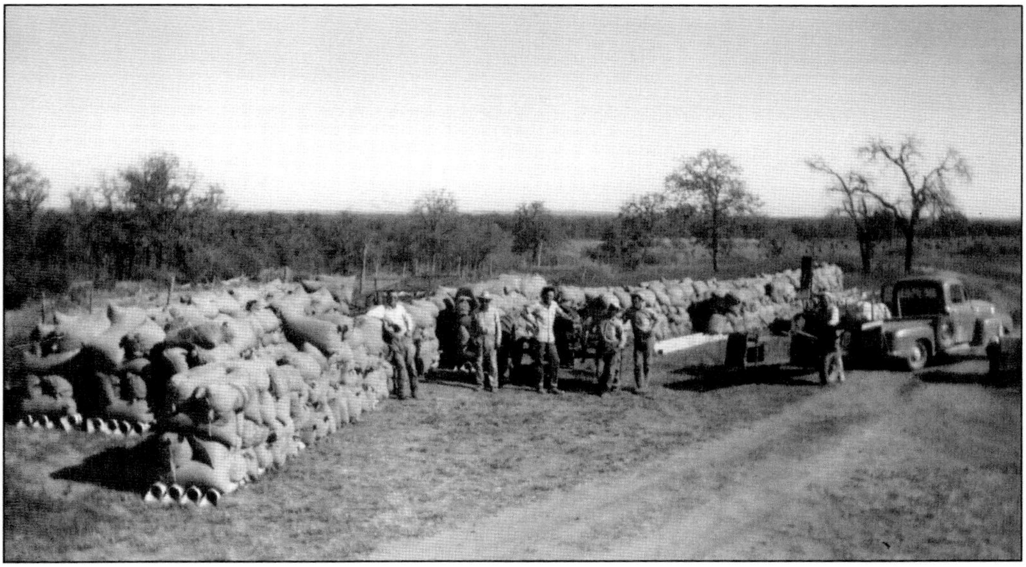

Beginning in the 1940s, peanuts became one of the most important crops in Mason County. The above image, taken in 1955, shows a large harvest of peanuts drying at the Homer Geistweidt Ranch near Streeter before being taken to market. Hooked to the back of the pickup truck was a hay baler. When processing peanuts, little of the plant was wasted. After the plants were plowed up, they were bundled, thrown onto a wooden sled, and taken to a stationary threshing machine where the hay and peanuts were separated. In the bottom image, taken in 1949 on the Wilbur Durst Ranch in eastern Mason County, the machine is making square bales and is being fed hay from the thresher by Wilbur (on the left). Sam Metzger is sitting on a bale and tying twine around each bale. Earl McDaniel is standing opposite Sam. (Above photograph courtesy of the Homer Geistweidt family; bottom photograph courtesy of Doris Dannheim.)

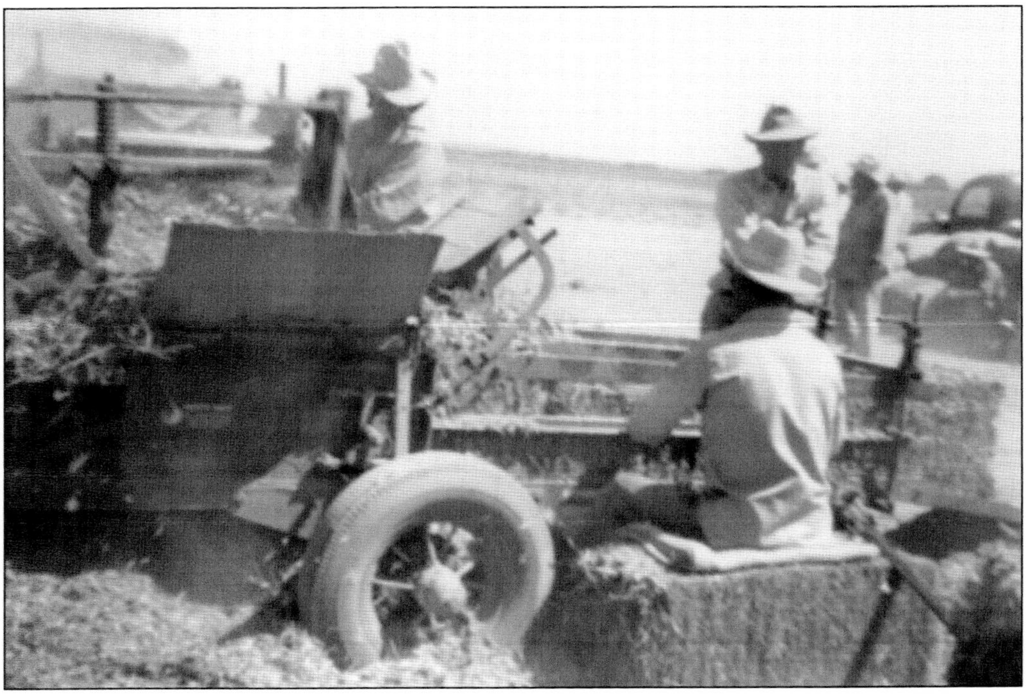

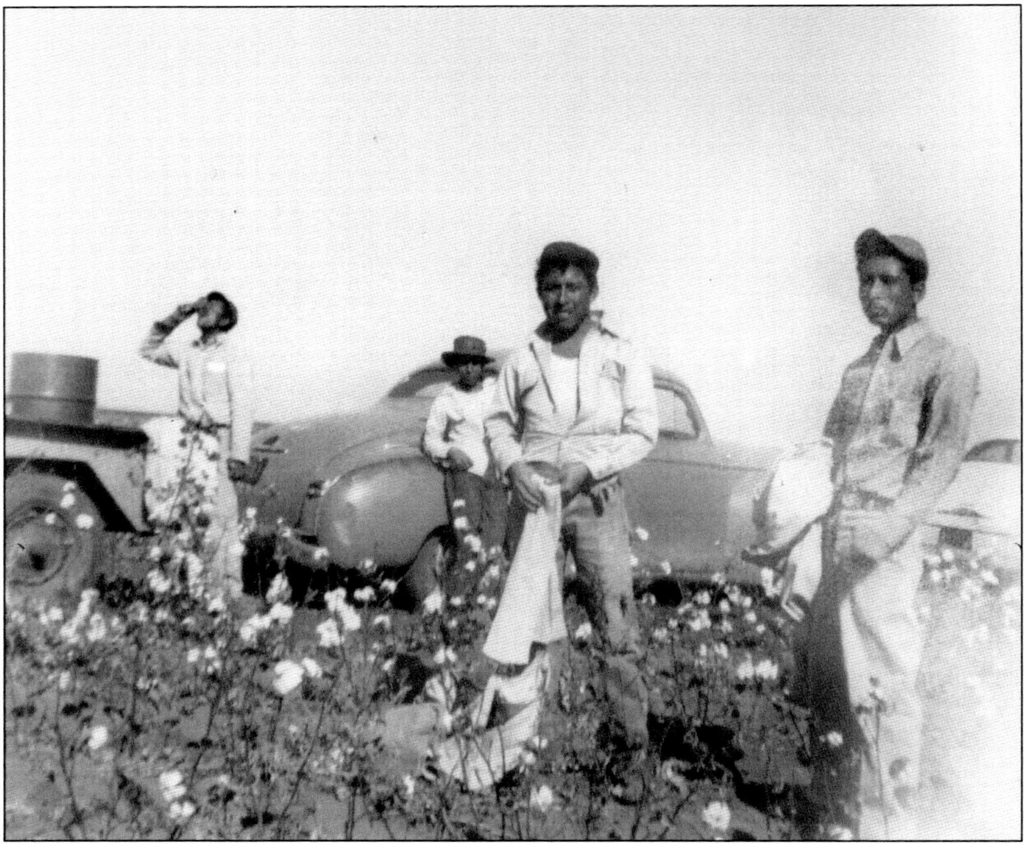

These men are picking cotton in the Katemcy area in the fall of 1956. From left to right are unidentified, Benito Gonzalez, Santiago Torrez, and Pete Martinez. (Courtesy of Candy Luna.)

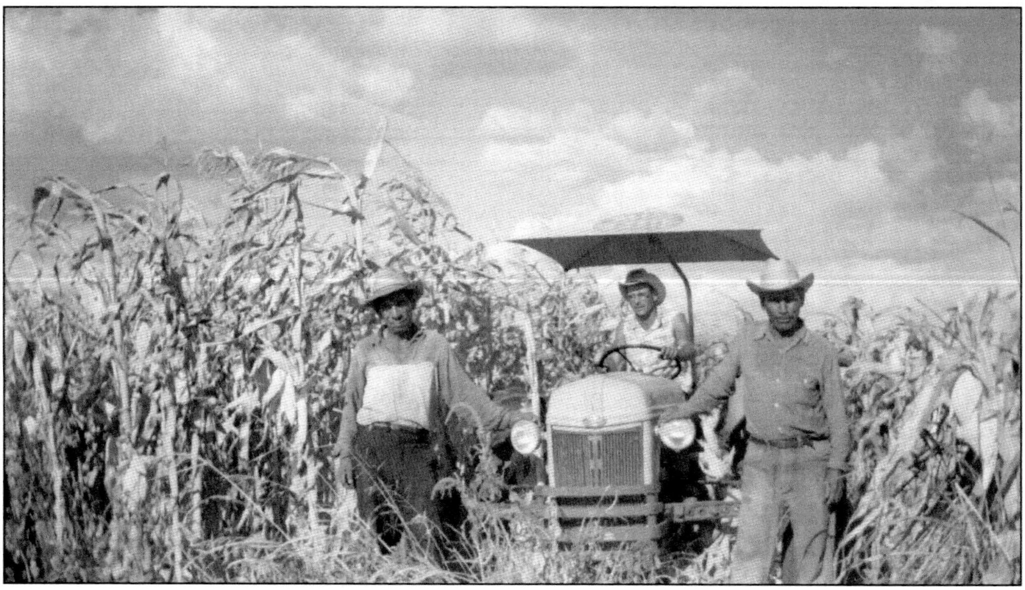

Homer Geistweidt is shown in 1956 on his Ford 8N tractor in a cornfield at his Streeter homestead. He moved there with his family in 1950. (Courtesy of the Homer Geistweidt family.)

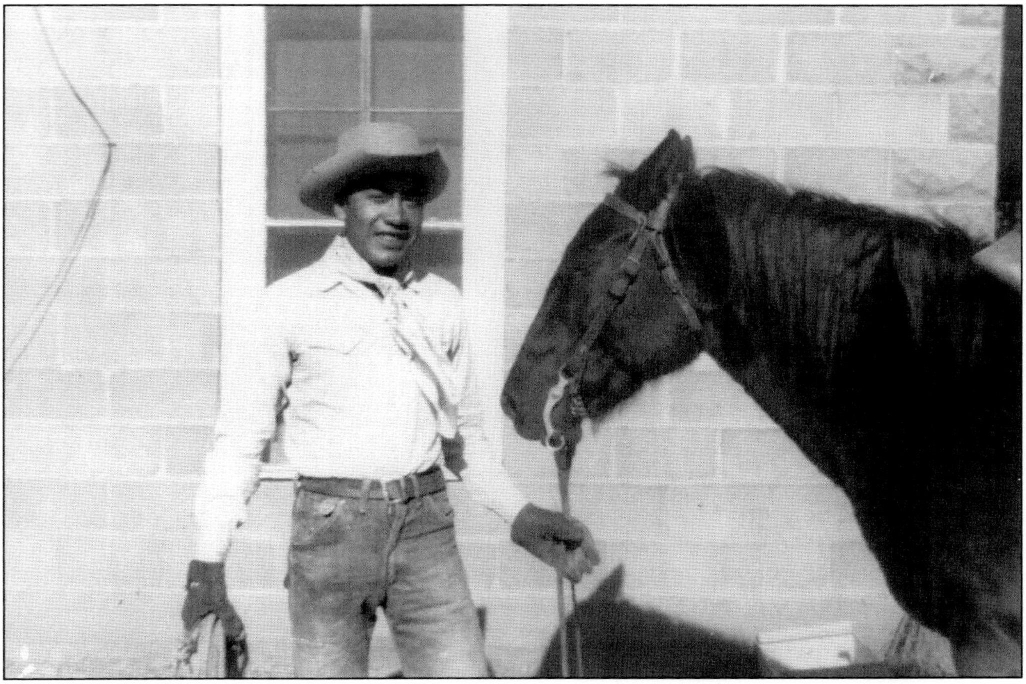

Macario Agustin Orozpe came to Mason in 1956 from Temamalta Edo de Mexico and worked as a cowboy on several ranches during the first 12 years he lived in the county. He is pictured here at the Seth Martin Ranch at age 20 in August 1957. (Courtesy of Amanda Orozpe.)

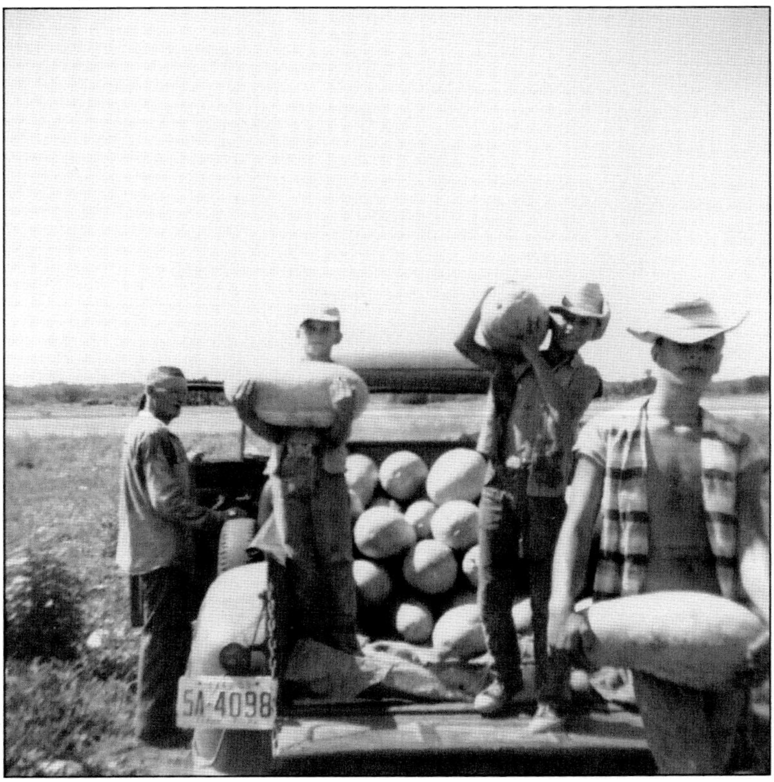

These industrious fellows are picking watermelons on the Homer Geistweidt place at Streeter in the late 1950s. From left to right are Ervin Geistweidt, Gene Geistweidt, Joe D. Geistweidt, and Rodney Leifeste. (Courtesy of the Homer Geistweidt family.)

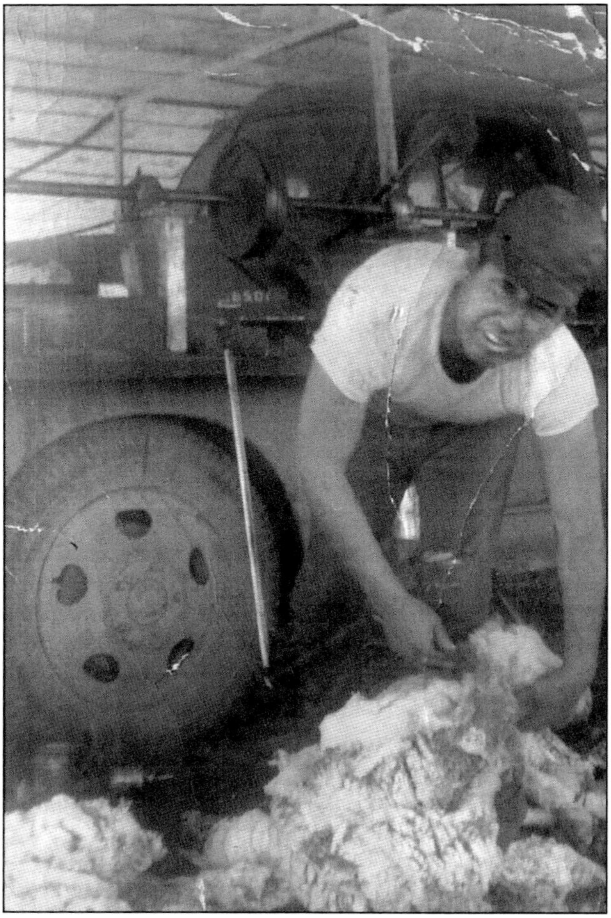

Savino Menchaca, born in Mason County in 1880, started a shearing business that his sons and grandsons continued, working throughout the state. For many years, the Menchaca shearing crews were an integral part of ranch life in Mason County. An experienced crew member averaged about 150 goats or sheep per day. At left, Enrique Menchaca is pictured shearing an Angora goat in 1958, with the motorized shearing rig in the background. In the bottom photograph, Mary Menchaca, wife of Alfred Menchaca Sr., sits on a sack of mohair at the Arthur Geistweidt Ranch in the late 1950s. Mary prepared meals on-site for the crew. (Left photograph courtesy of Dolores Menchaca; bottom photograph courtesy of the Alfred Menchaca family.)

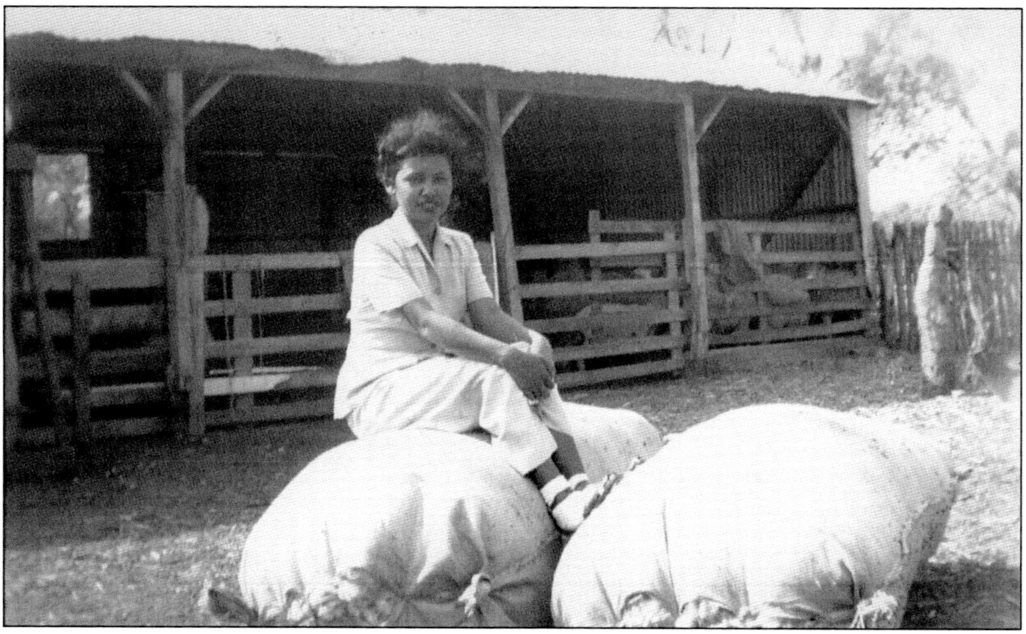

Eight

At Play

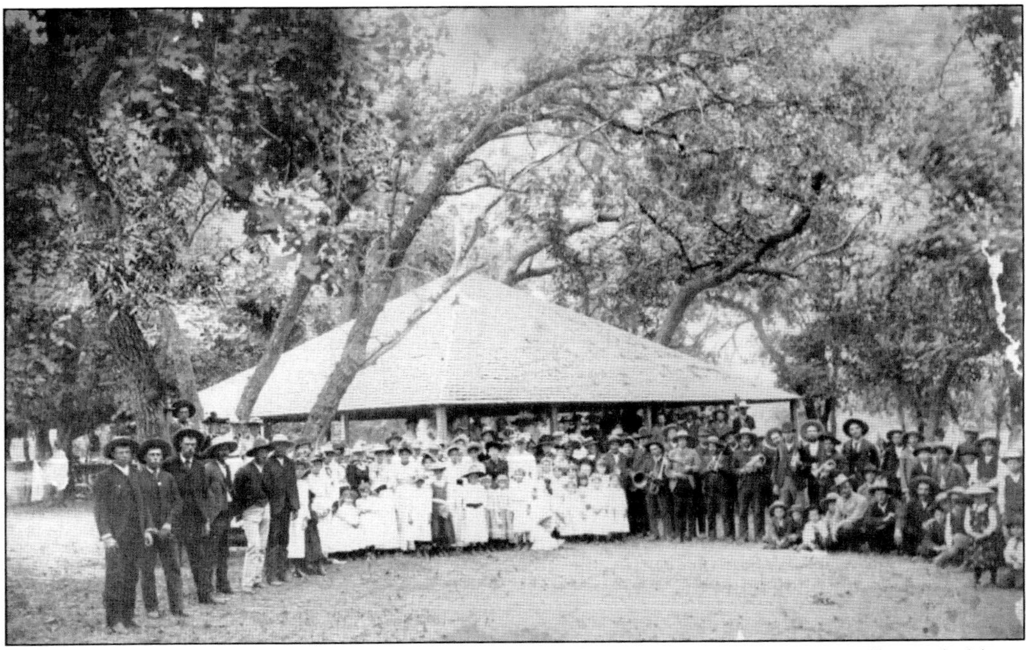

This community gathering took place at a bandstand in a pecan grove in Simonsville, probably in the 1890s. Band members are posing with brass instruments to the right of the children dressed in white. In its heyday, Simonsville was known for its marksmanship contests, picnics, horse races, and dances that lasted until late into the night. A permanent dance pavilion was erected in the Dangers bottom near the Robert Zesch homestead in 1884. It was eventually destroyed by fire. (Courtesy of Charles Kettner.)

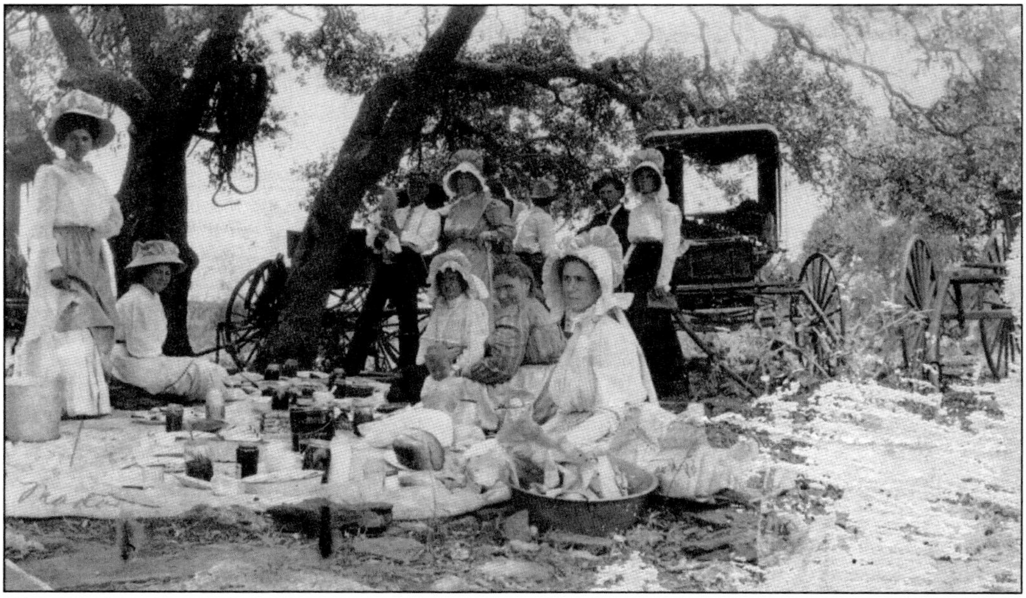

The Reichenau family is enjoying a picnic near their home on the Llano River around 1912. Mada Reichenau is standing on the left, and Erna Reichenau (Watkins) is sitting next to her. Standing second from the right in the dark suit is Willie Reichenau, and Max Reichenau is in the center, wearing a band cap. Grandmother Johanna Moldenhauer Reichenau is seated on the quilt, dressed in a striped blouse. (Courtesy of Charles Reichenau.)

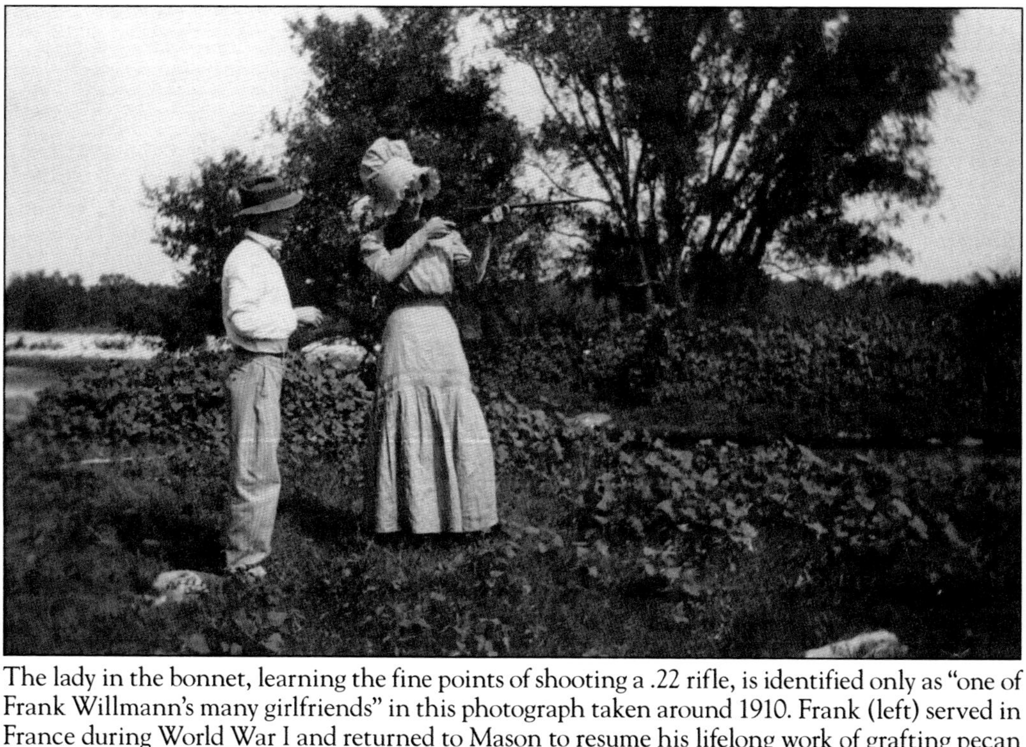

The lady in the bonnet, learning the fine points of shooting a .22 rifle, is identified only as "one of Frank Willmann's many girlfriends" in this photograph taken around 1910. Frank (left) served in France during World War I and returned to Mason to resume his lifelong work of grafting pecan trees. He finally selected one special girlfriend and married Marguerite Schroeder of La Grange in 1931. (Courtesy of Doug and Sherry Willmann.)

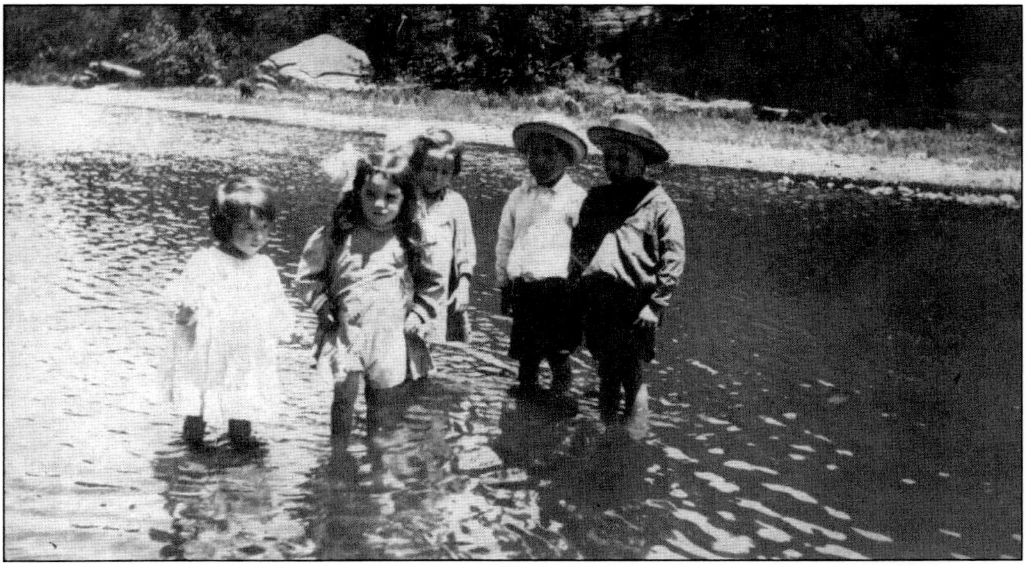

These children appear to be dressed in their Sunday best, but that did not stop them from splashing in the Llano River around 1911. The girls are, from left to right, Ruth, Benellen, and Dixie Hey, daughters of Ben and Maud Hey. Their companions are two Keller boys. (Courtesy of Peggy Laverty.)

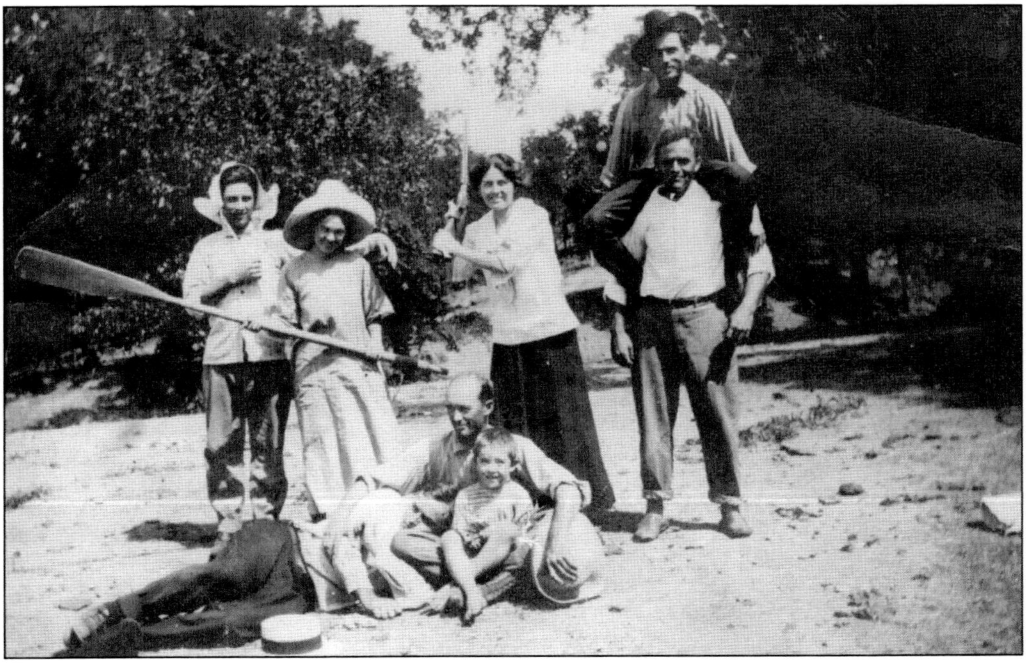

These folks obviously spent a fun day on the Llano River in 1912. From left to right in the back row are Irl Larrimore, wearing a woman's sunbonnet, with his arm draped over Caroline "Carrie" Willmann (Howard), who is wearing Irl's hat and ready to swat someone with a boat oar. (Irl was a publisher of the *Mason County News* from 1920 until 1944.) Next is Carrie's sister Alma Willmann (Grosse), ready to do business with her Winchester .22 rifle. T. J. Dent is perched on the shoulders of Oscar Shearer. In front is Oscar's twin brother, Otis Shearer, with his head on the leg of C. C. Willmann, and Lee "Buck" Shearer in C. C.'s lap. (Courtesy of Beverly Baker.)

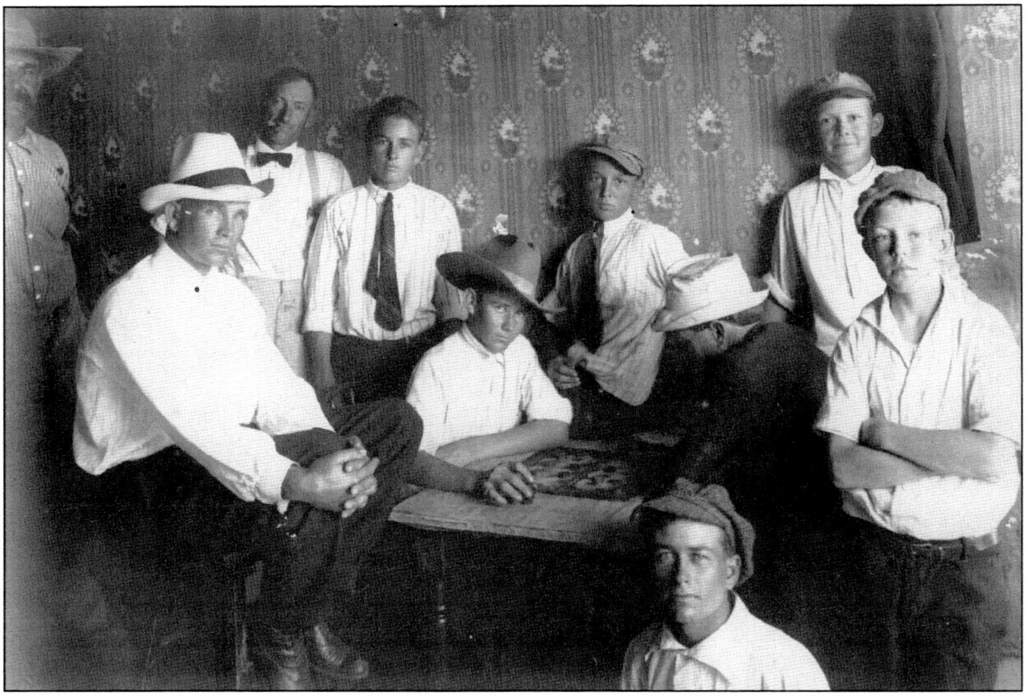

This group pauses from a checker game in the back of C. L. "Charlie" Hofmann's Café in 1915. The first four from the left are Charlie Haler, Jap Emry, Charlie Hofmann, and Carson Henrich. Henry "Slick" McDougall stands to the right with his arms folded. The others, not positively identified, include Clarence Williams, Allan Doell, Ben Evans, and Herbert Ogle. Located on the northeast block of the square (present-day Mason Square Museum), the café was known for its 10¢ hamburgers with meat an inch thick, spread with mustard, onions, and pickles. (Courtesy of the Mason County Museum.)

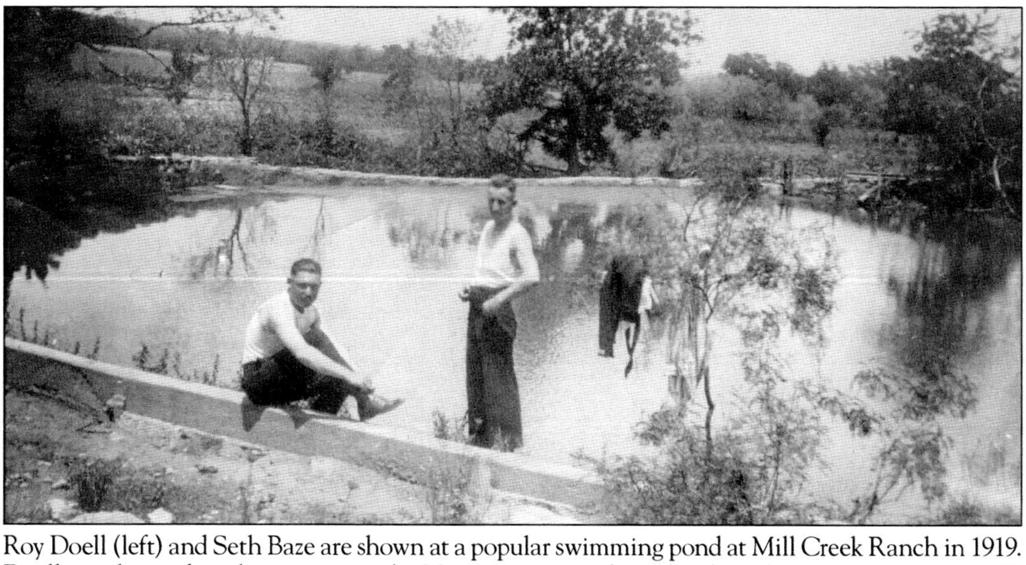

Roy Doell (left) and Seth Baze are shown at a popular swimming pond at Mill Creek Ranch in 1919. Doell, just home from his service in the U.S. Navy, started a tailor shop that year in the back of J. S. King's jewelry store. Seth joined him in the business in 1926, and they operated Baze and Doell Style Headquarters for Men on the northeast block of the square. (Courtesy of MCHC.)

Frank John Willmann is shown with a buck he shot with his trusty Savage Model 1899 after returning home from service in World War I. Willmann served in France in the 36th Division in Battery C of the 132nd Field Artillery. In addition to exhibiting this handy way of packing out his deer, Frank sports his military boots and pants. (Courtesy of Doug and Sherry Willmann.)

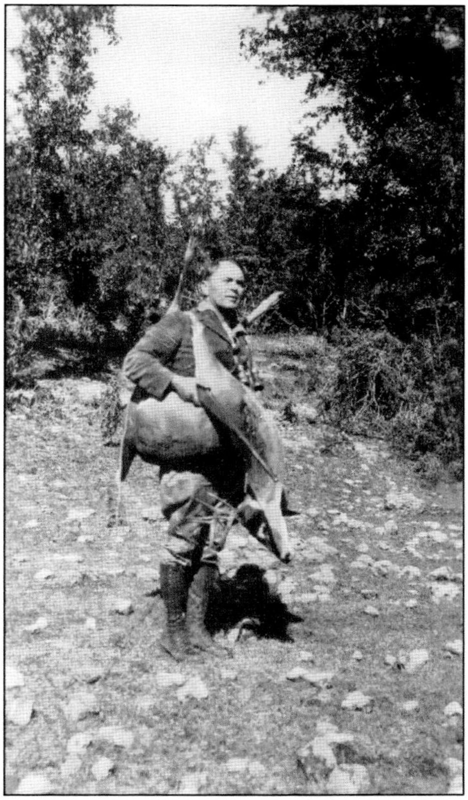

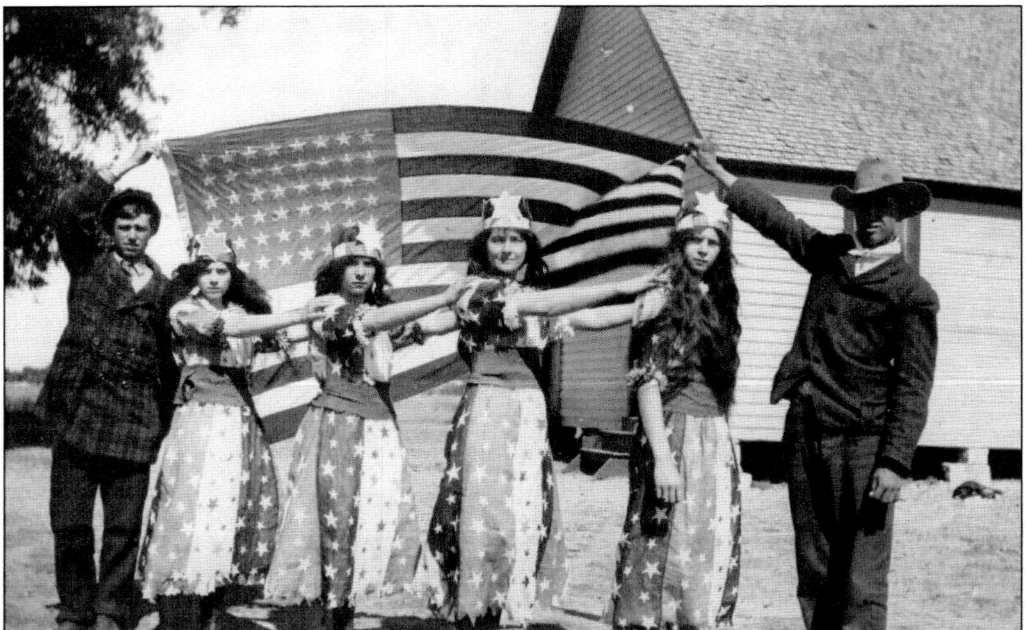

This group of proud American citizens may be commemorating Memorial Day, celebrating the end of the school year, or simply practicing for an event to be presented at school. The flag has 48 stars, so the photograph was taken after 1912, possibly around 1920. (Courtesy of Wilburn Shearer.)

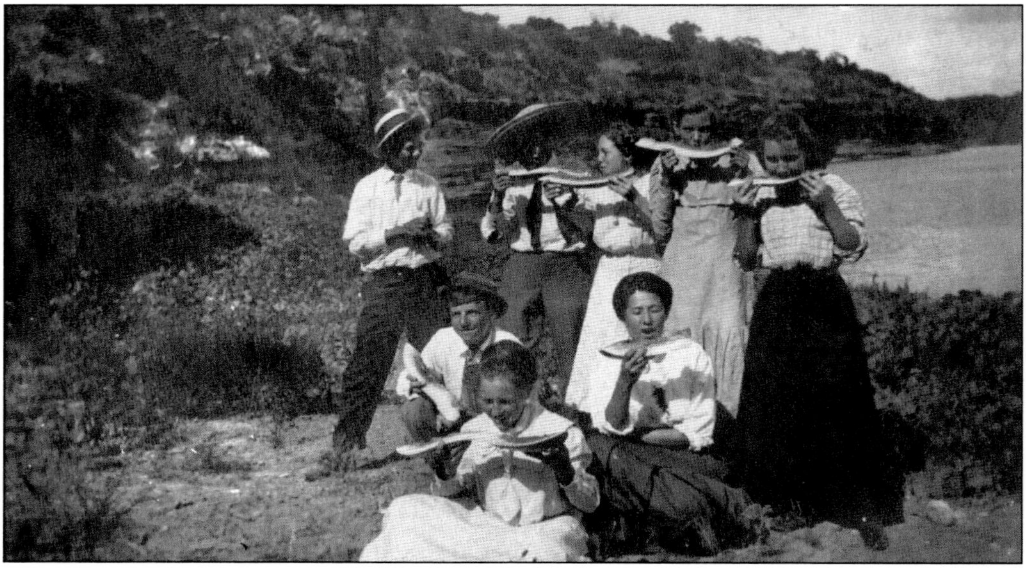

This photograph, taken around 1920, captures a group of smiling, happy watermelon eaters as they picnic near the confluence of the Llano and James Rivers. A Texas German custom, possibly unique to this area, was the preparation of a pulpy jam, *wassermelonenschmier*, made by cooking watermelon until it thickened into a sweet, reddish mass that was stored in five- and 10-gallon crocks. It was then eaten with bread and butter, or on *schmierkas*, a homemade cottage cheese. (Courtesy of Wilburn Shearer.)

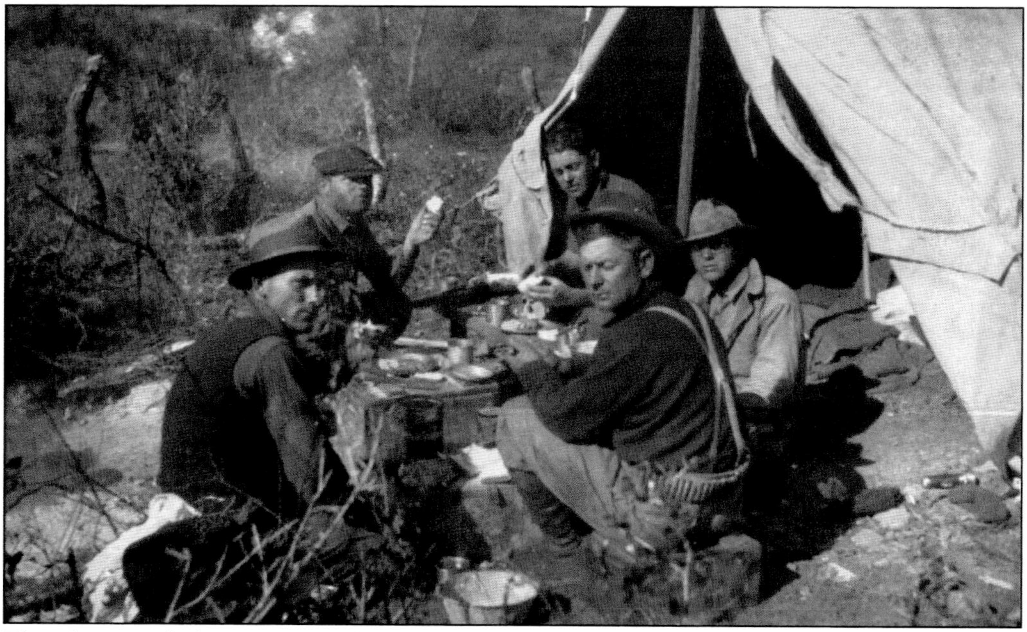

This photograph depicts a typical hunting camp in southern Mason County, around 1920. From left to right are (first row) Hugh Shearer and Charlie Willmann; (second row) Kimsey Shearer, Ed Willmann, and Frank Willmann. The Shearer brothers were Mason County residents; the Willmann brothers had jobs elsewhere but managed to return for the hunting trips. (Courtesy of Wilburn Shearer.)

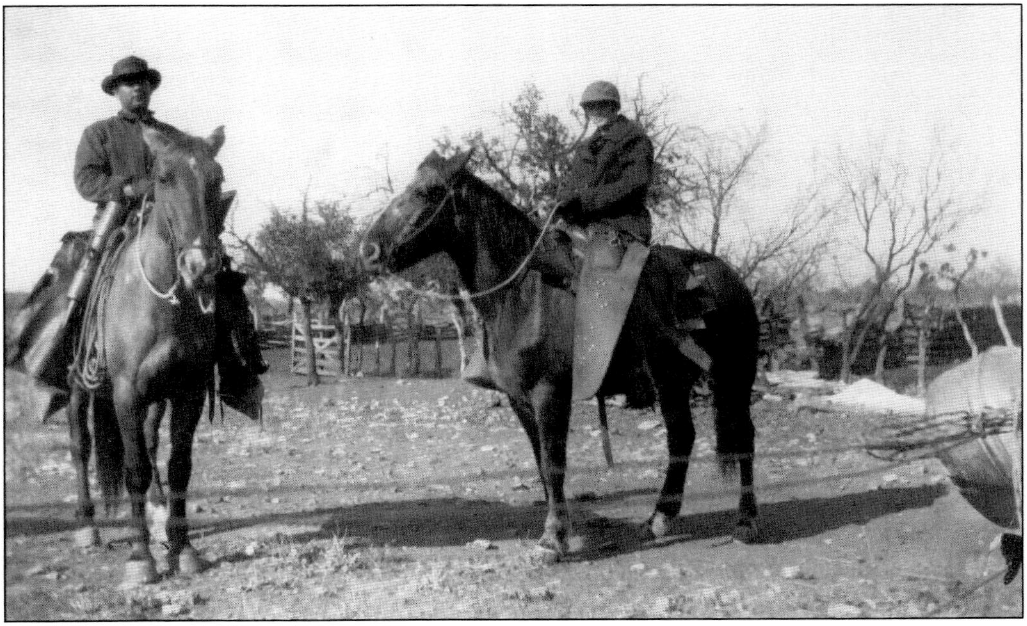

Emeth and Susie Keller are shown in 1924. During the first year of their marriage, they went hunting together and sometimes stayed out until after sundown. Susie was concerned that she might get separated from Emeth and could not find her way home. Emeth told her that if that happened, she should give the horse the reins, and he would find their way home. (Courtesy of Rosemary Kruckemeyer.)

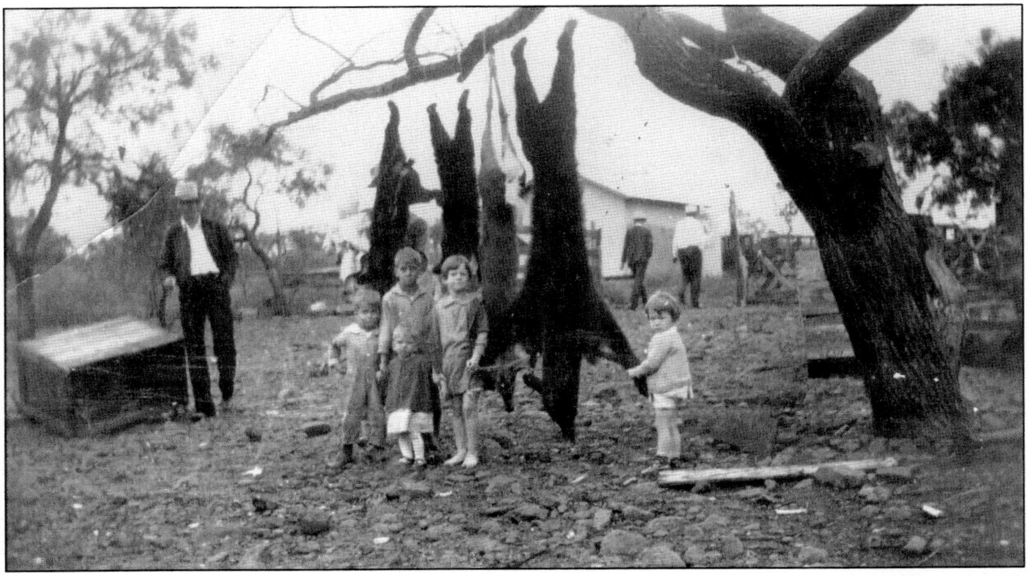

In 1929, a group of intrepid hunters ventured into Mexico and returned with these three black bears (a sow and two cubs) and a buck, suspended from a tree in the backyard of Wilson "Mick" Hey. The large hunting party included Leonard Wood (left), Pete Schmidt (in the dark clothes walking away), C. C. King (in the white shirt with Schmidt), Mick Hey (not pictured), and J. Hugh Shearer (not pictured). Shearer was the bear slayer. The children are Wilson (Mickey) Hey Jr. in the foreground and, behind him from left to right, John Hey, Jim Hey, C. C.'s daughter Mary Francis, and Leonard's daughter Gail. (Courtesy of Beverly Baker.)

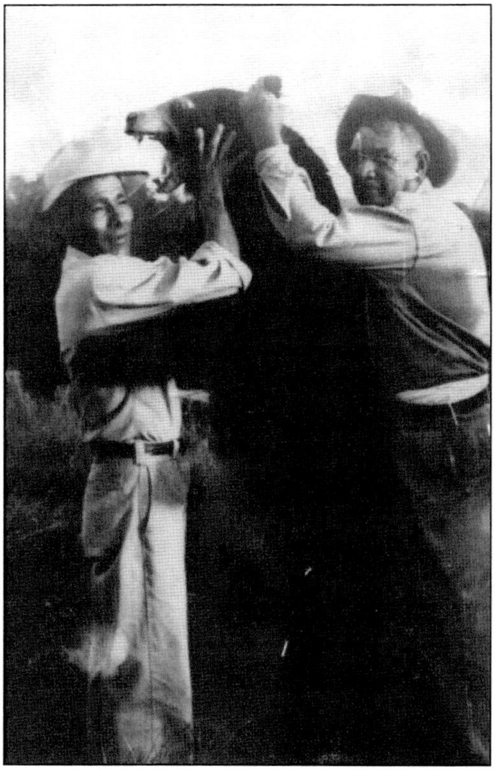

Cornelio Lopez (left) and Savino Menchaca pose with a bear when a carnival came through Mason in the 1930s. Savino was a son of Raphael Menchaca, who settled in Mason in 1876 and married Annie King. In 1881, the family purchased 154 acres south of town and built a large stone house there. The place became known as "Raphael's Hill." (Courtesy of the Alfred Menchaca family.)

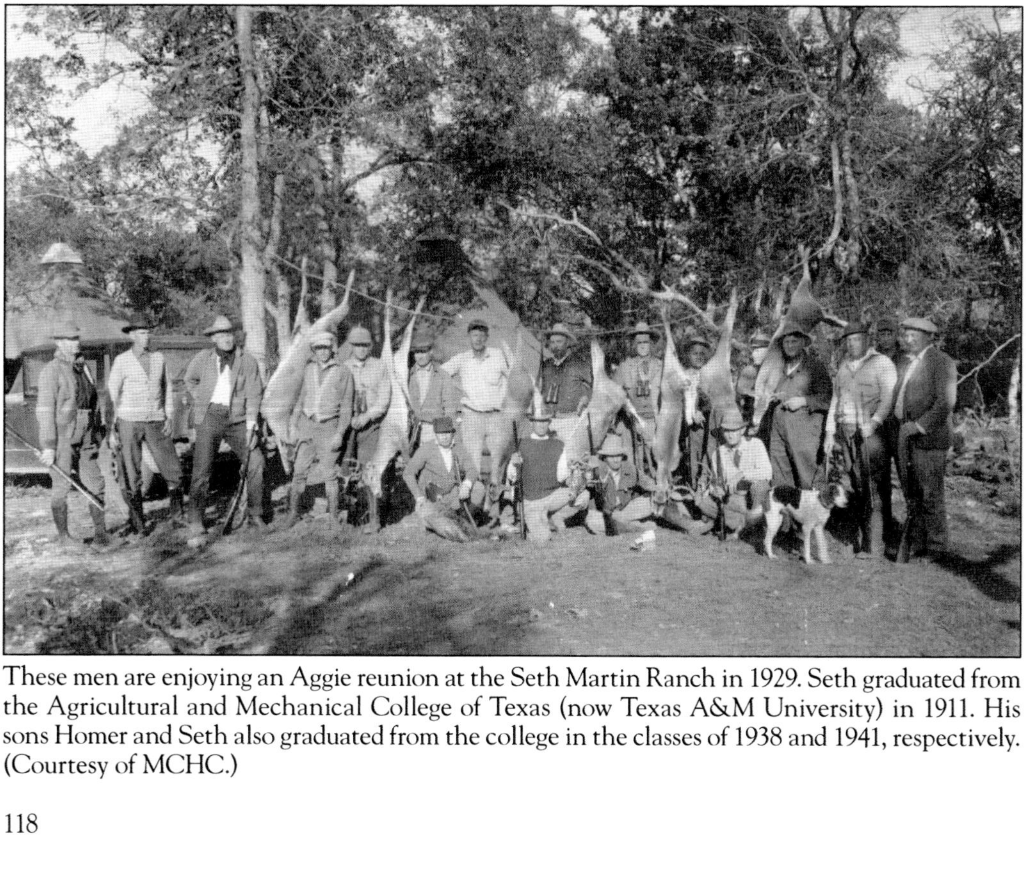

These men are enjoying an Aggie reunion at the Seth Martin Ranch in 1929. Seth graduated from the Agricultural and Mechanical College of Texas (now Texas A&M University) in 1911. His sons Homer and Seth also graduated from the college in the classes of 1938 and 1941, respectively. (Courtesy of MCHC.)

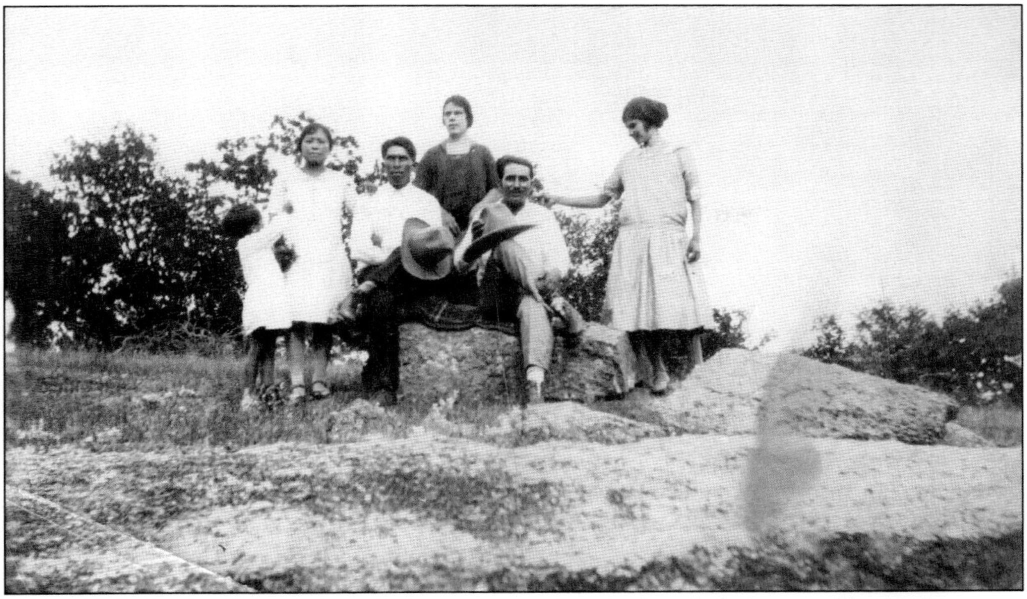

Pictured from left to right at this early 1940s outing are unidentified, Carmen Florez, Florentino Florez, unidentified, Seferino Ruiz, and Petra Ruiz. Carmen and her husband, Florentino, swam the Rio Grande to escape the turmoil of the Mexican Revolution and spent most of their lives in Mason County. (Courtesy of Amanda Orozpe.)

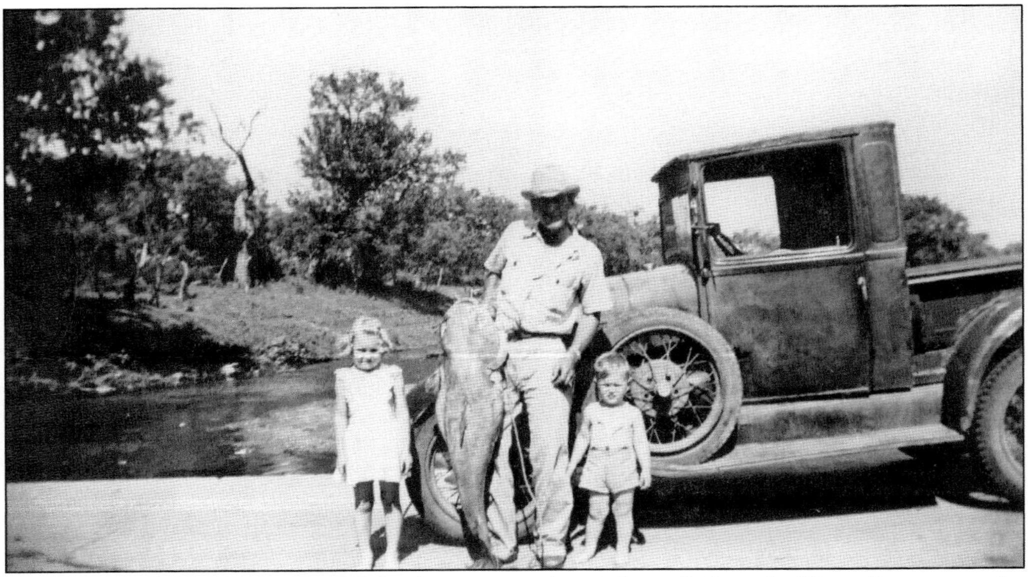

Walter C. (Pinkie) Willmann caught this 62-pound catfish in 1942 in the Llano River near the Comanche Creek junction. Pictured with Pinkie are his children Sue (Oates Caldwell), age four, and Doug, age two. After working for Gulf Oil in west Texas, Pinkie returned to Mason, where he, like his older brother Frank, engaged in his real love of propagating pecan and fruit trees. (Courtesy of Doug and Sherry Willmann.)

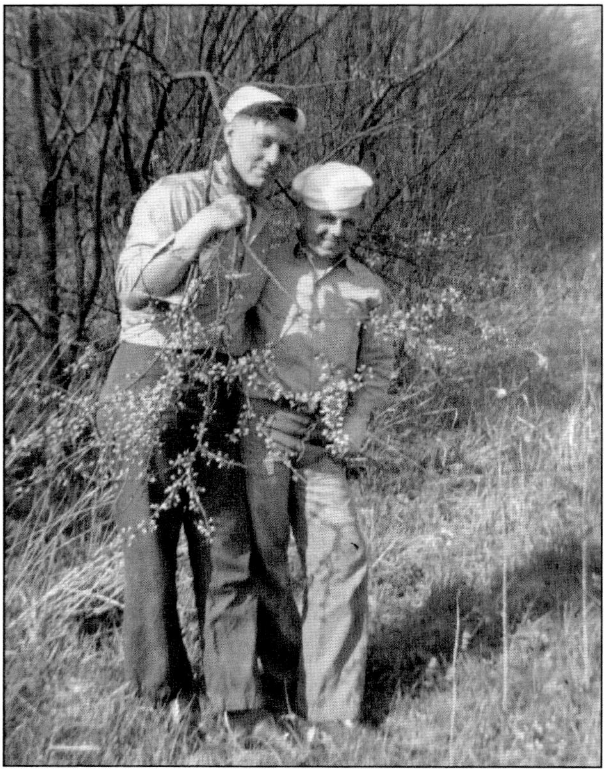

Alex Grosse (left) and Jack Hofmann enjoy a lighthearted moment during their military service. They joined the U.S. Navy at Corpus Christi Naval Air Station on October 2, 1943, and stayed together throughout their navy time until they were discharged in 1946. (Courtesy of Florene Hofmann.)

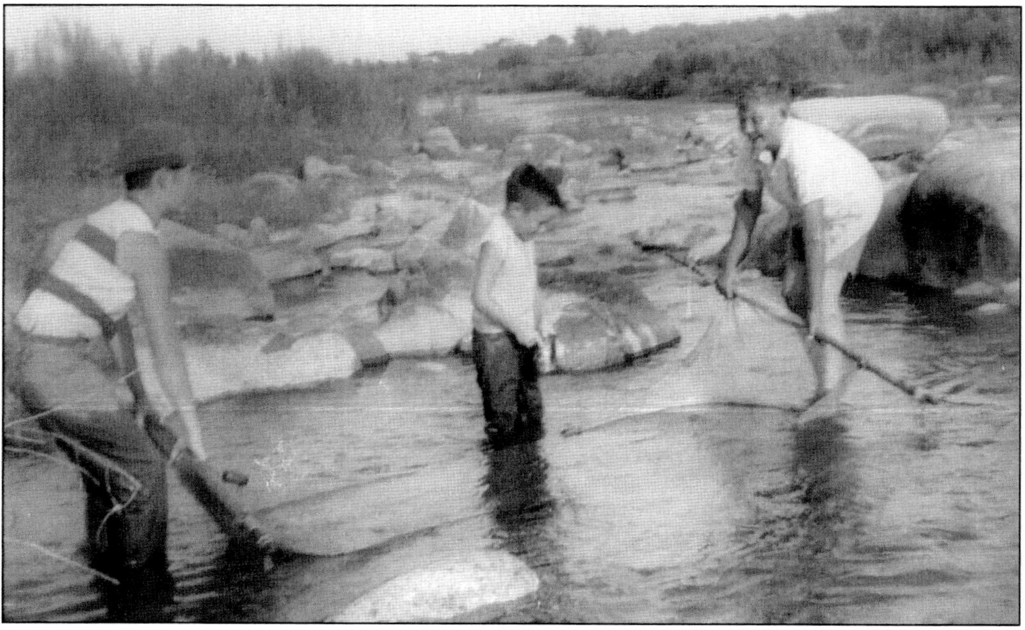

From left to right, Charles Eckert, Dewey Eckert, and Mortimer Kothmann are seining for minnows in the Llano River around 1950, getting bait so they could go catch "the big ones." They may look more like three Huckleberry Finns than serious students, but the boys went on to earn advanced degrees in theology (Charles), civil engineering (Dewey), and range management (Mortimer). (Courtesy of Charles Eckert.)

From left to right, Dovie Morris, Elvie Morris, Fae Danz, Gordon Danz, Earlene Morris (Bode), Boogie Morris (in the dark hat), Betty Morris, and Dorothy Starts are in the yard at the Morris house in the summer of 1955. Fae is teasing her mother, Dovie, because she refused to wear dresses that showed her knees. The family lived on Morris Street, north of the Mason Auction Company. (Courtesy of Fae Danz.)

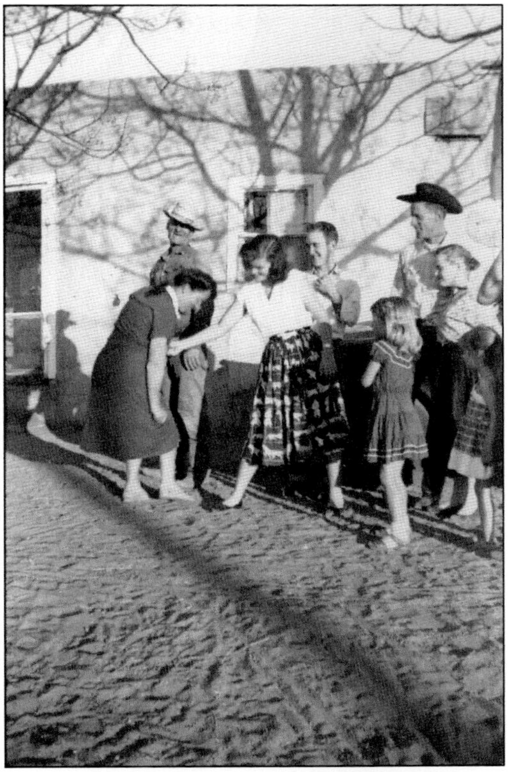

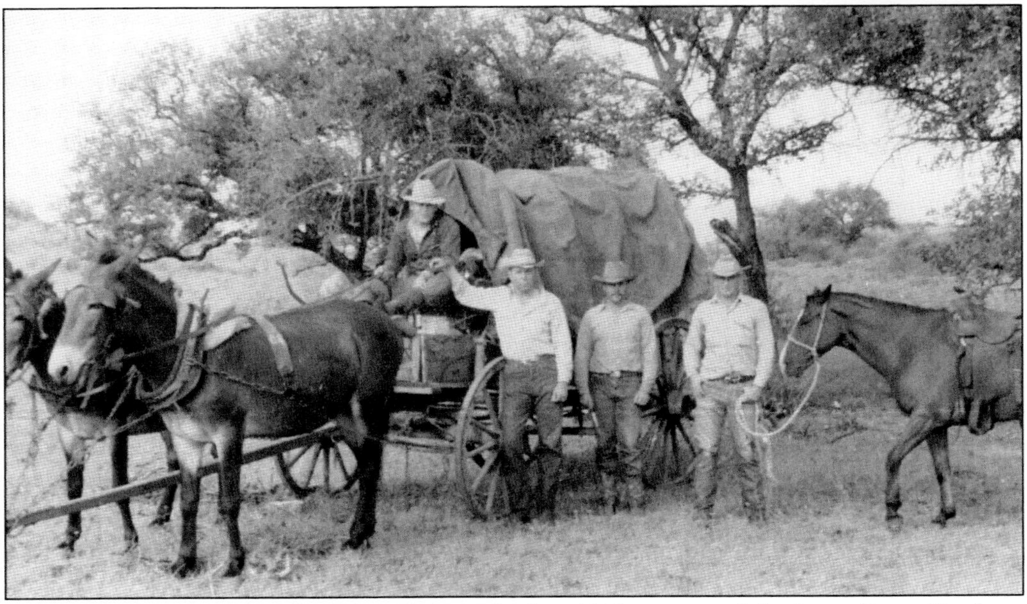

A group of Mason High School friends from the late 1940s organized the James River Cowboys around 1951 and held a three-day ride in May 1958. They started at the August Simon place on the Llano River, followed the Mill Creek Road, crossed James River and Devil's River, and returned by way of James River Road. From left to right are Wayne Keller, Charles Pluenneke, Gene Zesch, and Douglas Owen. Others who went on the ride were Buzzy Keller, George Keller, Max Hey, and Harvey Zesch. (Courtesy of Gene Zesch.)

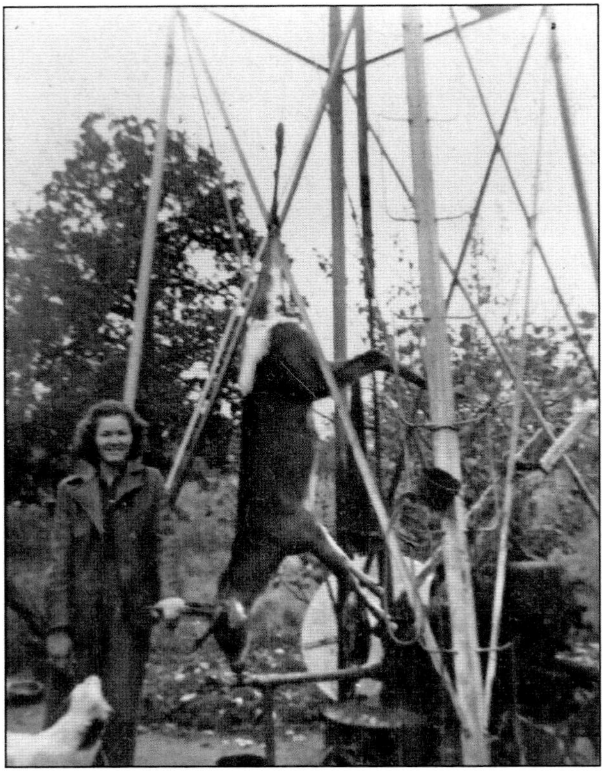

The women of Mason County were actively involved in farm and ranch work from the earliest times, and many of them took up hunting and fishing as well. During the postwar years, it also became more common for men to take part (occasionally) in the household chores. In these two photographs, Elvie Zesch (Donop) of Grossville is seen bringing in a deer (at left) and a turkey (below) in 1945. (Courtesy of Elvie Donop.)

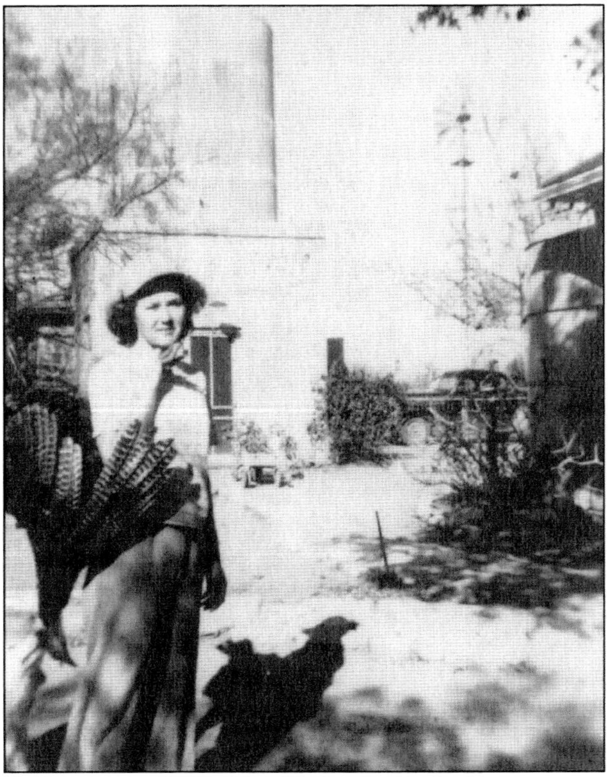

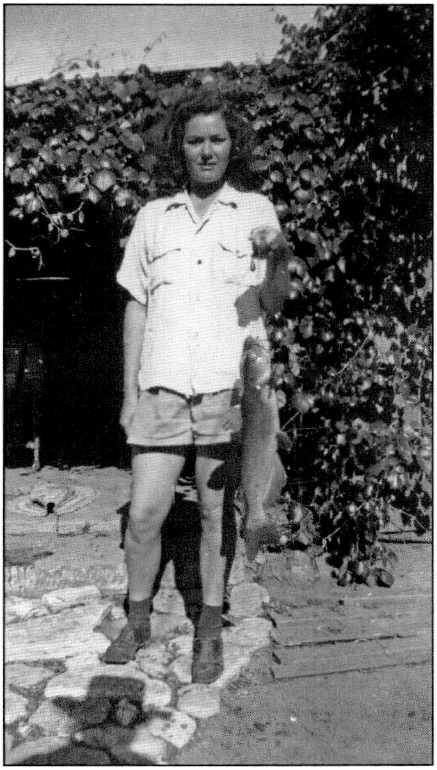

Continuing from the previous page, Elvie Zesch (Donop) displays a fish she caught (at right), also in 1945. In the photograph below, the photographer catches Elvie's brother R. C. Zesch hanging out the diapers in 1951, the year after his son Bobby was born. During World War II, R. C. had served for 16 months in the Pacific on the USS *Lander*. (Courtesy of Elvie Donop.)

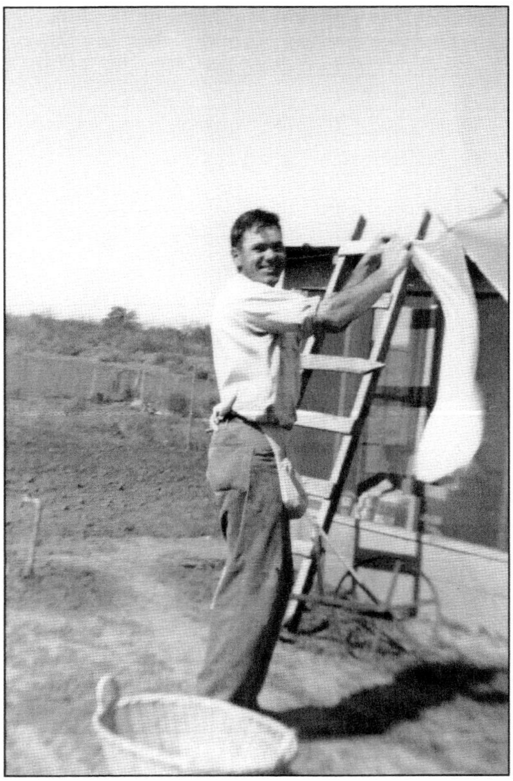

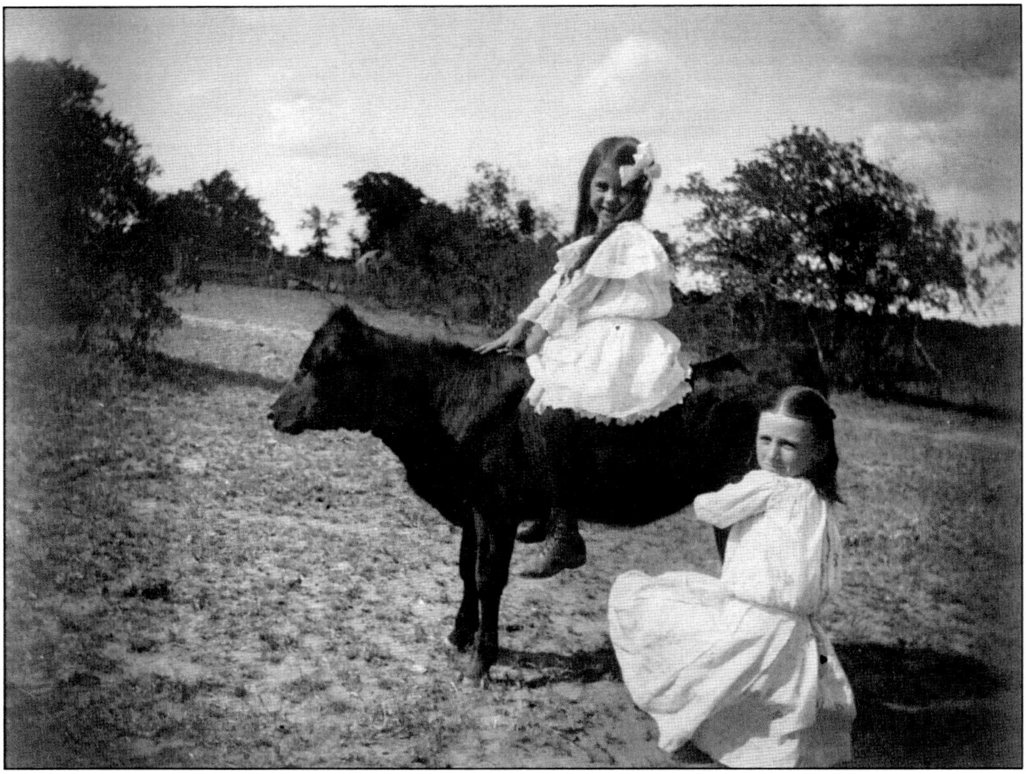

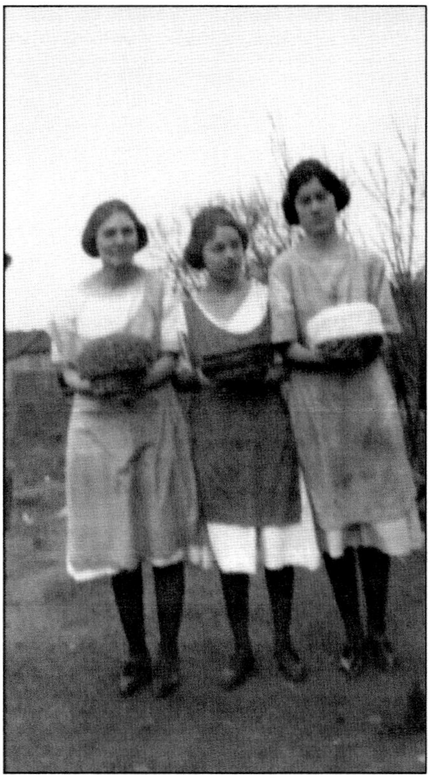

This pictorial history concludes with eight images of gals having fun in Mason County. In the above photograph, taken around 1908 at the Georg and Katherine Ischar farm at Simonsville, Katie Ischar (Hohmann) sits on a very patient calf while her older sister Hattie (Reichenau) holds it in place. At left, three young cousins, still in their cooking aprons, proudly display cakes that they just baked for the evening's cakewalk at the Grit Tabernacle around 1920. From left to right are Lucy Cavness (Koerner), Lydia Keith (Kothmann), and Lela Cavness (Gamel). At the Grit cakewalk, couples walked to music over numbered squares; when the music stopped, the lucky couple on the winning number got the cake. (Above photograph courtesy of the Mason County Museum; left photograph courtesy of Emma Gene Jackson.)

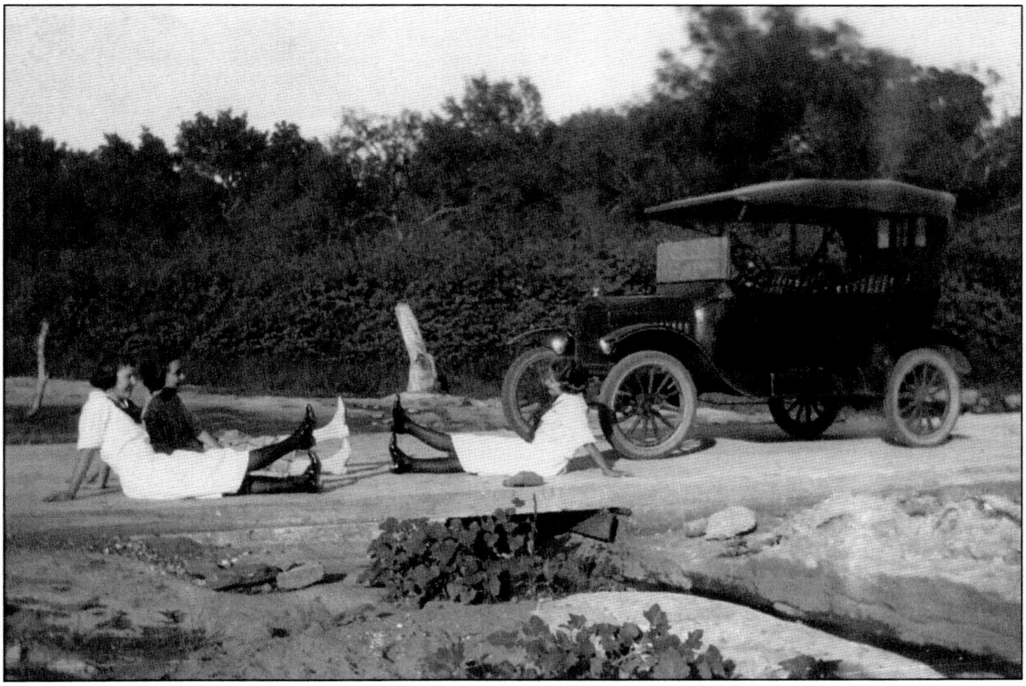

What a delightful way for these winsome young ladies to spend a moment on a summer day, driving a Ford Model T to a nearby creek crossing and showing off the latest in mid-1920s footwear. (Courtesy of Wilburn Shearer.)

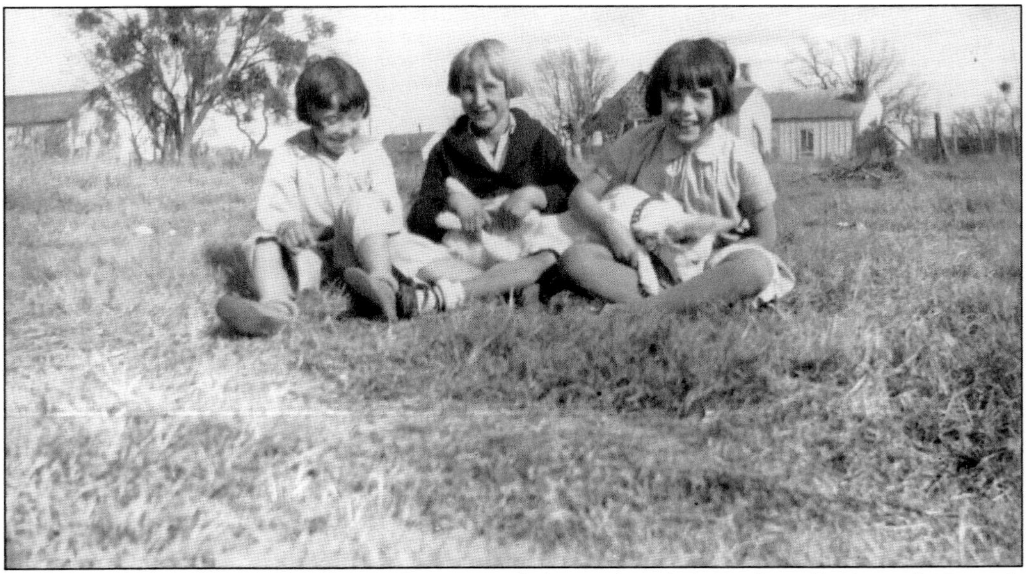

Pictured in 1927 are, from left to right, Lena Sibyl Hey (Snyder), Ruth Nell "Boosie" Henrich (Pitman), Johanna Hey (Wupperman), and their dog Dynamite in the yard of the second Wilson and Hannah Hey house on Highway 87 with the Runge house in the background. The Hey girls' oldest sister, Dixie Fae, wrote in her diary that Johanna and Lena Sibyl were known as "the meanest kids in town," always picking fights and teasing tourist kids, "full of pep and mischief," and "about as popular as scarlet fever." But they look so sweet and happy in the photograph! (Courtesy of Peggy Laverty.)

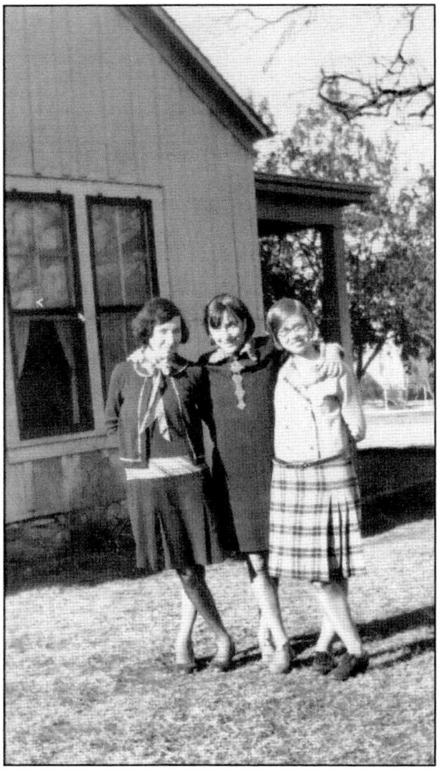

Some country kids who wanted to attend high school had to travel more than 20 miles, so many of them lived with relatives in town and went home on the weekends. Florine Loeffler (Magee), in the center of this coquettish threesome in 1929, lived in the Hilda community, 16 miles southeast of Mason. During the week, she stayed with her aunt Bertha Bickenbach, whose house is in the background. (Courtesy of Jan Appleby.)

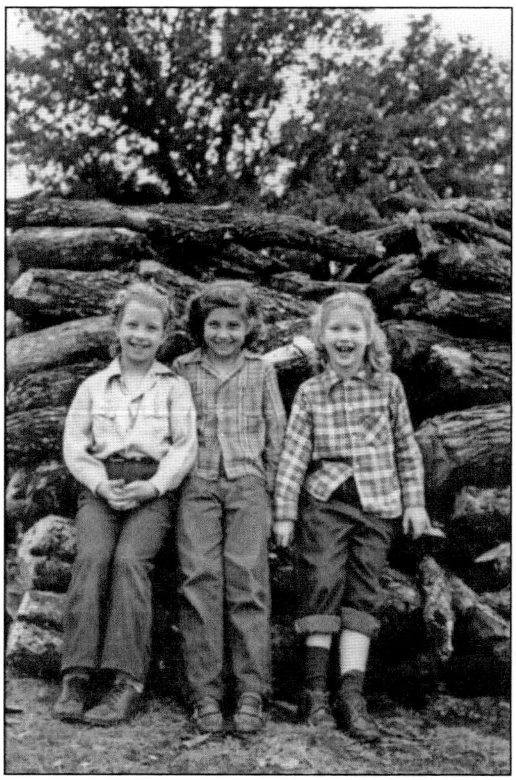

From left to right are Doris Durst (Dannheim), Jimmie Black (Schmidt), and Cissy Cifers (Elkins), obviously enjoying themselves in this 1948 photograph. They are leaning on a large woodpile in the backyard of Doris's parents, Wilbur and Lois Durst. In those days, a large supply of wood was needed year-round, since most rural homes had no hot running water and used woodstoves for cooking and fireplaces for heat. (Courtesy of Doris Dannheim.)

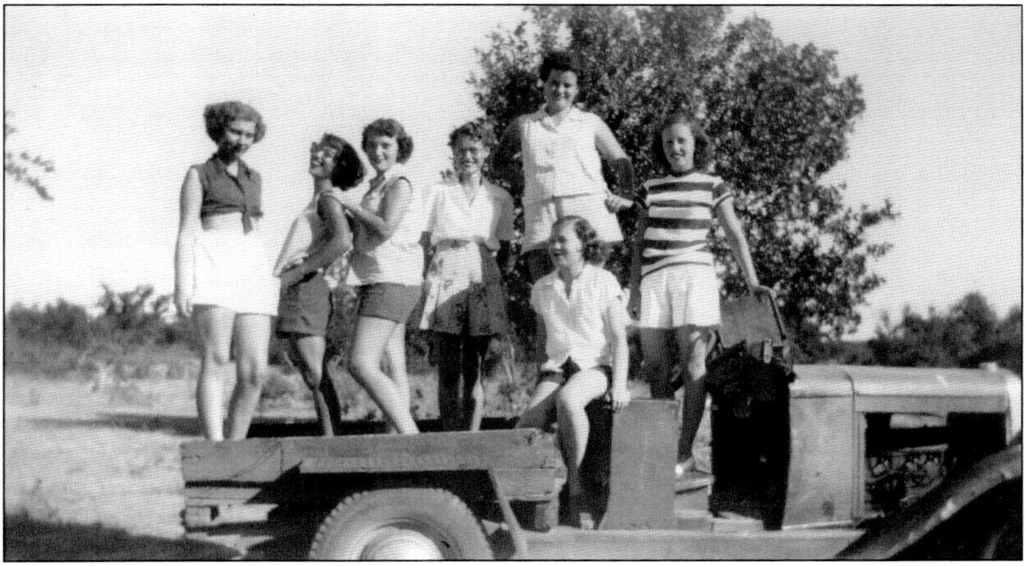

The girls of Mason High School's class of 1949 made the most of their senior year. These charming young ladies were wrapping up a slumber party in the spring of 1949 at the home of Meta Eckert at Ranch Branch. They are, from left to right, Gertrude Thaxton (Morris), Pearlene Kruse (Segars), Sara Eckert (Banta), Lois Jordan (Koock), Ruth Jordan, Bonnie Kruse (Hannah), and Lyndith Leifeste (Kuhne). (Courtesy of Sara Banta.)

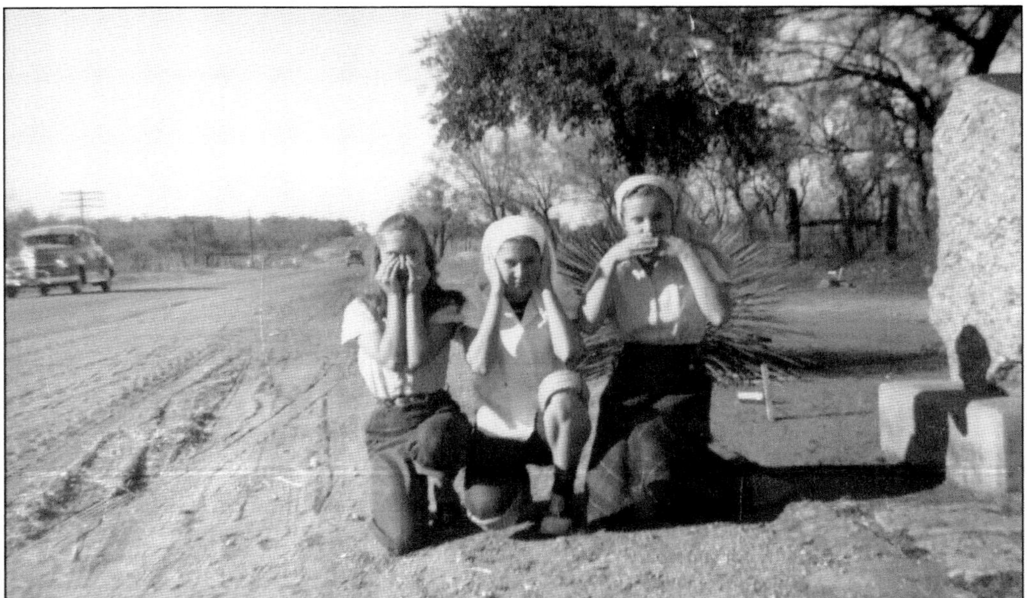

This pictorial walk through Mason County's past concludes with the message "See No Evil" (Frankie Mueller [Hendley]), "Hear No Evil" (Sally Capps), and "Speak No Evil" (Beth Reardon [Leifeste Alm]). These young ladies are posed in 1948 or 1949 on Highway 9 (near the present-day Highway 87) north of Mason. At that time, the Brady Highway ran behind the Crosby Cemetery, located to the right of the car headed away. The granite marker on the right was later moved to the roadside park south of town. A 1948 Chevrolet is coming toward the camera. (Courtesy of Sally Capps.)